# Communications
# in Computer and Information Science    **2004**

## Rationale

The CCIS series is devoted to the publication of proceedings of computer science conferences. Its aim is to efficiently disseminate original research results in informatics in printed and electronic form. While the focus is on publication of peer-reviewed full papers presenting mature work, inclusion of reviewed short papers reporting on work in progress is welcome, too. Besides globally relevant meetings with internationally representative program committees guaranteeing a strict peer-reviewing and paper selection process, conferences run by societies or of high regional or national relevance are also considered for publication.

## Topics

The topical scope of CCIS spans the entire spectrum of informatics ranging from foundational topics in the theory of computing to information and communications science and technology and a broad variety of interdisciplinary application fields.

## Information for Volume Editors and Authors

Publication in CCIS is free of charge. No royalties are paid, however, we offer registered conference participants temporary free access to the online version of the conference proceedings on SpringerLink (http://link.springer.com) by means of an http referrer from the conference website and/or a number of complimentary printed copies, as specified in the official acceptance email of the event.

CCIS proceedings can be published in time for distribution at conferences or as postproceedings, and delivered in the form of printed books and/or electronically as USBs and/or e-content licenses for accessing proceedings at SpringerLink. Furthermore, CCIS proceedings are included in the CCIS electronic book series hosted in the SpringerLink digital library at http://link.springer.com/bookseries/7899. Conferences publishing in CCIS are allowed to use Online Conference Service (OCS) for managing the whole proceedings lifecycle (from submission and reviewing to preparing for publication) free of charge.

## Publication process

The language of publication is exclusively English. Authors publishing in CCIS have to sign the Springer CCIS copyright transfer form, however, they are free to use their material published in CCIS for substantially changed, more elaborate subsequent publications elsewhere. For the preparation of the camera-ready papers/files, authors have to strictly adhere to the Springer CCIS Authors' Instructions and are strongly encouraged to use the CCIS LaTeX style files or templates.

## Abstracting/Indexing

CCIS is abstracted/indexed in DBLP, Google Scholar, EI-Compendex, Mathematical Reviews, SCImago, Scopus. CCIS volumes are also submitted for the inclusion in ISI Proceedings.

## How to start

To start the evaluation of your proposal for inclusion in the CCIS series, please send an e-mail to ccis@springer.com.

Jun Shao · Sokratis K. Katsikas · Weizhi Meng
Editors

# Emerging Information Security and Applications

4th International Conference, EISA 2023
Hangzhou, China, December 6–7, 2023
Proceedings

 Springer

*Editors*
Jun Shao 🆔
Zhejiang Gongshang University
Hangzhou, China

Sokratis K. Katsikas 🆔
Norwegian University of Science
and Technology
Gjøvik, Norway

Weizhi Meng 🆔
Technical University of Denmark
Kongens Lyngby, Denmark

ISSN 1865-0929           ISSN 1865-0937 (electronic)
Communications in Computer and Information Science
ISBN 978-981-99-9613-1           ISBN 978-981-99-9614-8 (eBook)
https://doi.org/10.1007/978-981-99-9614-8

This Springer imprint is published by the registered company Springer Nature Singapore Pte Ltd.
The registered company address is: 152 Beach Road, #21-01/04 Gateway East, Singapore 189721, Singapore

Paper in this product is recyclable.

# Preface

This volume contains the papers that were selected for presentation and publication at The Fourth International Conference on Emerging Information Security and Applications (EISA 2023), which was organized by Zhejiang Gongshang University, China on 6–7 December 2023.

With the recent evolution of adversarial techniques, intrusions that may threaten the security of various assets, including information and applications, have become more complex. In addition, coordinated intrusions like worm outbreaks will continue to be a major threat to information, system and network security in the near future. The popularity of the Internet generates a large volume of different types of sensitive information. Therefore, there is a need for emerging techniques, theories and applications to protect information and practical security. EISA aims to provide a platform for both researchers and practitioners across the world, from either academia or industry, to exchange their ideas. It seeks original submissions that discuss practical or theoretical solutions to enhance information and application security in practice.

This year's Program Committee (PC) consisted of 34 members with diverse backgrounds and broad research interests. A total of 35 papers were submitted to the conference under a single-blinded reviewing mode. Papers were selected based on their originality, significance, relevance, and clarity of presentation as assessed by the reviewers. Most papers were reviewed by three or more PC members. Finally, 11 full papers were selected for presentation at the conference, resulting in an acceptance rate of 31.4%.

For the success of EISA 2023, we would like to first thank the authors of all submissions and all the PC members for their great efforts in selecting the papers. We also thank all the external reviewers for assisting the reviewing process. For the conference organization, we would like to thank the general chairs - Anthony T. S. Ho, Rongxing Lu and Fagen Li; the publicity chairs – Yunguo Guan, Cong Zuo and Long Meng; and the publication chair – Wei-Yang Chiu. Finally, we thank everyone else, speakers and session chairs, for their contribution to the program of EISA 2023.

December 2023

Jun Shao
Sokratis K. Katsikas
Weizhi Meng

# Organization

## General Chairs

Anthony T. S. Ho — University of Surrey, UK
Rongxing Lu — University of New Brunswick, Canada
Fagen Li — University of Electronic Science and Technology of China, China

## Program Chairs

Jun Shao — Zhejiang Gongshang University, China
Sokratis K. Katsikas — Norwegian University of Science and Technology, Norway
Weizhi Meng — Technical University of Denmark, Denmark

## Steering Committee

Jiageng Chen — Central China Normal University, China
Liqun Chen — University of Surrey, UK
Steven Furnell — University of Nottingham, UK
Anthony T. S. Ho — University of Surrey, UK
Sokratis K. Katsikas — Norwegian University of Science and Technology, Norway
Javier Lopez — University of Malaga, Spain
Weizhi Meng (Chair) — Technical University of Denmark, Denmark

## Publicity Chairs

Yunguo Guan — University of New Brunswick, Canada
Cong Zuo — Beijing Institute of Technology, China
Long Meng — University of Surrey, UK

## Publication Chair

Wei-Yang Chiu                      Technical University of Denmark, Denmark

## External Reviewers

Hanzhi Zhang
Dimah Almani
Shuai Shang
Fei Zhu
Fudong Deng

## Program Committee

Cong Zuo                      Beijing Institute of Technology, China
Wun-She Yap                   Universiti Tunku Abdul Rahman, Malaysia
Shoichi Hirose                University of Fukui, Japan
Yicheng Zhang                 University of California, Riverside, USA
Chingfang Hsu                 Central China Normal University, China
Haiyang Xue                   Hong Kong Polytechnic University,
                                 Hong Kong SAR, China
Wenjuan Li                    Hong Kong Polytechnic University,
                                 Hong Kong SAR, China
Mingjun Wang                  Xidian University, China
Albert Levi                   Sabanci University, Turkey
Weizhi Meng                   Technical University of Denmark, Denmark
Jun Shao                      Zhejiang Gongshang University, China
Xiong Li                      Hunan University of Science and Technology,
                                 China
Beibei Li                     Sichuan University, China
Giovanni Livraga              University of Milan, Italy
Je Sen Teh                    Universiti Sains Malaysia, Malaysia
Xingye Lu                     Hong Kong Polytechnic University,
                                 Hong Kong SAR, China
Zhe Xia                       Wuhan University of Technology, China
Xue Yang                      Tsinghua University, China
Gao Liu                       Chongqing University, China
Qianhong Wu                   Beihang University, China
Yunhe Feng                    University of North Texas, USA
Xin Jin                       Ohio State University, USA

| Reza Malekian | Malmö University, Sweden |
| Steven Furnell | University of Nottingham, UK |
| Lei Wu | Shandong Normal University, China |
| Mahmoud Nabil | North Carolina A&T University, USA |
| Ahmed Sherif | University of Southern Mississippi, USA |
| Chunhua Su | University of Aizu, Japan |
| Debiao He | Wuhan University, China |
| Stefanos Gritzalis | University of Piraeus, Greece |
| Jiangang Shu | Peng Cheng Laboratory, China |
| Sokratis Katsikas | Norwegian University of Science and Technology, Norway |
| Cheng Huang | University of Waterloo, Canada |
| Alessandro Brighente | University of Padua, Italy |

# Contents

# PtbStolen: Pre-trained Encoder Stealing Through Perturbed Samples

Chuan Zhang[1], Haotian Liang[1], Zhuopeng Li[1], Tong Wu[2], Licheng Wang[1(✉)], and Liehuang Zhu[1]

[1] Beijing Institute of Technology, Beijing 100081, China
{chuanz,haotianl,zhuopengl,lcwang,liehuangz}@bit.edu.cn
[2] University of Science and Technology Beijing, Beijing 100081, China

**Keywords:** Pre-trained encoders · Encoder stealing attacks · Perturbed samples

## 1 Introduction

Recent years have witnessed the huge success of adopting the self-supervised learning paradigm into pre-train effective encoders [1]. Compared to conventional supervised learning, these pre-trained encoders can learn feature vectors from the inputs, even with little or no labeled data [33]. Therefore, these encoders are widely applied to extract important information representations [2]. Moreover, through the integration of respective downstream classifiers, a singular pre-trained encoder can be utilized across a multitude of downstream classification assignments [3]. This approach facilitates the sharing of a single pre-trained encoder for diverse downstream classification tasks, enhancing overall efficiency and resource utilization. For example, with the use of unlabeled data from ImageNet, an encoder pre-trained via SimCLR combined with the corresponding downstream classifier can perform better than AlexNet in the supervised learning setting [4].

Although it is promising to adopt pre-trained encoders into various downstream tasks, the training cost (i.e., the requirement of abundant data and resources) of a well-performed encoder is also unaffordable for most individual developers [20,23]. Consequently, many big AI enterprises tend to treat their pre-trained encoders as intellectual property and only provide services via their cloud APIs to gain commercial profit. Hence, the concept of Encoder-as-a-Service (EaaS) has become more and more popular in recent years [7,18,27]. For instance, OpenAI has made the API access for their GPT-3 model available. This offering caters to many real-world natural language processing (NLP) tasks, encompassing activities like code generation and language translation [18].

This work is supported by the National Natural Science Foundation of China (Grant Nos. 62232002 and 62202051), the China Postdoctoral Science Foundation (Grant Nos. 2021M700435 and 2021TQ0042), the Shandong Provincial Key Research and Development Program (Grant No. 2021CXGC010106), the Guangdong Provincial Key Labo-

J. Shao et al. (Eds.): EISA 2023, CCIS 2004, pp. 1–19, 2024.
https://doi.org/10.1007/978-981-99-9614-8_1

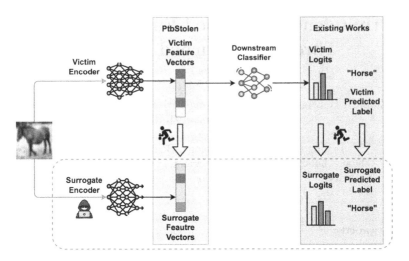

**Fig. 1.** Comparison between PtbStolen (ours) and model stealing attacks (existing). Existing works aim at using predicted labels or softmax outputs to steal the classifiers. In contrast, PtbStolen focuses on stealing the encoders using the feature vectors.

Unfortunately, recent investigations [16,17,26,27,29] have uncovered that merely granting API access falls short in safeguarding the confidentiality of pretrained encoders. Many studies have illustrated that attackers can exploit information received from the API query to perform model stealing attacks. These attacks could not only violate the copyright of these encoders but also provide potentially useful information for further adversarial attacks [7,18,27] (i.e., membership inference, backdoor injections, etc.). Compared to works [16,26,29] that mainly focused on supervised classifiers, where the attacker uses the prediction results or softmax outputs (shown in Fig. 1), Liu et al. [18] first introduced the StolenEncoder, an attack that concentrates on stealing the functionality of encoders via the feature vectors returned from the API. Furthermore, Sha et al. [27] propose the Cont-Steal that utilizes the concept of contrastive learning to improve the performance of encoder stealing attacks. However, these attacks all ignored the robustness of the pre-trained encoders. From intuition, a well-trained commercial encoder ought to be robust enough to handle samples with small perturbations. In fact, small perturbation to image samples is reasonable as one cannot always get perfect image inputs and send them to the cloud platform without any loss [8]. Therefore, the behavior to handle such perturbed inputs by the victim encoder is also valuable enough for the attacker to steal, as the main idea of encoder stealing is to let a surrogate encoder mimic the behaviors of the victim encoder.

To better utilize this characteristic to enhance the performance of encoder stealing attacks, we introduce PtbStolen, a pre-trained encoder stealing attack

ratory of Novel Security Intelligence Technologies (Grant No. 2022B1212010005), and the Beijing Institute of Technology Research Fund Program for Young Scholars.

through perturbed samples. Specifically, we first utilize the perturbation operation to expand the shadow dataset of the attacker to steal the victim encoder. Subsequently, through the utilization of these modified instances, the attacker can instruct its surrogate encoder to steal the functionality of the victim encoder, thereby enabling it to process the perturbed samples effectively. Furthermore, as using perturbed samples may result in additional queries to API, we adopt the approximation technique to reduce the query budget of PtbStolen further. This technique is inspired by the intuition that the feature vectors of the original and perturbed sample from the victim encoder should be similar enough. The experiments conducted on real-world datasets also prove that PtbStolen achieves good performance with high efficiency. In a real-life scenario, an attacker can use the PtbStolen method to initiate queries for the surrogate dataset to the encoder's API to achieve the purpose of stealing functions.

In summary, our contribution can be summarized as follows:

- We introduce PtbStolen, an encoder stealing attack that first exploits the characteristic of the robustness of well-trained encoders.
- We utilize the approximation technique based on the robustness of the encoder to reduce the query budget for PtbStolen further.
- We conducted extensive experiments on a range of real-world datasets, revealing the good performance and operational efficiency of PtbStolen.

The rest of our paper is organized as follows: Sect. 2 will describe the encoder pre-training process using self-supervised learning and its application to downstream tasks. We will introduce the threat model of PtbStolen in Sect. 3 and explain in detail the problem formulation and algorithm of its stealing attack in Sect. 4. We will conduct experiments to demonstrate the good performance of PtbStolen on real-world datasets and present the results in Sect. 5. In addition, important related work in contrastive learning and model stealing attacks is introduced in Sect. 6. Finally, we will summarize our work in the last section of this paper.

## 2 Preliminaries

Making use of the inherent information embedded in unlabeled data, self-supervised learning has been employed to pre-train encoders, as highlighted in prior research [4,11,24]. These pre-trained encoders serve as versatile feature vector extractors for different downstream tasks. In this section, we first commence by providing an overarching explanation of the encoder pre-training process. Then, we discuss its application in downstream tasks.

### 2.1 Encoder Pre-training

Generally, to pre-train an encoder, the contrastive learning algorithm utilizes abundant image-text pairs or unlabeled images. In particular, a crucial element of contrastive learning involves the data augmentation technique that consists of a series of augmentation procedures at random. These processes include random horizontal image flipping, random adjustments of brightness, contrast, and saturation, as well as the stochastic conversion of an image to grayscale. Upon receiving an image as input, the data augmentation technique produces two distinct augmented views at random, denoted as positive pairs. Conversely, augmented views stemming from different inputs are referred to as negative pairs. In essence, the encoder is engineered to produce similar feature vectors for positive pairs while ensuring the divergence of feature vectors for negative pairs. Here, we mainly concentrate on two contrastive learning algorithms that are widely adopted in self-supervised learning: SimCLR [4] and MoCo [11].

**SimCLR.** The concept of SimCLR [4] consists of three major parts: the image encoder $E$, the projection head $ph$, and the data augmentation. For a determined input image sample $img$, the image encoder $E$ first obtains the corresponding feature vector $E(img)$. Next, these feature vectors are mapped to compute the contrastive loss via the projection head $ph$. Generally, $ph$ is a fully connected network composed of hidden layers. When given a mini-batch image set $\{img_1, img_2, ..., img_U\}$ randomly sampled, SimCLR produces two augmented views for each $img_i$ $i \in \{1, \cdots, U\}$. The set of $2U$ augmented images can be denoted as $\{i\tilde{m}g_1, i\tilde{m}g_2, ..., i\tilde{m}g_{2U}\}$. For a positive pair $\{i\tilde{m}g_i, i\tilde{m}g_j\}$, $i\tilde{m}g_i$, and other $2(U-1)$ images from negative pairs. The algorithm calculates the contrastive loss for the determined positive pair $\{i\tilde{m}g_i, i\tilde{m}g_j\}$ according to Eq. (1).

$$\ell_{i,j} = -\log \frac{exp\left(f_s\left(ph(E(i\tilde{m}g_i)), ph(E(i\tilde{m}g_j))\right)/\tau\right)}{\sum_{k=1, k\neq i}^{2U} exp\left(f_s\left(ph(E(i\tilde{m}g_i)), ph(E(i\tilde{m}g_k))\right)/\tau\right)}, \quad (1)$$

where $f_s$ represents the similarity function, and $\tau$ signifies a hyperparameter. The final loss is computed as the summation of $\ell_{i,j}$ across all positive pairs. The algorithm conducts pre-training by jointly optimizing the encoder $E$ and the projection head $ph$ through the minimization of this final contrastive loss.

**MoCo.** The MoCo [11] framework mainly comprises four components: the query encoder $E_q$, the momentum encoder $E_m$, the stochastic data augmentation module, and the dictionary $\mathcal{D}$. Utilizing identical architectures, MoCo employs two neural networks $E_q$ and $E_m$, for the extraction of feature vectors from both input images and their corresponding augmented perspectives. For the augmented views of corresponding input images, we denote the feature vectors from the momentum encoder $E_m$ as key vectors. Dictionary $\mathcal{D}$ is essentially a queue that stores key vectors. During the training, key vectors are iteratively updated to the dictionary $\mathcal{D}$, with new keys added and the oldest keys removed. Like SimCLR, MoCo generates two augmented views for all $U$ input image $\{img_1, img_2, ..., img_U\}$, resulting in 2U augmented images $\{i\tilde{m}g_1, i\tilde{m}g_2, ..., i\tilde{m}g_{2U}\}$. For each pair of augmented views that originate from the same input image (e.g., $\{i\tilde{m}g_i, i\tilde{m}g_j\}$ from image $img$), one view is treated as the query and the other as the key. The query view (e.g., $i\tilde{m}g_i$) is passed through the query encoder $E_q$ to get the query feature vector $E_q(\tilde{img}_i)$ while the key view (e.g., $\tilde{img}_j$) is taken as the input to the momentum encoder $E_m$ to get the key feature vector $E_m(\tilde{img}_j)$. Next, the key vector $E_m(\tilde{img}_j)$ is enqueued to the dictionary $\mathcal{D}$. The contrastive loss in MoCo is defined as follows:

$$\ell_{i,j} = - \log \frac{exp\left(f_s\left(E_q(\tilde{img}_i), E_m(\tilde{img}_j)\right)/\tau\right)}{\sum_{k \in \mathcal{D}} exp\left(f_s\left(E_q(\tilde{img}_i), k\right)/\tau\right)}, \tag{2}$$

where $f_s$ represents the similarity function and $\tau$ is a hyperparameter. The summation of individual losses $\ell_{i,j}$ across all $U$ positive pairs yields the ultimate contrastive loss. MoCo conducts the pre-training of encoder $E$ by optimizing for the minimization of this final contrastive loss.

## 2.2 Application in Downstream Tasks

Pre-trained image encoders can obtain feature vectors that are useful for different downstream tasks, which we mainly aim at classification tasks in PtbStolen. We can first utilize the encoder already pre-trained to perform feature vector extraction from training inputs. Subsequently, adhering to the principles of supervised learning, we proceed to train a corresponding classifier using these feature vectors and labels. For a testing input image, we employ the image encoder to get its corresponding feature vector. Next, we utilize the downstream classifier to obtain the prediction result. This process is conducted using a dataset designated as the downstream dataset, which serves for both training and testing purposes.

## 3 Threat Model

Here, we concentrate on the scenario with two parties: The *service provider* and the *attacker*. Specifically, a service provider could usually be an organization or an enterprise with enough resources (e.g., OpenAI, Meta, and Google). The service provider first utilizes the self-supervised learning paradigm to pre-train an encoder (referred to as victim encoder) on a pre-train dataset. Then, it deploys the pre-trained encoder on the cloud platform to provide EaaS services for commercial profits. As for the user (e.g., an attacker), it can use its images as input for querying the API to get the corresponding feature vectors. Concretely, the user first submits an image as the input to the EaaS API. After that, the pre-trained encoder computes the corresponding feature vector according to the input image and sends it back to the user. Notably, based on the total API query numbers from the user, the service provider may charge a certain amount of money according to its pricing policy. Next, we illustrate the threat model in three aspects: The attacker's objectives, capability, and background knowledge.

### 3.1 Objectives

The objectives of the attacker can be taxonomized as follows:

1. **Acquiring the victim encoder's functionality.** In this objective, the attacker focuses on stealing the victim encoder to make its surrogate encoder acquire the victim encoder's functionality. Specifically, the classifiers based on the surrogate encoder are required to perform at least comparable to that achieved by classifiers built upon the victim encoder across a range of diverse downstream tasks.
2. **Minimizing the query budget.** As illustrated before, the amount of queries to API is closely related to the monetary cost for the attacker. Hence, in this objective, the attacker concentrates on how to minimize the query budget while successfully stealing the victim encoder.

### 3.2   Capability

In PtbStolen, we make the assumption that the attacker can only access the victim encoder in a black-box manner, meaning it can only use its images as inputs to get the corresponding feature vectors via querying the API.

### 3.3   Background Knowledge

Here, we discuss the background knowledge regarding the shadow dataset and the architecture of the encoder. It is noteworthy that because PtbStolen does not leverage any contrastive algorithms to optimize the surrogate encoder, the attacker does not require any information or knowledge about the contrastive algorithm utilized to pre-train the victim encoder.

**Shadow Dataset.** PtbStolen assumes that the attacker has access to a limited set of unlabeled images, known as the *shadow dataset*. Considering this assumption and the attacker's knowledge of the pre-training dataset used for the victim encoder, we examine three distinct scenarios related to the shadow dataset.

1. **Pre-train dataset's subset.** In this situation, the shadow dataset is a pre-train dataset's subset. For example, if AI enterprises use the data collected from public websites to pre-train its encoder, the attacker is able to use a similar way to build its shadow dataset.
2. **Pre-train dataset's same distribution.** In this situation, despite the absence of overlap between the shadow dataset and the dataset used for pre-training, they exhibit an identical distribution.
3. **Pre-train dataset's different distribution.** In this situation, the distribution of the shadow dataset is entirely dissimilar to that of the dataset used to pre-train the victim encoder. Essentially, this indicates that the attacker possesses no knowledge or information regarding the dataset employed in pre-training the encoder. This case is sensible as many pre-train datasets are derived from the service provider's private data [27].

**Architecture of the Encoder.** This part of background knowledge represents whether the attack possesses information about the network architecture of the victim encoder. According to real-world EaaS scenarios, the attacker may face two cases:

1. **Architecture is known.** In this case, the attacker can acquire information about the victim encoder's architecture and know its details. For instance, some service providers may open source their encoder's architecture to improve trust and transparency [18]. Consequently, the attacker can employ an identical architecture when constructing its surrogate encoder.
2. **Architecture is unknown.** In this case, the attacker lacks knowledge concerning the structural details of the victim encoder. To overcome this challenge, the attacker may select a deeper or more expressive network architecture for the surrogate encoder, which is more likely to acquire the functionality from the victim encoder. For example, if the victim encoder is based on ResNet18, the attacker can choose ResNet34 as the architecture for its surrogate encoder.

## 4   Details of PtbStolen

### 4.1   Overview

The main idea of PtbStolen revolves around formulating the encoder stealing attack as a minimization optimization problem. Subsequently, we utilize the widely adopted stochastic gradient descent technique to address this problem. As mentioned before, in PtbStolen, the attacker concentrates on achieving two objectives simultaneously. For the first objective, the feature vector obtained from the surrogate encoder should be similar to the one from the victim encoder when given an image from the shadow dataset. Furthermore, due to the relatively small size of the shadow dataset, we utilize the random noise to perturb images in the shadow dataset. Importantly, both the surrogate encoder and the victim encoder should yield similar feature vectors for these perturbed images. Nevertheless, because the attacker has to get feature vectors of these perturbed images from the victim encoder, it may lead to abundant queries to the EaaS API, which violates the second objective. To tackle this challenge, we take the feature vector of the original image obtained from the victim encoder as the alternate approximation for the feature vector of the perturbed image from the victim encoder. Employing this technique allows for a reduction in the number of queries made to the EaaS API for obtaining the feature vectors of perturbed images. Consequently, the attacker is able to achieve both two objectives simultaneously.

### 4.2   Problem Formulation

Here, we denote the victim and surrogate encoder as $E_v$ and $E_s$. The shadow dataset of the attacker is defined as $\mathcal{D}$, and $img$ is an input image that satisfies $img \in \mathcal{D}$. The corresponding feature vectors produced by $E_v$ and $E_s$ for

$img$ are denoted as $E_v(img)$ and $E_s(img)$, respectively. Then, we introduce the loss function for the attacker's two objectives, and combine them to formulate PtbStolen as a minimization optimization problem.

**Achieving the First Objective.** When it comes to the first objective, the attacker concentrates on acquiring the functionality of the victim. Generally speaking, the effectiveness of a pre-trained encoder is assessed through the accuracy of diverse classifiers built upon it. Unfortunately, the attacker may not know any information about the possible downstream classifiers during its stealing process. Therefore, it is not sensible to directly leverage the accuracy from downstream tasks to evaluate the performance of the first objective. To overcome this challenge, we adopt the similarity between the feature vectors from pre-trained encoders to evaluate the performance, which is commonly adopted in various related works [7,18,27]. Specifically, when the feature vector produced by the surrogate encoder closely resembles that of the victim encoder, the downstream classifiers built upon these feature vectors would yield similar accuracy outcomes.

Concretely, the surrogate encoder should obtain similar feature vectors as the ones from the victim encoder for images in the shadow dataset $\mathcal{D}$ of the attacker. Therefore, we introduce the first loss function $\mathcal{L}_0$ as follows:

$$\mathcal{L}_0 = -\frac{1}{|\mathcal{D}|} \cdot \sum_{img \in \mathcal{D}} f_s(E_v(img), E_s(img)), \tag{3}$$

where $E_v$ represents the victim encoder and $E_s$ denotes the surrogate encoder. $img$ is the image that belongs to the shadow dataset $\mathcal{D}$. $f_s$ is the similarity function (e.g., cosine similarity) to evaluate the similarity between $E_v(img)$ and $E_s(img)$, which are obtained from the victim and surrogate encoder for the given input $img$, respectively. When the feature vector obtained from the surrogate encoder $E_s$ gradually becomes similar to the one from the victim encoder $E_v$, the loss $\mathcal{L}_0$ will also become smaller.

According to the threat model, the attacker is assumed to acquire a shadow dataset with a small amount of images. It is reasonable because the attacker is always an entity whose resource is insufficient to pre-train its encoder individually. Consequently, only utilizing such a small shadow dataset to minimize the loss function $\mathcal{L}_0$ may result in a surrogate encoder that exhibits suboptimal performance, as demonstrated in our experimental findings. To tackle this problem, we first leverage the data perturbation technique to expand the shadow dataset. Then, we require that, for perturbed input images, the surrogate encoder should output feature vectors similar to the one from the victim encoder. This is inspired by the intuition that well-pre-trained encoders are robust enough to the data perturbed with a small magnitude of noise. In particular, we obtain a perturbed image by leveraging various types of random noise (e.g., Gaussian noise, Laplacian noise). For simplicity, we denote $\mathcal{P}$ as the perturbation operation and $\mathcal{P}(img)$ as the perturbed image with $img$ as the input. Based on these perturbed images, the corresponding feature vectors obtained from the surrogate encoder should be similar to the ones from the victim encoder. Therefore, we introduce the second loss function $\mathcal{L}_1$ as follows:

$$\mathcal{L}_1 = -\frac{1}{|\mathcal{D}|} \cdot \sum_{img \in \mathcal{D}} f_s(E_v(\mathcal{P}(img)), E_s(\mathcal{P}(img))), \tag{4}$$

where $\mathcal{P}(img)$ is an perturbed image obtained from $img \in \mathcal{D}$. By combining both the loss function terms in Eq. (3) and Eq. (4), the first objective can be achieved via optimizing the surrogate encoder $E_s$ by solving the minimization optimization problem in Eq. (5).

$$\min_{E_S} \mathcal{L} = \mathcal{L}_0 + \eta \cdot \mathcal{L}_1. \tag{5}$$

where $\eta$ represents the hyperparameter that governs the trade-off between the influences of the two loss terms.

**Achieving the Second Objective.** Upon initiating the resolution of the minimization optimization problem defined in Eq. (5) utilizing the Stochastic Gradient Descent (SGD) technique, it first randomly initializes the parameters of the surrogate encoder (denoted as $\theta_{E_s}$). Then, it leverages a small batch of images from the shadow dataset to compute the gradient of the loss function $\mathcal{L}$ about the surrogate encoder's parameters and optimize the parameters via SGD with the determined learning rate. The aforementioned optimization process iterates until the specified threshold (loss or epochs) is attained.

As we can observe, the attacker must make one query to the victim encoder for each image in the shadow dataset, resulting in the acquisition of corresponding feature vectors. These feature vectors can be stored offline and later utilized for the computation of the loss function $\mathcal{L}_0$ throughout the optimization process. In other words, calculating the loss function $\mathcal{L}_0$ requires $|\mathcal{D}|$ times of query. Moreover, in order to acquire feature vectors for the perturbed images, the attacker must also make queries to the victim encoder. However, this could result in a substantial query expenditure, especially when using different perturbed images in each epoch during the optimization process to improve the surrogate encoder's performance. In particular, suppose the desired number of epochs is $n$. The attacker needs to perform $n \cdot |\mathcal{D}|$ times of query to the victim encoder to obtain the feature vectors of the perturbed images for computing the loss term $\mathcal{L}_1$ during the optimization process. Hence, the total query budget is $(n+1) \cdot |\mathcal{D}|$.

Because performing one query to the victim encoder for each image in the shadow dataset is necessary, the query budget to compute the loss $\mathcal{L}_0$ is already minimal and has no need for further improvement. Therefore, we mainly focus on reducing the query budget of computing the loss $\mathcal{L}_1$. Notably, according to our observation, the well-trained encoders always obtain similar feature vectors for a given image and its perturbed version. That is to say, the value of $E_v(\mathcal{P}(img))$ can be approximately replaced by $E_v(img)$. By applying this key observation, we can get the improved loss function $\mathcal{L}_{1_{impr}}$ as follows:

$$\mathcal{L}_{1_{impr}} = -\frac{1}{|\mathcal{D}|} \cdot \sum_{img \in \mathcal{D}} f_s(E_v(img), E_s(\mathcal{P}(img))), \tag{6}$$

Similarly, we leverage $\mathcal{L}_{1_{impr}}$ to replace $\mathcal{L}_1$, and the minimization optimization problem illustrated in Eq. (5) can then be transformed as follows:

$$\min_{E_s} \mathcal{L}_{impr} = \mathcal{L}_0 + \eta \cdot \mathcal{L}_{1_{impr}}, \tag{7}$$

where $\eta$ is the hyperparameter. As demonstrated by the experimental results, the surrogate encoder obtained by solving the minimization optimization problem in Eq. (5) and Eq. (7) shows similar accuracy performance in various downstream classification tasks. Notably, the loss function $\mathcal{L}_{1_{impr}}$ does not necessitate additional queries to the victim encoder. This is because the feature vectors, denoted as $E_v(img)$, have already been acquired and are stored locally for the computation of the loss function term $\mathcal{L}_0$. Therefore, the total query budget for solving the optimization problem in Eq. (7) is only $|\mathcal{D}|$, which is much less than the one for Eq. (5).

---

**Algorithm 1.** PtbStolen

---

**Input:** Shadow dataset $\mathcal{D}$, similarity function $f_s$, total epochs $e$, learning rate $\mu$,
   hyperparameter $\eta$, perturbation operation $\mathcal{P}$, batch size $b$.
**Output:** Trained surrogate encoder $E_s$.
1: /*Query the victim encoder to obtain feature vectors.*/
2: $Vec(img) \leftarrow E_v(img), \; img \in \mathcal{D}$
3: /*Initialize the parameters of the surrogate encoder at random.*/
4: $\theta_{E_s} \leftarrow RandInit()$
5: **for** $i \leftarrow 1, 2, \cdots, e$ **do**
6:    **for** $j \leftarrow 1, 2, \cdots, \lfloor |\mathcal{D}/b| \rfloor$ **do**
7:       $\mathcal{B} \leftarrow SmallBatch(\mathcal{D})$
8:       $\mathcal{L}_0 \leftarrow \frac{1}{|\mathcal{B}|} \cdot \sum_{img \in \mathcal{B}} f_s(Vec(img), E_s(img))$
9:       $\mathcal{L}_{1_{impr}} \leftarrow \frac{1}{|\mathcal{B}|} \cdot \sum_{img \in \mathcal{B}} f_s(Vec(img), E_s(\mathcal{P}(img)))$
10:      $\mathcal{L}_{impr} = \mathcal{L}_0 + \eta \cdot \mathcal{L}_{1_{impr}}$
11:      $\theta_{E_s} \leftarrow \theta_{E_s} - \mu \cdot \nabla_{\theta_{E_s}} \mathcal{L}_{impr}$
12:    **end for**
13: **end for**

---

### 4.3   Algorithm of PtbStolen

As mentioned before, the solution to the minimization optimization problem in Eq. (7) represents the desired surrogate encoder for the attacker. The algorithm of PtbStolen is illustrated in Algorithm 1. First, the attacker queries the victim encoder to obtain the corresponding feature vectors $E_v(img)$ for each image in $\mathcal{D}$ and stores them locally as $Vec(img)$ (Line 2 in Algorithm 1). Then, it leverages the function $RandInit()$ to randomly initialize the parameters of the surrogate encoder $E_s$ (Line 4 in Algorithm 1). To solve the optimization problem according to Eq. (7), the attack utilizes the SGD technique. During each epoch, the attacker first obtains small batches of the shadow dataset with the use of the function $SmallBatch$ (Line 7 in Algorithm 1). Next, for each image in the small batch $\mathcal{B}$, the attacker leverages all images in $\mathcal{B}$ to iteratively calculate the loss function term $\mathcal{L}_0$ and $\mathcal{L}_{1_{impr}}$ (Line 8 and 9 in Algorithm 1). After that, it utilizes the gradient descent method to update the parameters $\theta_{E_s}$, as shown in Line 10 and 11. Notably, the data perturbation $\mathcal{P}(img)$ introduces a stochastic modification to the input image $img$.

## 5  Experiments

### 5.1  Attack Settings

**Pre-train Datasets and Victim Encoders.** In the experiment, we utilize CIFAR10 [14] and SVHN [34] datasets as the pre-training datasets. Note that we do not take the images in the testing part of the datasets into training encoders. This is because these images are reserved for measuring PtbStolen under the setting where the attacker's shadow dataset exhibits the same underlying distribution as the pre-training dataset but remains non-overlapping. For the contrastive learning algorithm, we use SimCLR [4] by default. We take the ResNet18 as the architecture of the victim encoder.

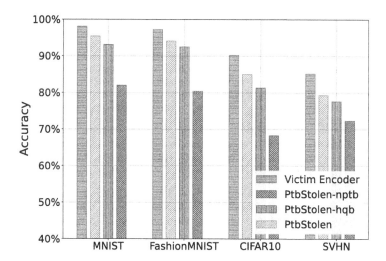

**Fig. 2.** The performance of the PtbStolen attack against victim encoders and comparison with various baselines. The victim encoder is pre-trained on the CIFAR10 dataset. The x-axis represents various datasets of corresponding downstream tasks, while the y-axis indicates the accuracy of the downstream tasks.

**Parameter Settings.** Regarding the shadow dataset, we randomly select unlabeled images from the STL10 [6] dataset, and its size is set as 5% of the pre-train dataset. Moreover, we leverage ResNet34 as the architecture of the surrogate encoder. For the perturbation operation $\mathcal{P}$, we here take the Gaussian noise by default. Regarding the similarity function, we utilize the cosine similarity due to its good performance in many related works [7,18,27]. Furthermore, the hyperparameter $\eta$ is set to 1, total epochs $e$ is set to 100, learning rate $\mu$ is set to $10^{-3}$, and batch size $b$ is set to 64.

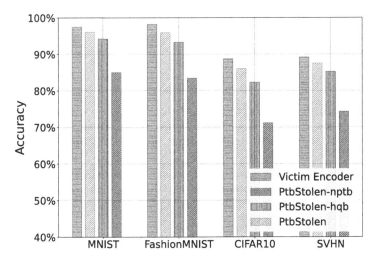

**Fig. 3.** The performance of the PtbStolen attack against victim encoders and comparison with various baselines. The victim encoder is pre-trained on the SVHN dataset.

**Downstream Task Settings.** For the downstream task, we utilize MNIST [15], FashionMNIST [32], CIFAR10, and SVHN as datasets. The images in pretrain and downstream datasets are all resized to $32 \times 32$. Moreover, we extend images in MNIST and FashionMNIST into three channels for convenience. For each downstream task, we leverage the victim or surrogate encoder to perform feature extraction. Then, we implement a fully connected network as the classifier. Specifically, it includes two hidden layers that are composed of 512 and 256 neurons, respectively. We utilize the Adam optimizer with a learning rate of $10^{-4}$ and train the downstream classifier for a total of 500 iterations.

**Baselines for Comparison.** To better measure the performance of PtbStolen, we compare PtbStolen with two baselines.

- **PtbStolen without perturbed images (PtbStolen-nptb):** To better illustrate the factor of these perturbed images in advancing the stealing performance of the surrogate encoder, we measure a variant of PtbStolen without utilizing the perturbed images. In essence, it is equivalent to the method proposed by Cong et al. [7].

- **PtbStolen with high query budget (PtbStolen-hqb):** Note that we utilize the approximation to reduce the query budget. To ensure that it has no negative effect on the performance of PtbStolen, we measure another variant of PtbStolen, which employs perturbed images for querying the API to get the corresponding feature vectors.

**Evaluating Metrics.** In this part, we evaluate three metrics for evaluating PtbStolen: *Victim Accuracy (VA), Surrogate Accuracy (SA), and Query Budget.*

### 5.2 Experimental Results

**Performance of PtbStolen.** Figures 2 and 3 demonstrate the performance of PtbStolen on various downstream tasks with the victim encoder pre-trained on CIFAR10 and SVHN. As can be seen, PtbStolen can extract and maintain the functionality of the victim encoder. Moreover, PtbStolen also outperforms the other two baselines mentioned before. Notably, for most downstream classification tasks, the SA of PtbStolen is superior to PtbStolen-nptb for at least 10%. This demonstrates the improvement brought by the perturbed sample that leverages the characteristic of robustness. In conclusion, The experimental results indicate that PtbStolen effectively steals and preserves the victim encoder's functionality, surpassing other baselines.

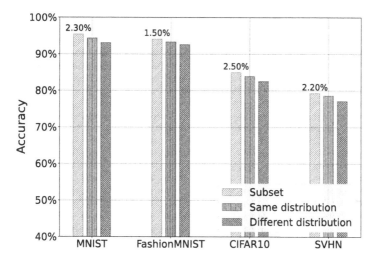

**Fig. 4.** The impact of the shadow dataset's distribution on PtbStolen's SA performance. The victim encoder is pre-trained on the CIFAR10 dataset.

**Impact of the Shadow Dataset.** In this part, we explore how the distribution of the shadow dataset affects the attacker's performance in PtbStolen. Figure 4 demonstrates the SAs of PtbStolen when the distribution of the shadow dataset varies. Specifically, we consider three situations. For the situation where the shadow dataset is the **pre-train dataset's subset**, we randomly select images from the training part of the pre-train dataset to form it. For the situation where the shadow dataset is the **pre-train dataset's same distribution**, we opt for a random selection of images from the corresponding testing dataset associated with the pre-training dataset. Finally, for the situation where the shadow dataset is the **pre-train dataset's different distribution**, we randomly sample images from other datasets (e.g., STL10). The experimental results show that the accuracy for different downstream tasks is relatively similar under three situations. Thus, the attacker can utilize PtbStolen to effectively extract the functionality of the victim encoder even if he has no knowledge about the pre-train dataset.

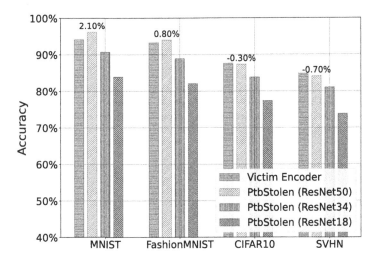

**Fig. 5.** The impact of the architecture of the surrogate encoder. The architecture of the victim encoder is ResNet34.

**Impact of Encoder Architecture.** Because the attacker has no knowledge about the architecture of the victim encoder, it can choose a more expressive architecture for the surrogate encoder. Figure 5 demonstrates the SAs when the surrogate encoder varies, and the victim encoder is based on ResNet34. The experiments demonstrate that PtbStolen is effective when the surrogate encoder's architecture varies. In such cases, the surrogate accuracy (SA) performs comparably or even better (e.g., +2.10% for MNIST) than the victim accuracy (VA). However, when the surrogate encoder (e.g., ResNet18) has lower expressive capability than the victim encoder (e.g., ResNet34), the corresponding surrogate accuracy (SA) exhibits inferior performance compared to the victim accuracy (VA).

**Impact of Similarity Function.** Regarding the impact of the similarity function, the experimental results are demonstrated in Fig. 6. Here, the victim encoder is pre-trained on CIFAR10. In this case, we discuss three commonly used functions: cosine similarity, $\ell_1$ distance, and $\ell_2$ distance. As can be seen, cosine similarity outperforms the other two functions. Moreover, $\ell_2$ distance is also superior to $\ell_1$ distance in terms of SAs.

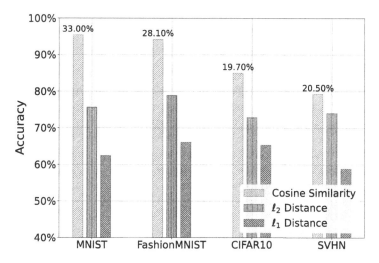

**Fig. 6.** The impact of the similarity function on SA of PtbStolen. The victim encoder is pre-trained on the CIFAR10 dataset.

## 5.3   Cost Analysis

In addition to performance, the cost of the PtbStolen is also worth noticing. Here, we compare the query budget and the corresponding SA for PtbStolen to the baselines mentioned before, as shown in Table 1. The victim encoder is pre-trained on CIFAR10, and the downstream tasks are performed on Fashion-MNIST and SVHN. Experimental results indicate that PtbStolen outperforms PtbStolen-nptb in terms of SA while requiring a significantly reduced query budget (100× fewer) compared to PtbStolen-hqb.

**Table 1.** Comparison of PtbStolen variants regarding SAs in different downstream tasks and query budgets.

| Method | SA (%) (FashionMNIST) | Query Budget (FashionMNIST) | SA (%) (SVHN) | Query Budget (SVHN) |
|---|---|---|---|---|
| PtbStolen-nptb | 82.14 | 5,250 | 72.31 | 5,250 |
| PtbStolen-hqb | 94.36 | 530,250 | 77.63 | 530,250 |
| **PtbStolen** | **95.41** | **5,250** | **79.34** | **5,250** |

## 6  Related Works

### 6.1  Contrastive Learning

With the growing demand for pre-training effective encoders, many works focusing on improving the contrastive algorithm have been proposed [4,5,10,11,21, 31]. Among them, SimCLR, MoCo, BYOL, and SimSiam are some mainstream paradigms widely adopted in real-world scenarios. Furthermore, as security and privacy concerns are also raised in self-supervised learning, many works have focused on the security of the pre-trained encoders. For instance, researchers have proposed that the encoders are threatened by membership inference attacks [12,17], backdoor attacks [9,13,25], and model stealing attacks [18,27]. As indicated, the pre-trained encoders face serious security and privacy threats, and the related topics need more attention and further research.

### 6.2  Model Stealing Attack

In 2016, Tramer et al. [28] initially introduced the model-stealing attack approach by employing API queries in a black-box manner. Since then, numerous efforts have been made to improve the model stealing attack in various aspects. For example, Wang et al. [30] introduced the first attack that focuses on stealing the hyperparameters, while Oh et al. [19] presented an enhanced version that can also support stealing the model architecture. For the functionality, the knockoff nets proposed by Orekondy et al. [22] first concentrated on stealing the victim model's functionality. When it comes to the recently popular pre-trained encoders, Liu et al. [18] introduced the StolenEncoder attack in their initial work, which aimed to replicate a pre-trained encoder's functionality through optimization. Meanwhile, a similar method is also discussed by Cong et al. [7]. To better utilize the relationship between feature vectors, Sha et al. [27] introduced the Cont-Steal attack, which showed superior performance compared to the previous encoder stealing attacks. However, these works all ignored the inner characteristics of the victim encoder (e.g., robustness), while we leverage such factors to improve further the performance of encoder stealing attacks with high efficiency.

# 7   Conclusion

In this paper, we demonstrate that an attacker can query a pre-trained encoder to steal its functionality. Specifically, this attack can be represented as an optimization problem aiming for minimization, with the solution itself serving as the surrogate encoder. Moreover, we found that leveraging perturbed samples can improve the stealing performance without additional budgets. The experimental outcomes illustrate the attacker's capacity to efficiently steal the functionality of a victim encoder, even when resources are constrained. This means the threat to the pre-trained image encoders is heavily ignored and underestimated. In addition, based on Ptbstolen's excellent performance in image encoder stealing attacks, further interesting directions can be put on how to exploit the inherent robustness of various data types (text, speech, etc.), which will extend the application of PtbStolen to more complex tasks (NLP, audio recognition, etc.). We hope our work could raise the awareness of developing more effective methods to defend against our proposed attack.

# References

1. Assran, M., et al.: Self-supervised learning from images with a joint-embedding predictive architecture. In: Proceedings of the IEEE/CVF Conference on Computer Vision and Pattern Recognition, pp. 15619–15629 (2023)
2. Baevski, A., Hsu, W.N., Xu, Q., Babu, A., Gu, J., Auli, M.: Data2vec: a general framework for self-supervised learning in speech, vision and language. In: International Conference on Machine Learning, pp. 1298–1312. PMLR (2022)
3. Bardes, A., Ponce, J., LeCun, Y.: VICRegl: self-supervised learning of local visual features. In: Advances in Neural Information Processing Systems 35, pp. 8799–8810 (2022)
4. Chen, T., Kornblith, S., Norouzi, M., Hinton, G.: A simple framework for contrastive learning of visual representations. In: International Conference on Machine Learning, pp. 1597–1607. PMLR (2020)
5. Chen, X., He, K.: Exploring simple Siamese representation learning. In: Proceedings of the IEEE/CVF Conference on Computer Vision and Pattern Recognition, pp. 15750–15758 (2021)
6. Coates, A., Ng, A., Lee, H.: An analysis of single-layer networks in unsupervised feature learning. In: Proceedings of the Fourteenth International Conference on Artificial Intelligence and Statistics, pp. 215–223. JMLR Workshop and Conference Proceedings (2011)
7. Cong, T., He, X., Zhang, Y.: SSLGuard: a watermarking scheme for self-supervised learning pre-trained encoders. In: Proceedings of the 2022 ACM SIGSAC Conference on Computer and Communications Security, pp. 579–593 (2022)
8. Fawzi, A., Moosavi-Dezfooli, S.M., Frossard, P.: The robustness of deep networks: a geometrical perspective. IEEE Signal Process. Mag. **34**(6), 50–62 (2017)
9. Feng, S., et al.: Detecting backdoors in pre-trained encoders. In: Proceedings of the IEEE/CVF Conference on Computer Vision and Pattern Recognition, pp. 16352–16362 (2023)
10. Grill, J.B., et al.: Bootstrap your own latent-a new approach to self-supervised learning. In: Advances in Neural Information Processing Systems 33, pp. 21271–21284 (2020)

11. He, K., Fan, H., Wu, Y., Xie, S., Girshick, R.: Momentum contrast for unsupervised visual representation learning. In: Proceedings of the IEEE/CVF Conference on Computer Vision and Pattern Recognition, pp. 9729–9738 (2020)

12. He, X., Zhang, Y.: Quantifying and mitigating privacy risks of contrastive learning. In: Proceedings of the 2021 ACM SIGSAC Conference on Computer and Communications Security, pp. 845–863 (2021)

13. Jia, J., Liu, Y., Gong, N.Z.: BadEncoder: backdoor attacks to pre-trained encoders in self-supervised learning. In: 2022 IEEE Symposium on Security and Privacy (SP), pp. 2043–2059. IEEE (2022)

14. Krizhevsky, A.: Learning multiple layers of features from tiny images. Master's thesis, University of Tront (2009)

15. LeCun, Y., Cortes, C., Burges, C., et al.: MNIST handwritten digit database (2010)

16. Lin, Z., Xu, K., Fang, C., Zheng, H., Ahmed Jaheezuddin, A., Shi, J.: QUDA: query-limited data-free model extraction. In: Proceedings of the 2023 ACM Asia Conference on Computer and Communications Security, pp. 913–924 (2023)

17. Liu, H., Jia, J., Qu, W., Gong, N.Z.: EncoderMI: membership inference against pre-trained encoders in contrastive learning. In: Proceedings of the 2021 ACM SIGSAC Conference on Computer and Communications Security, pp. 2081–2095 (2021)

18. Liu, Y., Jia, J., Liu, H., Gong, N.Z.: StolenEencoder: stealing pre-trained encoders in self-supervised learning. In: Proceedings of the 2022 ACM SIGSAC Conference on Computer and Communications Security, pp. 2115–2128 (2022)

19. Oh, S.J., Schiele, B., Fritz, M.: Towards reverse-engineering black-box neural networks. In: Samek, W., Montavon, G., Vedaldi, A., Hansen, L.K., Müller, K.-R. (eds.) Explainable AI: Interpreting, Explaining and Visualizing Deep Learning. LNCS (LNAI), vol. 11700, pp. 121–144. Springer, Cham (2019). https://doi.org/10.1007/978-3-030-28954-6_7

20. Oliynyk, D., Mayer, R., Rauber, A.: I know what you trained last summer: a survey on stealing machine learning models and defences. ACM Comput. Surv. **55**, 1–41 (2023)

21. Oord, A.v.d., Li, Y., Vinyals, O.: Representation learning with contrastive predictive coding. arXiv preprint arXiv:1807.03748 (2018)

22. Orekondy, T., Schiele, B., Fritz, M.: Knockoff nets: stealing functionality of black-box models. In: Proceedings of the IEEE/CVF Conference on Computer Vision and Pattern Recognition, pp. 4954–4963 (2019)

23. Peng, W., et al.: Are you copying my model? Protecting the copyright of large language models for EaaS via backdoor watermark. arXiv preprint arXiv:2305.10036 (2023)

24. Radford, A., et al.: Learning transferable visual models from natural language supervision. In: International Conference on Machine Learning, pp. 8748–8763. PMLR (2021)

25. Saha, A., Tejankar, A., Koohpayegani, S.A., Pirsiavash, H.: Backdoor attacks on self-supervised learning. In: Proceedings of the IEEE/CVF Conference on Computer Vision and Pattern Recognition, pp. 13337–13346 (2022)

26. Sanyal, S., Addepalli, S., Babu, R.V.: Towards data-free model stealing in a hard label setting. In: Proceedings of the IEEE/CVF Conference on Computer Vision and Pattern Recognition, pp. 15284–15293 (2022)

27. Sha, Z., He, X., Yu, N., Backes, M., Zhang, Y.: Can't steal? Cont-steal! Contrastive stealing attacks against image encoders. In: Proceedings of the IEEE/CVF Conference on Computer Vision and Pattern Recognition, pp. 16373–16383 (2023)

28. Tramèr, F., Zhang, F., Juels, A., Reiter, M.K., Ristenpart, T.: Stealing machine learning models via prediction APIs. In: 25th USENIX security symposium (USENIX Security 2016), pp. 601–618 (2016)
29. Truong, J.B., Maini, P., Walls, R.J., Papernot, N.: Data-free model extraction. In: Proceedings of the IEEE/CVF Conference on Computer Vision and Pattern Recognition, pp. 4771–4780 (2021)
30. Wang, B., Gong, N.Z.: Stealing hyperparameters in machine learning. In: 2018 IEEE Symposium on Security and Privacy (SP), pp. 36–52. IEEE (2018)
31. Wu, Z., Xiong, Y., Yu, S.X., Lin, D.: Unsupervised feature learning via non-parametric instance discrimination. In: Proceedings of the IEEE Conference on Computer Vision and Pattern Recognition, pp. 3733–3742 (2018)
32. Xiao, H., Rasul, K., Vollgraf, R.: Fashion-MNIST: a novel image dataset for benchmarking machine learning algorithms. arXiv preprint arXiv:1708.07747 (2017)
33. Yu, J., Yin, H., Xia, X., Chen, T., Li, J., Huang, Z.: Self-supervised learning for recommender systems: a survey. IEEE Trans. Knowl. Data Eng. **36**, 335–355 (2023)
34. Yuval, N.: Reading digits in natural images with unsupervised feature learning. In: Proceedings of the NIPS Workshop on Deep Learning and Unsupervised Feature Learning (2011)

# Towards Efficient Universal Adversarial Attack on Audio Classification Models: A Two-Step Method

Huifeng Li[1], Pengzhou Jia[2], Weixun Li[3], Bin Ma[3], Bo Li[4,5], Dexin Wu[6], and Haoran Li[6(✉)]

[1] State Grid Hebei Electric Power Research Institute, Shijiazhuang, Hebei, China
`dyy_lihf@he.sgcc.com.cn`
[2] State Grid Handan Electric Power Supply Company, Handan, Hebei, China
[3] State Grid Hebei Electric Power Co., Ltd., Shijiazhuang, Hebei, China
`{liwx,mab}@he.sgcc.com.cn`
[4] NARI Group Corporation (State Grid Electronic Power Research Institute),
Nanjing, China
`libo5@sgepri.sgcc.com.cn`
[5] Beijing Kedong Electric Power Control System Co., Ltd., Beijing, China
[6] Software College, Northeastern University, Shenyang, China
`lihaoran@stumail.neu.edu.cn`

**Abstract.** Audio classification models have witnessed remarkable progress in the past few years. As a counterpart, such models are also vulnerable to adversarial attacks by examples with indistinguishable perturbations that produce incorrect predictions. There are two types of perturbations, i.e., audio-dependent and audio-agnostic. Audio-dependent perturbations involve crafting perturbations for each clean example, while audio-agnostic attacks create a universal adversarial perturbation (UAP) that can fool the target model for almost all clean examples. However, the existing audio classification model-oriented attack methods still suffer from unideal efficiency. In this paper, we aim to bridge this gap. In order to achieve an efficient attack, we transformed the complex UAP generate problem into a superposition of two simple problems and proposed a two-step-based strategy. Specifically, in the first step, we generate audio-dependent (individual) perturbations for each target example. In the second phase, we aggregate the generated perturbations and fine-turn them into UAPs. By this strategy, we can optimize the desired UAPs at an ideal starting point, resulting in a remarkably efficient. Experiments show that the proposed method can generate UAP in 87.5% and 86.8% less time than similar methods for untargeted and targeted attacks while having a better SNR score.

**Keywords:** Universal Adversarial Perturbations · Adversarial Examples · Deep Neural Networks

© The Author(s), under exclusive license to Springer Nature Singapore Pte Ltd. 2024
J. Shao et al. (Eds.): EISA 2023, CCIS 2004, pp. 20–37, 2024.
https://doi.org/10.1007/978-981-99-9614-8_2

# 1  Introduction

Recent advances in Deep Neural Networks (DNNs) have enabled machines to achieve a superior performance in various tasks such as face recognition, dialog systems, recommend systems, drug discovery, etc. [10,14,29]. As an aspect of the exciting achievement, DNN-based audio classification models have also shown their fruitful performance and have been embedded into various audio-related applications [3,16,18,30,33] such as Siri, Google Assistant, and Alexa. Compared with traditional signal processing methods, these DNN-embedded applications are generally welcomed and widely used by users due to their advantages of high efficiency, high accuracy, and low time cost. Besides, these applications have also attracted considerable attention from the society and have been deployed in various real-world scenarios, e.g., Automated Driving Systems [28] and Smart Speakers [2].

As a counterpart, the lack of interpretability and robustness of DNNs makes them vulnerable to adversarial attacks [20,22], thus poses a great threat to the working conditions of the DNN-based real-world applications. Various pioneer works [6,13,31] have pointed out that the performance of a well-trained DNN can be significantly degraded by adversarial examples, which are carefully crafted inputs with a small magnitude of perturbations added. Most adversarial attack methods focus on making audio-dependent perturbations, that is, crafting perturbations individually for each target audio. Recently, the single audio-agnostic perturbation termed universal adversarial perturbation (UAP) has been proposed and received considerable attention [17,22,32]. In UAPs, the attacker only needs to optimize one fixed UAP in advance to add to each clean audio for performing a real-time attack [20]. The existence of UAPs reveals important geometric correlations among the high-dimensional decision boundary of DNNs. UAP generated for one model can adversely affect other unrelated models, exposing potential security breaches of DNNs. The emergence of UAPs further increases the vulnerability of DNNs deployed in the real world, and it is imperative to investigate UAPs.

There are already some pioneer works have been proposed based to generate UAPs on audio-related models. Most of them introduce a one-step strategy to build UAPs, which is not ideal to achieve efficient attacks. As shown in Fig. 1, we advocate that for each example, there is a corresponding adversarial space in which the adversarial examples are audio-dependent, and the very small intersection region of all adversarial spaces is the desired UAPs. Since UAPs are more difficult to craft than ordinary adversarial perturbations, this one-step strategy will take a considerable time to search for the optimized UAPs. The phenomenon is usually shown as an oscillating loss value in optimization.

In this paper, we propose UAP Efficient Attack (UAPEA), a novel framework to craft UAPs on audio classification models in an *efficient* manner. In UAPEA, unlike the existing methods that use one-step strategy to build UAPs, we model our attack as a two-phase optimization problem. In the first phase, we aim to build non-universal perturbations for each victim audio, which is not a difficult optimization process. In the second phase, we first normalize the generated non-

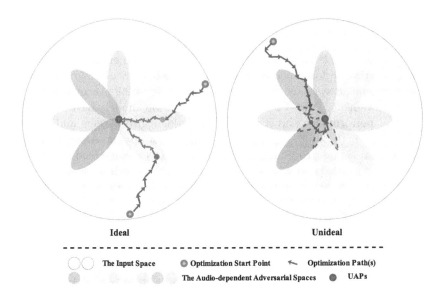

**Fig. 1.** The existing unideal method (shown as right) try to find the UAPs in the full input space directly, thus resulting in a *detoured and inefficient* optimization paths, since various local intersections (shown as red dotted lines) can interfere with the optimization process. In our ideal efficient approach (shown as left), we first generate audio-dependent perturbations for each example, followed by a novel normalization and fine-tuning strategy to avoid local intersections. (Color figure online)

universal perturbations and produce an ideal initial point, then we fine-tune these initial perturbations to craft UAPs.

We summarize our main contributions as follows:

- We propose an efficient optimization method to construct UAPs in an efficient manner, called UAPEA. Notably, the proposed UAPEA can be deployed in both the targeted and non-targeted attack settings.
- In order to achieve an efficient attack process, unlike existing approaches that model the attack process as a difficult optimization problem, we transform the process into two easy optimization problems. We first generate audio-dependent perturbations for each example, then normalize and fine-tune the perturbations to UAPs.
- Experiments show that the proposed method can generate UAP in 87.5% and 86.8% less time than similar methods for untargeted attack and targeted attack while having a better unnoticeability.

The rest of this paper is organized as follows. We first review related work and algorithms on UAP in Sect. 2. Section 3 details the proposed UAPEA. Experiments results of attacking audio classifiers are reported in Sect. 4, followed by the conclusions in Sect. 5.

## 2   Related Works

In this section, we revisit the existing input-dependent adversarial attacks and universal adversarial attacks.

### 2.1   Input-Dependent Adversarial Attacks

The input-dependent adversarial attack was first introduced on image-related models [31], which has demonstrated that the performance of a well-trained DNN can be significantly weakened by adversarial examples, which can be crafted by adding the human-imperceptible perturbation on the original input. After that, various gradient-based adversarial attack methods in the field of image classification were proposed, such as FGSM [11], PGD [19] and MIM [9]. C&W attack [5] is an iterative algorithm, which introduced new forms of loss function under $\ell_0$, $\ell_2$ and $\ell_\infty$ norms-based metrics respectively for generating small magnitude of perturbation by encoding the domain constraint as a change of variable.

On audio-related models, Carlini et al. [6] proposed the first targeted attack method on the automatic speech recognition model DeepSpeech [13], in which an iterative approach is deployed to generate threatening adversarial examples on a white-box setting. Carlini et al. [6] are confirming for the first time to prove the feasibility and existence of the adversarial attacks on audio data. Thereafter, Alzantot et al. [24] proposed a genetic algorithm-based method to generate audio adversarial examples that would not change the listener's perception of the audio segment. Taori et al. [23] built on this research by using an optimized and dynamic mutation mechanism-embedded genetic algorithm fused with gradient evaluation to transform the clean audio into specified target phrases. In [23], the attacker arbitrarily selected 100 public speech audio samples from a public speech dataset for experiments, the success rate of the generated target adversarial examples was 35%. In 2019, Du et al. [25] proposed a particle swarm optimization-based target and non-target audio adversarial attack method, and the effectiveness is verified in a series of application scenarios, e.g., speech recognition, speaker recognition, and music genre classification. The attack success rate of this method can reach 99.45%, and this method is effective in both black-box and white-box end-to-end acoustic systems. In 2019, Abdoli [4] et al. implemented a generalized audio adversarial attack method based on the greedy iteration algorithm and the penalty algorithm, and the success rates under the targeted and untargeted attacks is 85% and 83.1%, respectively. However, this method can only be applied to audio classifiers under white-box settings.

### 2.2   Universal Adversarial Attacks

Universal Adversarial Attacks has been extensively studied in image-related tasks, yet rarely in audio. The existence of image-agnostic perturbations, also known as universal adversarial perturbations (UAPs), which is a fixed perturbations that can be added directly to various clean images, resulting in incorrect results when these victim images have been fed into the target model.

UAP was first introduced by Moosavi-Dezfooli et al. [20], in which they proposed an algorithm based on the image-dependent DeepFool attack [21]. The core idea is to calculate the minimum perturbation from each example to the decision boundary and iteratively accumulate these perturbations to find a universal perturbation. To solve the negative influence brought by the minimum perturbation, Dai et al. [8] choose the perturbation whose orientation is similar to that of the current universal perturbation to maximize the magnitude of the aggregation of both the perturbations. However, these methods are cumbersome and lead to an ineffective and iterative process. Thereafter, Generative adversarial perturbations (GAP) [26] utilized generative adversarial networks (GANs) to provide a unifying framework for generating image-agnostic perturbations and image-dependent perturbations for image classification tasks and semantic segmentation tasks. GAP was the first to propose the targeted universal perturbations on the ImageNet dataset.

This paper aims to present a universal and efficient audio adversarial example design, which results in a comparable or even advanced performance as previous methods in both targeted & non-targeted attack settings.

## 3   The Proposed Method

This section presents a detailed account of the proposed UAPEA to craft UAPs for conducting non-targeted and targeted attacks in an efficient and unnoticeable manner.

### 3.1   Preliminaries

To be clear, before detailing our method, we first briefly introduce the notation of our goal, which is to misclassify the clean examples as many as possible by adding a universal noise on target examples.

Mathematically, let $\mathcal{X}$ to be the set of target examples, our objective can be expressed as follows:

$$\arg\max_{\delta} \sum_{x \in \mathcal{X}} \mathbb{I}(f(x + \delta) \neq y_x), \tag{1}$$

where $\delta$ is the desired UAP, which can fool target audio classifier $f(\cdot)$ when added to the target example $x \in \mathcal{X}$. $f(x)$ is the predict of $x$, and $y_x$ is the ground-truth label of $x$. Note that we assume $f(x) = y_x$.

For a straightforward illustration, we denote the adversarial example $x + \delta$ as $x'$.

The attacker expects the adversarial perturbation used in the attack to have as little effect as possible on the audio, thus the magnitude of the perturbations should be considered. Specifically, in this paper, we use $\ell_2$ norm to measure the difference between the clean example and the adversarial example to not only control the magnitude of the generated perturbations but also reduce the possibility of the adversarial perturbation to be detected by the human ear in the time domain, and to improve the signal-to-noise ratio (SNR) score of the adversarial examples.

The $\ell_2$ norm characterizes the Euclidean distance between $x$ and $x'$ via measures of the total difference between all data points in the audio. Intuitively, a very small perturbation of each data point will also keep the Euclidean distance small. The computation of the $\ell_2$ norm is:

$$||x - x'||_2 = (\sum_{i=0}^{n} |x_i - x_i'|^2)^{\frac{1}{2}}. \tag{2}$$

Hence, the remaining issue to us is to optimize $\delta$ based on our two-step strategy, which is introduced in the next subsection.

## 3.2 Craft Individual Perturbations

As we mentioned, in the proposed method, we first craft input-dependent perturbations for each example $x \in \mathcal{X}$.

In the target attack, the attacker expects that the classification result of the classifier can be output according to the specified label $y_{tar}$ on the basis of the classification error. In this paper, by introducing the cross entropy as the loss term of the model, it is possible to evaluate the gap between the model classification result $f(x_i')$ and the target result $y_{tar}$:

$$\mathcal{L}_{CE} = CE(f(x_i'), t), \tag{3}$$

where $CE(\cdot)$ denote the cross-entropy loss. For the untargeted attack, the above loss function can be modified as:

$$\mathcal{L}_{CE} = -CE(f(x_i'), y_i). \tag{4}$$

The complete loss can be described as:

$$\mathcal{L}_{TOTAL} = \alpha \mathcal{L}_{CE} + \mathcal{L}_{LIM}, \tag{5}$$

where $\alpha$ is a hyper-parameter. A higher $\alpha$ would make the starting point of the iterative process more focused on increasing the attack success rate than on the size of the perturbation. We define $\mathcal{L}_{LIM} := ||\delta||_2$.

For the $\lambda$-th iteration, the optimize process of the desired $\delta$ can be described by:

$$\delta_{\lambda+1} = \delta_\lambda + \eta \nabla \frac{\partial \mathcal{L}_{TOTAL}}{\partial \delta_\lambda}, \tag{6}$$

where $\eta$ is the learning rate.

In the process of iterative optimization, for each input original audio sample, we first initialize a random noise that has the same length as this sample. In each iteration (epoch) of optimization, we greedily adjust the coefficients of the loss function based on the results of the previous epoch to speed up the iteration and then stop iterating when the attack succeeds to save the adversarial sample. The first phase of the proposed UAPEA can be described by the Algorithm 1.

---

**Algorithm 1:** UAPEA (first-phase)

---

**Input:** target model $f(\cdot)$, clean example $x$, ground-truth label $y_x$, target label
$y_{tar}$, iterations $\tau$, learning rate $\eta$, hyper-parameters $\alpha$

**Output:** the adversarial example $x'$

1 Let $\lambda = 1$
2 Randomly initialize the desired perturbation $\delta$
3 **while** $\lambda \leq \tau$ **do**
4 | let $x_\lambda = x + \delta$
5 | feed $x_\lambda$ into the target model to get logits $f(x_\lambda)$
6 | execute FFT on $x_\lambda$ and $x$, then get $x_{ij}^s$ and ${x_{ij}^s}'$
7 | compute $\mathcal{L}_{CE}, \mathcal{L}_{LIM}$
8 | compute $\mathcal{L}_{TOTAL}$
9 | update $\delta$ via Eq. 6
10 | $\lambda$ ++

11 **return** $\delta$

---

### 3.3    Fine-Turn Universal Perturbations

As for now, we have crafted multiple $\delta_x$ for each example $x \in \mathcal{X}$. Hence, the remaining issue to us is to fine-turn these individual $\delta_x$ to UAPs. We denote the desired UAP as $\delta_U$ for a simple illustration.

There are two optional normalization methods to initialize the UAP. The first method is the spherical paradigm constraint normalization. This normalization method is often employed by UAP generation methods [1]. Specifically, this method maps the UAP to a high-dimensional spherical space after each update. The process can be expressed as follows:

$$\delta^u = \sum_x^{\mathcal{X}} \delta_x * min(1, \frac{r}{||\sum_x \delta_x||_2}), \tag{7}$$

where $r$ is a hyper-parameter that indicts the constraint radius, and $r$ is fixed as 10 in this paper. Another normalization method is to directly average the generated perturbations:

$$\delta^u = \frac{\sum_x^{\mathcal{X}} \delta_x}{|\mathcal{X}|} \tag{8}$$

In Eq. 7, $\delta^u$ is normalized by recalculating the individual values with reference to the size of its overall $\ell_2$ norm. However, when data samples of varying lengths are sliced and diced to attack $\delta^u$, this normalization method can potentially over-normalize values that are seldom added to the original audio. Therefore, our normalization method should consider the weight of audio length on the original values. In Eq. 8, the normalizing process based on the total number of samples enables $\delta^u$ to be normalized to a reasonable range while preserving the original weights. The comparison results of the two normalization methods is provided in the next section.

Recall that in the first phase, we have crafted a series of individual perturbations $\delta_x$ for each target example $x \in \mathcal{X}$. Intuitively, through these perturbations has been fused in above, we devote the fused initial $\delta^u$ is a ideal start point to construct the UAP. Following this intuition, we fine-turn the $\delta^u$ to UAP in a straightforward manner. Different from the first phase, in order to make the generated perturbation universal, the loss function of multiple examples needs to be considered. Thus, the loss function needs to support batch computation. Regarding this, a batch loss function based on the MSS is developed in this paper, which can characterize the overall effect of the perturbation under multiple examples.

The proposed batch loss that be used to fine-tune the $\delta^u$ can be expressed as follows:

$$\mathcal{L}_{BATCH} = \frac{1}{|\mathcal{X}|} \sum_{x \in \mathcal{X}} \mathcal{L}_{TOTAL}(x + \delta^u). \tag{9}$$

That is, we add $\delta^u$ to each target example $x \in \mathcal{X}$, and minimize $\mathcal{L}_{BATCH}$ as follows:

$$\delta^u_{\lambda+1} = \delta^u_\lambda + \eta \nabla \frac{\partial \mathcal{L}_{BATCH}}{\partial \delta^u_\lambda}, \tag{10}$$

which the optimization process is similar to the first phase.

With these steps above, we can generate universal adversarial perturbations with strong attack capability.

# 4   Experiments

In this section, relevant experiments are conducted to evaluate the performance of the proposed UAPEA method in terms of untargeted attacks and targeted attacks.

## 4.1   Settings

**Dataset.** The experimental dataset uses a subset of the Task 2 dataset of the DCASE 2019 competition[1], i.e., 799 mono samples out of 4,970 samples, labeled with a total of 12 types: accordion, acoustic guitar, bass drum, bass guitar, electric guitar, female singing, glockenspiel, gong, harmonica, hi-hat, male singing, and marimba and xylophone. The divide of the dataset is provided by [27].

**Target Model.** In order to get an unhacked attack performance, the same target model in [27] is adopted in our experiments, in which the model uses 16kHz audio samples as input. For the mono audio classification, the target classification model uses $5 \times 5$ and $3 \times 3$ convolutional and ReLU activation layers along with batch normalization and average pooling layers. The convolutional layer stride determines the padding value, and a drop-out operation is added to

---

[1] https://dcase.community/challenge2019/task-audio-tagging-results.

reduce model overfitting. The final layer contains a $1 \times 1$ convolutional kernel and a global pooling layer that performs average pooling in frequency and maximum pooling in timing. The unhacked classification accuracy of this target model reaches 93.2%.

**Metrics.** In the untargeted attack, the adversarial sample containing the adversarial perturbation is fed into the target classification model, and if the model misclassifies this sample as any label other than the true label, it is considered as the success of the untargeted attack.

The definition of attack success rate (ASR) under untargeted attack can be obtained as:

$$ASR_{nt} = \frac{\sum_{x \in \mathcal{X}} \mathbb{I}(f(x) \neq y_i)}{|\mathcal{X}|}, \tag{11}$$

where $y_i$ is the ground-truth label of $x_i$ and $f(\cdot)$ is the target audio classification model. $\mathbb{I}$ is the indicator function, $\mathbb{I}(z) = 1$ if $z$ is true, 0 for otherwise.

In the targeted attack, for different input examples, if the target label is $y_{tar}$ (and $y_i \neq t_i$), then the targeted attack is successful when the target model classifies this sample as target label $y_{tar}$. At this time, the attack success rate can be calculated as:

$$ASR_t = \frac{\sum_{x \in \mathcal{X}} \mathbb{I}(f(x_i) = y_{tar})}{|\mathcal{X}|}. \tag{12}$$

To evaluate the efficiency of the proposed method, we introduce the Average Generation Time (AGT) as a metric since the faster generation method is more suitable to be used in practical application scenarios under the same attack success rate. In this paper, the average generation time of the adversarial examples in the whole dataset is obtained from the number of the generated adversarial examples $N$ and the overall generation time $T$. It can be calculated as:

$$AGT = \frac{N}{T}. \tag{13}$$

For a comprehensive evaluation, we introduce signal-to-noise ratio (SNR) as another important metric, which characterizes the power of the of the clean audio and the adversarial audio. A higher SNR indicates that the perturbation has less effect on the original audio sample, so it is harder to detect by the human ear. The SNR can be obtained as follows:

$$SNR = 20 * log(\frac{1}{N} \sum_{n}^{N} v_n^2)^{\frac{1}{2}}, \tag{14}$$

where $v_n$ denote a signal with length $N$. In our experiments, we mainly use the Avg. SNR and peak SNR (PSNR) to measure the quality of the adversarial examples, which can be calculated by referring to [7,15].

**Baselines.** In this setting, our baselines is FGSM [20], PGD [15], C&W [5], and Multi-Scale C&W [12] four attack methods.

- FGSM is one of the simplest and most well-known techniques for generating adversarial examples. FGSM achieves its attack by determining the direction in which the input data should be perturbed to increase the loss and cause a misclassification. The sign of the gradient determines this direction.
- PGD is an iterative attack method. The general idea is that FGSM is to do just one iteration with one big step, while PGD is to do multiple iterations with one small step each time, and each iteration clips the perturbation to a specified range.
- C&W and Multi-Scale C&W is a powerful attack method that reaches the attack by bringing the adversarial examples closer to the decision boundary of the target model.

Note that the vanilla version of these baseline methods are not suitable for generating UAPs, thus we refactored their implementations as follows:

$$\mathcal{L}_{UAP} = \sum_{x \in \mathcal{X}} \mathcal{L}_{ori}, \tag{15}$$

where $\mathcal{L}_{ori}$ denote the original loss that the baseline methods involved.

## 4.2   Quantitative Evaluation on Untargeted Attack

In the untargeted attack, the goal of the attacker is to have the classifier misclassify the input samples as arbitrary labels other than the true label.

The hyper-parameters are shown in Table 1, where the FGSM and PGD methods only have values $\epsilon$ and the other methods only have values $\alpha$.

**Table 1.** Hyper-parameters Settings

| Attack Method | $\alpha$ | $\epsilon$ | $\eta$ | $\tau$ |
|---|---|---|---|---|
| FGSM | – | 0.1 | – | 50 |
| PGD | – | 0.0005 | 0.00001 | 50 |
| C&W | 0.1 | – | 0.0001 | 50 |
| Multi-Scale C&W | 15 | – | 0.00005 | 500 |
| UAPEA | 10 | – | 0.0001 | 50 |

The results are shown in Fig. 2. For a comprehensive description, we also evaluated the quality of the adversarial examples generated by these methods as well as their generation efficiency. The results are shown in Table 2.

Form Fig. 2 and Table 2 we can get the following observations:

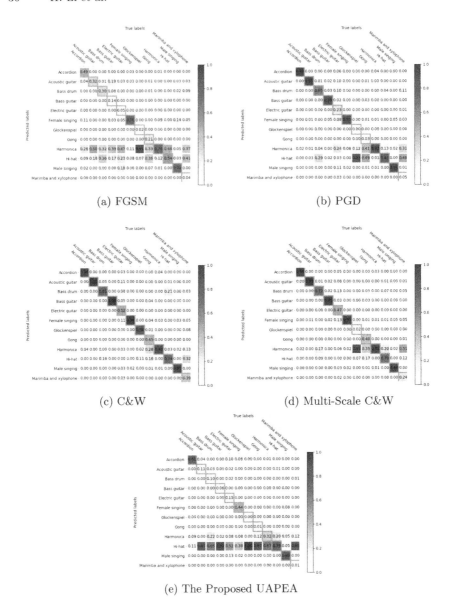

(a) FGSM

(b) PGD

(c) C&W

(d) Multi-Scale C&W

(e) The Proposed UAPEA

**Fig. 2.** The attack performance of the proposed UAPEA and baselines in the *untargeted* attack settings. The diagonal portion (orange frame) indicates the classified accuracy of the generated adversarial examples. The lighter the color and the smaller the value in the orange frame indicates better performance. (Color figure online)

**Table 2.** The attack performance of the proposed UAPEA and baselines. For ASR, Avg. SNR and PSNR, higher is better. For AGT, lower is better. For a straightforward illustration, we summarized these metrics by mix them together, denoted as Total, calculated as $ASR + Avg.SNR + PSNR - AGT$.

| Attack Method | $ASR_{nt}$ (%) | Avg. SNR (dB) | PSNR (dB) | AGT (s) | Total |
|---|---|---|---|---|---|
| FGSM | 63.58 | −5.52 | 22.42 | 0.22 | 80.26 |
| PGD | 37.80 | 9.76 | 40.06 | 3.27 | 84.35 |
| C&W | 18.39 | −11.25 | 25.83 | 2.70 | 30.27 |
| Multi-Scale C&W | 29.29 | −9.69 | 25.88 | 15.66 | 29.82 |
| UAPEA | 80.35 | 7.64 | 31.72 | 1.95 | **117.76** |

- The methods with the higher in attack success rate are FGSM, UAPEA. The FGSM method maintains the fastest average generation time of 0.22 s while improving the average SNR and PSNR to −5.52 dB and 22.42 dB, respectively.
- In addition, the proposed UAPEA method achieves the generalized attack effect, which are significantly higher than Multi-Scale C&W, and the average generation time of 1.91 s is kept within 2 s as well as UAPEA. Therefore, UAPEA has the highest attack success rate, the SNR performance is second only to PGD, and the generation speed is second only to FGSM.
- UAPEA has the best overall performance among the generalized adversarial perturbation generation methods under no-target attack.

### 4.3   Quantitative Evaluation on Targeted Attack

In the targeted attack, the goal of the attacker is to have the classifier misclassify the input samples to some manually defined target label. Note that since FGSM and PGD cannot be applied to the target attack, thus in this section, the UAPEA method is compared with C&W and Multi-Scale C&W only, and the parameters are shown in Table 3. The parameters of the two Multi-Scale C&W methods in Table 3 are the hyper-parameters from the literature [15] and the hyper-parameters that are adjusted to significantly improve the average generation time AGT. Note that we set the target label to be *accordion*.

Since the FGSM and PGD methods have some limitations in the target attack environment, in this section, we compare C&W, Multi-Scale C&W, and UAPEA methods in the experimental context of target attack. In order to better compare the advantages and disadvantages of the three methods, the same optimization process as that of UAPEA, (i.e., Stage 2: Optimization under multi-sample by adding a batch loss function on top of the UAP obtained from the first traversal) is added to the C&W and Multi-Scale C&W methods in the target attack in this section. The batch loss functions for the three methods under target attack are C&W, Multi-Scale C&W, and the loss function for the UAPEA method takes the mean value as the loss value. Among them, the normalization method for UAPEA is Eq. 7 and the remaining two methods use Eq. 8.

**Table 3.** Hyper-parameters Settings

| Attack Method | $\alpha$ | $\eta$ | $\tau$ |
|---|---|---|---|
| C&W | – | 0.0001 | 50 |
| Multi-Scale C&W | 15 | 0.00005 | 500 |
| Multi-Scale C&W (Adjust) | 10 | 0.0001 | 50 |
| UAPEA | 10 | 0.0001 | 50 |

**Table 4.** The attack performance of the proposed UAPEA and baselines. For ASR, Avg. SNR and PSNR, higher is better. For AGT, lower is better. For a straightforward illustration, we summarized these metrics by mix them together, denoted as Total, calculated as $ASR + Avg.SNR + PSNR - AGT$.

| Attack Method | $ASR_t$ (%) | Avg. SNR (dB) | PSNR (dB) | AGT (s) | Total |
|---|---|---|---|---|---|
| C&W | 25.28 | 1.65 | 28.27 | 3.39 | 51.81 |
| Multi-Scale C&W | 54.94 | −2.23 | 25.90 | 16.80 | 61.81 |
| Multi-Scale C&W (Adjust) | 91.24 | −0.75 | 25.18 | 3.81 | 111.86 |
| UAPEA | 88.74 | 8.10 | 34.44 | 2.21 | **129.07** |

The results are shown in Fig. 3 and Table 4, from which we can see that UAPEA method still maintains a high attack success rate of 88.74% in the context of target attack, and the average generation time of 2.21 s is also better than other methods.

### 4.4    Attack with Different Normalization Methods

In the target attack experiments, the methods have different normalization methods in addition to their respective loss functions, in order to explore the difference between the two normalization methods, this section conducts an experimental study on the performance changes of the three methods under target attack using different normalization methods (Table 5).

**Table 5.** Hyper-parameters Settings

| Attack Method | Normalization | $\alpha$ | $\epsilon$ | $\eta$ | $\tau$ |
|---|---|---|---|---|---|
| C&W | Eq. 7 | – | 0.1 | 0.0001 | 50 |
| C&W | Eq. 8 | – | 0.1 | 0.001 | 50 |
| Multi-Scale C&W | Eq. 7 | 15 | – | 0.00005 | 500 |
| Multi-Scale C&W | Eq. 8 | 15 | – | 0.00005 | 500 |
| UAPEA | Eq. 7 | 10 | – | 0.001 | 50 |
| UAPEA | Eq. 8 | 10 | – | 0.001 | 50 |

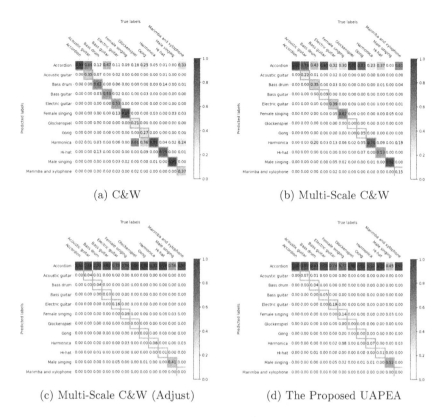

(a) C&W

(b) Multi-Scale C&W

(c) Multi-Scale C&W (Adjust)

(d) The Proposed UAPEA

**Fig. 3.** The attack performance of the proposed UAPEA and baselines in the *targeted* attack settings. The diagonal portion (orange frame) indicates the classify accuracy of the generated adversarial examples. The lighter the color and the smaller the value in the orange frame the better performance. (Color figure online)

From Table 6 and Fig. 4, we can clearly seen that, with the same loss function in each case, the attack methods normalized by Eq. 7 have different degrees of improvement in the Avg. SNR, with the three methods improving by 18.98 dB, 14.84 dB, and 8.57 dB, respectively. However, in terms of the ASR and the AGT, the use of the Eq. 8 normalization method leads to the latter two methods having different degrees of decrease, in which the ASR of the two methods decreases from 54.94% to 47.56 dB and from 92.74% to 88.74%, respectively, and the AGT improves by 0.14 s and 0.07 s, respectively.

In addition, C&W method in Table 6 shows an improvement in all four metrics after adopting the Eq. 8 normalization, with an increase in attack success rate by 21.78 dB, Avg. SNR by 18.98 dB, PSNR by 21.26 dB, and the average generation time decrease by 0.12 s. Considering that the normalization method using the Eq. 8 results in a very low SNR for the adversarial examples, which are 1.65 dB, −2.23 dB, and −0.47 dB, thus the best attack method across experiments is UAPEA and Eq. 8.

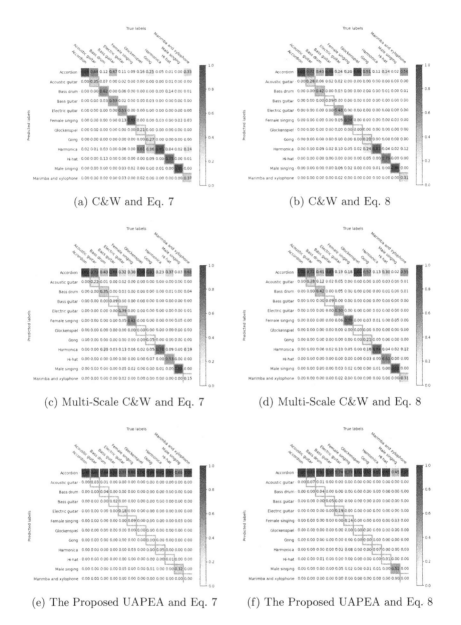

(a) C&W and Eq. 7

(b) C&W and Eq. 8

(c) Multi-Scale C&W and Eq. 7

(d) Multi-Scale C&W and Eq. 8

(e) The Proposed UAPEA and Eq. 7

(f) The Proposed UAPEA and Eq. 8

**Fig. 4.** The attack performance of the proposed UAPEA and baselines with different normalization method.

**Table 6.** The attack performance of the proposed UAPEA and baselines with different Normalization Methods.

| Attack Method | Normalization | $ASR_t$ (%) | Avg. SNR (dB) | PSNR (dB) | AGT (s) | Total |
|---|---|---|---|---|---|---|
| C&W | Eq. 7 | 25.28 | 1.65 | 28.27 | 3.39 | 51.81 |
| C&W | Eq. 8 | 47.06 | 20.63 | 49.53 | 3.27 | 113.95 |
| Multi-Scale C&W | Eq. 7 | 54.94 | −2.23 | 25.9 | 16.8 | 61.81 |
| Multi-Scale C&W | Eq. 8 | 47.56 | 12.64 | 41.02 | 16.94 | 84.28 |
| UAPEA | Eq. 7 | 92.74 | −0.47 | 26.25 | 3.52 | **115.00** |
| UAPEA | Eq. 8 | 88.74 | 8.1 | 34.44 | 3.59 | **127.69** |

## 5    Conclusions

In this paper, a method of generating UAPs called UAPEA is designed and described in detail, including the detailed steps of generating the generalized adversarial samples, the designed loss function, and the normalization method. In the experimental part, we compares UAPEA with a variety of attack methods of the same type, and the effect in the untargeted attack, target attack, and so on is experimentally verified. The adversarial examples are analyzed in the time and frequency domains, respectively, to verify the effect of the UAPEA method as well as the normalization method in the audio attack.

**Acknowledgments.** This work was supported in part by the National Natural Science Foundation of China under Grant Nos. 62372069 and 62173101, in part by the Fundamental Research Funds for the Central Universities under Grant N2017012.

## References

1. Abdoli, S., Hafemann, L.G., Rony, J., Ayed, I.B., Cardinal, P., Koerich, A.L.: Universal adversarial audio perturbations. arXiv abs/1908.03173 (2019)
2. Alom, M.Z., Aspiras, T.H., Taha, T.M., Asari, V.K.: Skin cancer segmentation and classification with NABLA-N and inception recurrent residual convolutional networks. arXiv abs/1904.11126 (2019)
3. Antón, S.D., Kanoor, S., Fraunholz, D., Schotten, H.D.: Evaluation of machine learning-based anomaly detection algorithms on an industrial Modbus/TCP data set. In: ARES (2018)
4. Brown, T.B., Mané, D., Roy, A., Abadi, M., Gilmer, J.: Adversarial patch. arXiv abs/1712.09665 (2017)
5. Carlini, N., Wagner, D.A.: Towards evaluating the robustness of neural networks. In: 2017 IEEE S&P (2017)
6. Carlini, N., Wagner, D.A.: Audio adversarial examples: targeted attacks on speech-to-text. In: IEEE S&P (2018)
7. Chen, G., et al.: Towards understanding and mitigating audio adversarial examples for speaker recognition. IEEE Trans. Dependable Secure Comput. **20**(5), 3970–3987 (2023)

8. Dai, J., Shu, L.: Fast-UAP: an algorithm for expediting universal adversarial perturbation generation using the orientations of perturbation vectors. Neurocomputing **422**, 109–117 (2021)
9. Dong, Y., et al.: Boosting adversarial attacks with momentum. In: IEEE/CVF Conference on Computer Vision and Pattern Recognition (2018)
10. Durand, T., Mehrasa, N., Mori, G.: Learning a deep convnet for multi-label classification with partial labels. In: CVPR (2019)
11. Goodfellow, I.J., Shlens, J., Szegedy, C.: Explaining and harnessing adversarial examples. In: ICLR (2015)
12. Grosse, K., Trost, T.A., Mosbach, M., Backes, M., Klakow, D.: Adversarial initialization - when your network performs the way I want. arXiv abs/1902.03020 (2019)
13. Hannun, A.Y., et al.: Deep speech: scaling up end-to-end speech recognition. arXiv (2014)
14. He, K., Zhang, X., Ren, S., Sun, J.: Identity mappings in deep residual networks. In: Leibe, B., Matas, J., Sebe, N., Welling, M. (eds.) ECCV 2016. LNCS, vol. 9908, pp. 630–645. Springer, Cham (2016). https://doi.org/10.1007/978-3-319-46493-0_38
15. Koerich, K.M., Esmailpour, M., Abdoli, S., de S. Britto, Jr., A., Koerich, A.L.: Cross-representation transferability of adversarial attacks: From spectrograms to audio waveforms. In: IJCNN (2020)
16. Krizhevsky, A., Sutskever, I., Hinton, G.E.: ImageNet classification with deep convolutional neural networks. In: NIPS (2012)
17. Li, Z., Wu, Y., Liu, J., Chen, Y., Yuan, B.: AdvPulse: universal, synchronization-free, and targeted audio adversarial attacks via subsecond perturbations. In: CCS (2020)
18. Liu, S., Liu, S., Cai, W., Pujol, S., Kikinis, R., Feng, D.: Early diagnosis of Alzheimer's disease with deep learning. In: ISBI (2014)
19. Madry, A., Makelov, A., Schmidt, L., Tsipras, D., Vladu, A.: Towards deep learning models resistant to adversarial attacks. In: ICLR (2017)
20. Moosavi-Dezfooli, S.M., Fawzi, A., Fawzi, O., Frossard, P.: Universal adversarial perturbations. In: CVPR (2017)
21. Moosavi-Dezfooli, S., Fawzi, A., Frossard, P.: DeepFool: a simple and accurate method to fool deep neural networks. In: CVPR (2016)
22. Neekhara, P., Hussain, S., Pandey, P., Dubnov, S., McAuley, J., Koushanfar, F.: Universal adversarial perturbations for speech recognition systems. In: INTERSPEECH (2019)
23. van den Oord, A., et al.: WaveNet: a generative model for raw audio. In: ISCA (2016)
24. van den Oord, A., et al.: Parallel wavenet: fast high-fidelity speech synthesis. In: ICML (2018)
25. Papernot, N., McDaniel, P.D., Jha, S., Fredrikson, M., Celik, Z.B., Swami, A.: The limitations of deep learning in adversarial settings. In: IEEE EuroS&P (2016)
26. Poursaeed, O., Katsman, I., Gao, B., Belongie, S.J.: Generative adversarial perturbations. In: CVPR (2018)
27. Prinz, K., Flexer, A.: End-to-end adversarial white box attacks on music instrument classification. arXiv abs/2007.14714 (2020)
28. Ren, P., Dong, Y., Lin, S., Tong, X., Guo, B.: Image based relighting using neural networks. ACM Trans. Graph. **34**(4), 111:1–111:12 (2015)
29. Ren, P., Wang, J., Gong, M., Lin, S., Tong, X., Guo, B.: Global illumination with radiance regression functions. ACM Trans. Graph. **32**(4), 130:1–130:12 (2013). https://doi.org/10.1145/2461912.2462009

30. Simonyan, K., Zisserman, A.: Very deep convolutional networks for large-scale image recognition. In: ICLR (2015)
31. Szegedy, C., et al.: Intriguing properties of neural networks. In: ICLR (2014)
32. Vadillo, J., Santana, R.: Universal adversarial examples in speech command classification. arXiv abs/1911.10182 (2019)
33. Yan, W., Yu, L.: On accurate and reliable anomaly detection for gas turbine combustors: a deep learning approach. arXiv (2019)

# Privacy-Preserving Authenticated Federated Learning Scheme for Smart Healthcare System

Jun Tu and Gang Shen[✉]

School of Computer Science, Hubei University of Technology, Wuhan 430068, China
shengang@hbut.edu.cn

**Abstract.** With the rapid advancement of artificial intelligence and network technology, smart healthcare system provides patients with satisfactory medical experience and clinical diagnosis, thus alleviating the imbalance between limited medical resources and a large patient population. However, the patient privacy security in smart healthcare system is still facing severe challenges. Additionally, due to the signal interruption in the federated learning mechanism, the model parameters can not be transmitted normally between local user and central server. In response to these issues, we propose a privacy-preserving authenticated federated learning scheme for smart healthcare system. Specifically, there is a hybrid federated learning framework composed of peer-to-peer and server-client architecture in the proposed scheme. In the proposed scheme, data owners can interact directly with each other for federated training to overcome the data silos issue. In addition, we leverage a homomorphic cryptosystem and the Schnorr signature algorithm to ensure the security and integrity of local model parameters. Security analysis and experimental results show that the proposed scheme can not only protect the sensitive information of data owners, but also has high efficiency.

**Keywords:** Privacy preservation · Federated learning · Smart healthcare system · Authentication · Homomorphic encryption

## 1 Introduction

Online medical health diagnostic in the smart healthcare system can offer patients a positive healthcare experience and aid in clinical decision-making, effectively addressing the disparity between the scarcity of healthcare resources and the high patient volume. The training data for online healthcare diagnosis systems is frequently derived from large datasets provided by various medical institutions (MIs). These datasets may contain confidential patient information such as names, ages, genders, locations, and vaccination records. However, the extensive acquisition of data may raise privacy concerns among MIs.

Federated learning [1,2], an emerging distributed machine learning paradigm, can protect data security and overcome data silos. In conventional machine learning, the architecture of centralised processing of user data not only imposes a significant computational load on the central server, but also entails a high risk of data leakage. In federated learning, the client trains and uploads the gradient locally, which can prevent the leakage of local data set and alleviate the burden on the central server [26,27]. Nonetheless, as a result of the development of new technologies, federated learning has uncovered a number of additional concerns. For example, federated learning is unable to offer privacy protection against some attacks such as reconstruction attacks [3,4], inference attacks [5,6], and free-riding attacks [7,8]. Furthermore, large-scale iterations in federated learning can result in an excess of communication. During the iteration process, adversaries may obtain uploaded data and recover sensitive data using the acquired information [9,10]. As the complexity of real-world application scenarios increases, only one single federated learning framework may be insufficient to meet the demands. To guarantee user rights and privacy security, we require a more sophisticated privacy-preserving federated learning system.

In this work, we integrate peer-to-peer federated learning architecture with server-client federated learning architecture. And the proposed scheme can encrypt the parameters of MIs and validate their identities. MIs can train online healthcare diagnostic models in a secure environment. Our contributions include the following aspects:

- We propose a privacy-preserving authenticated federated learning scheme for smart healthcare system, which is a hybrid federated learning framework that combines peer-to-peer [11] and server-client architecture. This scheme can not only prevent external adversaries from obtaining the local datasets of MIs, but also effectively solve the problem that the model parameters of MIs can not be normally transmitted to the central server when the signal is bad [12].
- We leverage Boneh-Goh-Nissim (BGN) homomorphic cryptosystem [13] to encrypt the model parameter of MI and sign it with Schnorr signature [14]. The proposed scheme can not only effectively prevent external adversaries from deducing sensitive medical information by obtaining the model parameters of MI, but also verify the legitimate identity of the information sender. The multiplicative homomorphic property of BGN enables the execution of model parameter averaging operations while operating on ciphertext.
- Experiments demonstrate that the proposed scheme exhibits high efficiency and robustness. During the training phase, the proposed scheme reduces the delay time between the client and the server by a significant margin.

The rest of the paper is organised as follows. Section 3 presents the basic knowledge of this paper. Section 4 introduces the system architecture and security model. A specific scheme is proposed in Sect. 5. Section 6 and 7 are security analysis and performance analysis, respectively. Finally, the paper concludes in Sect. 8.

## 2  Related Work

We will begin this section by discussing federated learning. Yang et al. [25] proposed the pertinent definitions and classifications of federated learning. Federated learning can be classified into horizontal federated learning, vertical federated learning, and federated transfer learning based on the overlap between datasets' sample space and feature space. After the advent of federated learning, researchers have constructed a variety of secure and privacy-preserving federated learning frameworks using a variety of cryptographic techniques. Without exchanging plaintext, the server performs secure aggregation calculations. This includes the method of homomorphic encryption. The output of decrypting two ciphertexts after homomorphic operation is identical to the output of the same operation on unencrypted data. Wang et al. [28] proposed a privacy-preserving scheme for assessing disease risk based on Paillier homomorphic encryption and Naive Bayes algorithm. Le et al. [9] made it possible for all participating clients to share a secret key that is resistant to attacks from malicious servers. Simultaneously, it is essential to ensure that the ciphertexts will not be leaked among the clients. Based on the Paillier homomorphic encryption algorithm [29], Truex et al. [23] designed a more general and versatile scheme. The scheme employs secure multi-party computation to conceal the entire local perturbation parameter and secret sharing technology to control the timing of decryption. And ensure that the plaintext of the aggregation result is obtained by the central server only after sufficient noise protection has been applied. These methods conceal the computation inputs and intermediate variables to prevent adversaries from gaining access to sensitive information. This may affect the opponent's attacks or render their strategies ineffective. Due to computational burden being concentrated on the server and the inability to fully utilize the clients' computational capabilities, as well as the inherent complexity of the cryptographic protocols, the overall size of the training data will reduce training efficiency. In contrast, in a decentralized architecture, all participating nodes are also computing nodes, and the computation and communication loads are relatively heavy, necessitating a high level of demand on the nodes. This is suited for cross-silo federated learning scenarios involving numerous large organizations as participants.

This paper proposes a client authentication privacy protection scheme based on a mixed federated learning medical training architecture in response to these issues.

## 3   Preliminaries

### 3.1   Federated Learning

The concept of federated learning is put forward as early as 2016 [1], which includes two fundamental training architectures: client-server and peer-to-peer. In client-server architecture, each participant uploads their parameters to the server, and all the uploaded parameters are aggregated on the server to form a global model. The server then sends the global model parameters back to the participants. This architecture requires a trusted server. Different from client-server architecture, each participant in peer-to-peer architecture can transmit his/her training model parameters to each other to improve the effectiveness of model.

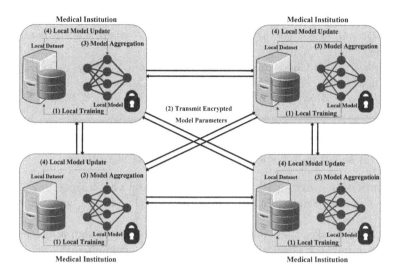

**Fig. 1.** Peer-to-peer federated learning architecture

The specific process of peer-to-peer federated learning is shown in Fig. 1. In the actual world, federated learning training typically employs a single mode, which may become inadequate to meet all requirements over time. Consequently, our scheme integrates the two architectures to create a hybrid framework that satisfies the privacy requirements of real-world scenarios. Specifically, a client cluster in the server-client architecture with a central node comprises a subset of the peer-to-peer federated learning architecture.

### 3.2 Boneh-Goh-Nissim (BGN) Cryptosystem

BGN cryptosystem [13] is a homomorphic cryptosystem, which can realize infinite additive homomorphic operation and a single multiplicative homomorphic operation of two ciphertexts. The following is a concise overview of BGN cryptosystem:

- $KeyGen(1^\kappa)$: Given a security parameter $\kappa$, and generate two cyclic groups $\mathbb{G}$, $\mathbb{G}_1$ with the identical order $N$, where bilinear map $e : \mathbb{G} * \mathbb{G} \to \mathbb{G}_1$, $N = q_1q_2$, and $q_1$, $q_2$ are two large prime numbers. Select two random generators $g$, $u \in \mathbb{G}$, and calculate $h = u^{q_2}$. Publish $pk = (N, \mathbb{G}, \mathbb{G}_1, e, g, h)$ as public key. And $sk = q_1$ is the secret key.
- $Enc(pk, m)$: User picks a message $m \in \mathbb{Z}_{q_2}$, then chooses a random integer $r \in (0, 1, 2, \ldots N)$ to encrypt message as $C = g^m h^r$.
- $Dec(sk, C)$: Compute $C' = C^{q_1} = (g^m h^r)^{q_1} = (g^{q_1})^m \bmod N$, it suffices to compute the discrete log of $C'$ base $g^{q_1}$ to recover $m = log_{g^{q_1}} C'$. Pollard's lambda method calculates efficiently discrete logarithm in a short interval length of $m$.

- *Add* $(pk, C_1, C_2)$: Secure sum module performs addition of two ciphertext $C_1$, $C_2$ as $C = C_1 \cdot C_2 \cdot h^r = g^{m_1+m_2} h^{r_1+r_2+r} mod\ N$, where $r \in \mathbb{Z}_N^*$ is a random number.
- *Mul* $(pk, C_1, C_2)$: Choose a random number $r \in \mathbb{Z}_N^*$, set $g_1 = e(g,g)$, $h_1 = e(g,h)$, where $g_1$ is order $n$ and $h_1$ is order $q_1$. Then $C = e(C_1, C_2) h_1^r \in= e(g^{m_1}h^{r_1}, g^{m_2}h^{r_2})h_1^r = g_1^{m_1 m_2} h_1^{m_1 r_2 + r_2 m_1 + \alpha q_2 r_1 r_2 + r} = g_1^{m_1 m_2} h_1^{\tilde{r}}$.

### 3.3  Schnorr Signature

The Schnorr signature scheme includes the following algorithms.

- *Setup*: Sender generates two big prime $p$, $q$, and chooses $g \xleftarrow{R} \mathbb{Z}_p^*$, where $g^q \equiv 1\ (mod\ p)$. Sender obtains a private key $x$ $(1 < x < q)$, and a public key $y \equiv g^x\ (mod\ p)$.
- *Sign*: Sender takes the following procedures in order to sign a message $m$: a random number $k$ is selected, where $1 < k < q$, computes $r \equiv g^k\ (mod\ p)$, $e = H(r,\ m)$, $s \equiv xe + k\ (mod\ q)$, and the resultant digital signature is $(e, s)$.
- *Verify*: Receiver calculates $r' \equiv g^s y^{-e}\ (mod\ p)$ and $H(r',\ m)$ after receiving the message $m$ and digital signature $(e, s)$ and then verifies using the following formula:

$$Ver(y, (e, s), m) = True \rightarrow H(r', m) = e$$

Its correctness can be demonstrated by the following formula:

$$r' = g^s y^{-e} \equiv g^{xe+k-xe} \equiv g^k \equiv r\ (mod\ p)$$

## 4  System Architecture and Security Model

In this section, we present the system architecture and security model.

### 4.1  System Architecture

As shown in Fig. 2, the proposed scheme architecture includes three entities, namely, medical institutions (MIs), computing service provider (CSP) and key generation center (KGC).

- *Medical Institution (MI)*. MI refers to medical and health center with private information. All MIs are divided into multiple groups by CSP, and they perform peer-to-peer federated learning within the group.
- *Computing Service Provider (CSP)*. CSP is honest-but-curious, that is, on the one hand, it can follow the protocol specifications, on the other hand, it may try to learn more about disallowed information by looking at the transcript of messages that it received and its internal status. CSP possesses the initial training model, performs model updates, and aggregates MIs' uploaded encrypted generated local model parameters.
- *Key Generation Center (KGC)*. KGC is a trusted third party that acts as a government agency or a trusted entity administered directly by the government. KGC is responsible for system initialization.

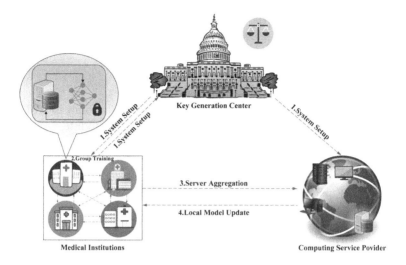

**Fig. 2.** System model

## 4.2 Security Model

In the proposed scheme, we do not consider the collusion of CSP and MI. In the meantime, we presume that all MIs will register with the KGC. Some dishonest MIs may attempt to join training as free-riding without registering, with the aim of disrupting the process. All MIs register with KGC will participate in the entire training process honestly, and there will be no collusion between any two MIs. In addition, our model takes into account an active adversary outside of the system (denoted **E**). **E** will use all available tools to attempt to decrypt the ciphertext from the data transmitted between CSP and MIs. **E** expects to acquire data whose value exceeds the cost of computation within a given budget. These data include MI's dataset or CSP's aggregation model.

## 4.3 System Requirements

Our proposed scheme takes into account the following system requirements:

*1)* Privacy preservation: A semi-honest CSP should be unaware of the model parameters uploaded by MIs. Nor should a semi-honest CSP be able to infer any private information about the MIs from the received information. Each round of encrypted data sent by MIs to CSP cannot be decrypted by the external adversary **E**. Concurrently, **E** is unable to access the aggregated model parameters returned by CSP to MIs.

*2)* Identity verification: MIs that are not registered with KGC can be defined as dishonest organisations. They may seek to join federated learning training process by sending packets with no data in order to obtain aggregated model parameters. During this procedure, CSP and MI receiving the information will identify dishonest MIs using signature-based validity checks and will reject their malicious messages.

## 5    Proposed Specific Scheme

In this section, we present our proposed scheme, which is comprised of system setup, group training, server aggregation and local model update.

### 5.1    System Setup

Given a security parameter $\kappa$, KGC executes KeyGen algorithm of BGN cryptosystem, generating $|p| = |q| = \kappa$, $e = \mathbb{G} * \mathbb{G} \rightarrow \mathbb{G}_1$, where $\mathbb{G}$ is a cyclic additive group of order $N$, $\mathbb{G}_1$ is a cyclic multiplicative group of order $N$, for details of the bilinear pairing [24]. Select two randomly-generated elements $g$, $u \in \mathbb{G}$, and calculate $N = pq$, $h = u^q$. KGC publishes public key $pk = \{N, \mathbb{G}, \mathbb{G}_1, e, g, h\}$ and private key $sk = p$. KGC transmits $sk$ to $MI_i$ via the secure channel and broadcasts $pk$ to MIs and CSP.

Likewise, under routine circumstances, all MIs should register with KGC. Through a secure channel, $MI_i$ submits its identity $ID_{vi}$ and password $PW$ to KGC. Government officials issued $ID_{vi}$ and $PW$ utilized here during the creation of $MI_i$, signifying government authentication. KGC initiates the generation of signature public-private key pairs $\{x_i, y_i\}$ in which $y_i = g^{x_i} mod \ p$. Through a secure channel, KGC transmits signature public-private key pair $\{x_i, y_i\}$ corresponding to each $MI_i$ to that $MI_i$.

Remark 1: The proposed scheme implies that all MIs must register with KGC, but only a subset of MIs will comply with the registration requirement. MIs who are dishonest may attempt to avoid registration and training. When choosing MIs to participate in training, the CSP will consider all MIs.

### 5.2    Group Training

CSP will divide up participating MIs based on their geographical location, communication environment, and type of medical institution. After the grouping process is completed by the CSP, each $MI_i$ conducts local training using local dataset. During the training procedure, convolutional neural network (CNN) is utilised. Meanwhile, MIs within $group[l]$ are trained using an peer-to-peer federated learning framework. After that, $MI_i$ transmits its model parameters encrypted with BGN and signed with Schnorr to other MIs within the same group. Local converge and global aggregation are the two slots that can be used to divide each training process. $MI_i$ trains their local model in computer time $T_i^{cmp}$. At time $T_i^{con}$, encrypted model parameters are transmitted to group members. The message is then transmitted to CSP at the time $T_i^{agg}$.

Step 1: If a MI is prepared to participate in the training, it submits its identity $ID_{vi}$ to the CSP. CSP classifies MIs based on network latency with the institutions and registered information such as geographic location and institution classification.

Step 2: CSP initializes a list using user sequence $U$, and updates skip list using Algorithm 1. The insertion and deletion procedures for skip list are described in [21]. Using Algorithm 2, CSP can conduct group queries for malicious MIs and then revoke them using Algorithm 1. Then CSP broadcasts MIs of user sequence $U$ and the number of users $N_{G_j}$ in each group.

Step 3: $MI_i$ selects model parameters $w_{u_i}$ to be encrypted as the broadcast message $m_i$ within the group. First, $MI_i$ uses $Enc(pk, m)$ algorithm to encrypt $m_i$. $MI_i$ selects $r_i$ and $k_i$ at random from $Z_n$ so that $0 < r_i < N$ and $0 < k_i < N$, and then computes $c_i = g^{m_i} h^{r_i} \ (mod \ N)$.

Step 4: $MI_i$ needs to send encrypted message $c_i$ to other MIs within the group after signing it with Schnorr signature scheme. $MI_i$ registered with KGC possesses a signature public-private key pair $\{x_i, y_i\}$ assigned by KGC. This key pair can be used to verify $MI_i$'s identity by other group members. Since enrolling with KGC would expose their dishonesty, dishonest MIs would not register. $MI_i$ calculates $r_{i_0} = g^{k_i} \ (mod \ p)$, $e_i = H\left(c_i || r_{i_0} || T\right)$ during signature procedure, where $T$ is current timestamp. Simultaneously, $MI_i$ calculates $s_i = (k_i + e_i x_i) \ mod \ q$ using $k_i$, $e_i$ and $x_i$. $MI_i$ sets the signature of $m_i$ as $\sigma_i = \{e_i, s_i\}$.

Step 5: Before receiving the message, receiving party $MI_i$ verifies the authenticity and validity of the message by checking the signature. After receiving the signature tuple $\{c_i, \sigma_i, T\}$, $MI_i$ verifies the validity of the timestamp $T$. $MI_i$ advances to the next verification phase if $(T > T_r - T_\nabla)$, where $T_r$ is time of receipt, $T_\nabla$ is predefined validity period, and $T$ is current time the message is sent. Upon receiving the signature tuple $\{c_i, \sigma_i, T\}$ for message $m_i$, the recipient first calculates $r'_{i_0} \equiv g^{s_i} y^{-e_i} \ (mod \ p)$, and then computes $H\left(c_i || r'_{i_0} || T\right)$. Using the public parameters and functions of the system, $MI_i$ receives encrypted message $c_i$ if the following equation holds true for the signature $\sigma_i = \{e_i, s_i\}$, where $\{i = 1, NG_j\}$:

$$H\left(c_i || r'_{i_0} || T\right) = e_i \tag{1}$$

Step 6: $MI_i$ performs homomorphic operations locally to obtain the aggregated model parameters after receiving an encrypted message from other MIs within the group. Using $sk = p$, $MI_i$ can promptly decrypt the aggregated result $[\![w_u^t]\!]$ to obtain $w_u^t = \sum_{i=1}^{m} w_{u_i}^t$. $MI_i$ then conducts a local mean aggregation operation to obtain $w_u^{t+1} = \dfrac{\sum_{i=1}^{m} w_{u_i}^t}{m}$. $MI_i$ then uses the new averaged model parameters $w_u^{t+1}$ as its own model parameters $w_{u_i}^t$ to continue training iteratively.

---

**Algorithm 1.** Group Refresh

---

**Input:** List of MIs, Num, and GroupThreshold.
**Output:** group of MIs *Group[n]*.
 1: cur = List→head, IntUser = 0
 2: **for** i = maxLevel to 0 **do**
 3:   **while** cur→next[i] and cur→next[i]→key  Num **do**
 4:     cur←cur→next [i]
 5:     IntUser←IntUser+1
 6:     update[i]=cur
 7:   **end while**
 8: **end for**
 9: **if** cur and cur→key is not Num **then**
10:   **if** (IntUser mod GroupThreshold is not 1) **then**
11:     rlevel = randomLevel
12:     newNode = createNode(rlevel, Num)
13:     **for** i=0 to rlevel **do**
14:       newNode→next[i]= updata[i]→next[i]
15:       update→next[i]=newNode
16:     **end for**
17:   **else**
18:     rlevel = maxLevel
19:     newNode = createNode(rlevel, Num)
20:     **for** i=0 to rlevel **do**
21:       newNode→next[i]= updata[i]→next[i]
22:       update→next[i]=newNode
23:     **end for**
24:     newNode→next=NULL
25:   **end if**
26: **end if**
27: p=List→head
28: **for** j=1 to n **do**
29:   p=p→next[maxLevel]
30:   groupNum=0
31:   **while** groupNum<GroupThreshold **do**
32:     groupNum=groupNum+1
33:     q=p→next[1]
34:     Group[j].append(q)
35:   **end while**
36: **end for**
37: **return** *Group[n]*

---

**Algorithm 2.** Client Search

---

**Input:** List of MIs, target Num.
**Output:** target MI List[i]
 1: cur = List→head
 2: **for** i = maxLevel to 0 **do**
 3:     **while** cur→next[i] and cur→next[i]→key < Num **do**
 4:         cur = cur→next[i]
 5:     **end while**
 6: **end for**
 7: **if** cur and cur→key is Num **then**
 8:     **return** cur
 9: **end if**

---

### 5.3  Server Aggregation

$MI_i$ encrypts its model parameters to obtain $[\![w_{u_i}^t]\!]$, signs $c_i = [\![w_{u_i}^t]\!]$ with Schnorr signature, and then transmits $\{c_i,\ \sigma_i,\ T\}$ to CSP. After receiving the encrypted model parameters $[\![w_{u_i}^t]\!]$ from each MI, the number of participating MIs $n^t$ is determined, and the identity of the $MI_i$ that sent the data is validated. Ensure that no illegal MIs impersonate legitimate ones or send fraudulent messages. CSP then uses encryption of BGN cryptosystem with the public key and system public parameters. CSP randomly selects two element $r', r_{csp} \in Z_n$ and computes $c_{csp} = Enc\left(pk, \frac{1000}{n}\right)$.

Secondly, when calculating the average model parameters, CSP first determines the sum of all MIs' model parameters $[\![w_u^t]\!] = g^{\sum\limits_{i=1}^{n} w_{u_i}^t} \cdot h^{\sum\limits_{i=1}^{n} r_i + r} \ mod\ N$. CSP then computes the multiplication of $[\![w_u^t]\!]$ and $c_{csp}$ utilizing the multiplicative homomorphic property of BGN cryptosystem. CSP selects $g_1 = e(g,g)$ and $h_1 = e(g,h)$, and two ciphertexts $c_1 = c_{csp} = g^{\frac{1000}{n}} \cdot h^{r_{csp}}$ and $c_2 = [\![w_u^t]\!] = g^{\sum\limits_{i=1}^{n} w_{u_i}^t} \cdot h^{\sum\limits_{i=1}^{n} r_i + r}$.

Last but not least, CSP transmits the averaged model parameters to the participating $MI_i$ for model aggregation.

### 5.4  Local Model Update

$MI_i$ receives the model parameter ciphertext $[\![w_u^t]\!]$ and decrypts it using $Dec(sk, C)$ to derive the average model parameter value $w_{csp}^t = \frac{[\![w_u^t]\!]^P}{1000} = \frac{(g^P)^{\sum\limits_{i=1}^{m} w_{u_i}^t}}{1000} mod\ N$. If the predetermined training epochs has not been completed, each participant continues training and moves on to the next epoch of global training. Otherwise, training concludes.

Remark 2: Each MI maintains a test dataset of identical, Non-IID. $MI_i$ compares the performance of the received aggregated model to the present model's performance on its local test dataset. If the present model's performance is superior, its parameters are retained. Otherwise, the aggregated model replaces the current model.

## 6  Security Analysis

In this section, we analyze the security of the proposed scheme.

### 6.1  Correctness

Theorem 1: MI can acquire the accurate parameters in Group Training and Server Aggregation if participants comply to the suggested approach.

Proof: First, our decryption procedure ensures that the model parameters obtained remain correct. Second, we demonstrate that the average values are the model parameters acquired following the Server Aggregation phase. Public key $pk$ is used for encryption in both the Server Aggregation and Group Training procedures. The homomorphic property is satisfied by the calculations that follow.

During the Group Training, MI can obtain the sum of model parameters using the homomorphic property of BGN Cryptosystem. MI is aware of the number of members in the group.

$$
\begin{aligned}
[\![w_u^t]\!] &= \prod_{i=1}^{m} [\![w_{u_i}^t]\!] h^r \ mod \ N \\
&= \prod_{i=1}^{m} g^{w_{u_i}^t} h^{r_i} h^r \ mod \ N \\
&= g^{\sum_{i=1}^{m} w_{u_i}^t} \cdot h^{\sum_{i=1}^{m} r_i + r} \ mod \ N
\end{aligned}
\tag{2}
$$

Hence, it is possible to calculate the average model parameters $w_u^{t+1} = \frac{\sum_{i=1}^{m} w_{u_i}^t}{m}$ during Group Training.

$$
\begin{aligned}
w_u^t &= [\![w_u^t]\!]^{p_i} \\
&= \left(g^{\sum_{i=1}^{m} w_{u_i}^t} \cdot h^{\sum_{i=1}^{m} r_i + r}\right)^{p_i} \\
&= \left(g^{\sum_{i=1}^{m} w_{u_i}^t}\right)^{p_i} u^{p_i q \sum_{i=1}^{m} r_i + r} mod \ N \\
&= \left(g^{p_i}\right)^{\sum_{i=1}^{m} w_{u_i}^t} mod \ N
\end{aligned}
\tag{3}
$$

Similarly, during the Server Aggregation, MI can directly acquire the average value of the model parameters throughout the multiplicative homomorphic property of BGN.

$$
\begin{aligned}
[\![w_{csp}^t]\!] &= e(c_1, c_2) \bmod N \\
&= e(g^{\frac{1000}{n}} h^{r_{csp}}, g^{\sum_{i=1}^n w_{u_i}^t} \cdot h^{\sum_{i=1}^n r_i + r}) \\
&= g_1^{\frac{1}{n} \sum_{i=1}^n w_{u_i}^t} h_1^{\frac{1000}{n}(\sum_{i=1}^n r_i + r) + r_{csp} \sum_{i=1}^n w_{u_i}^t + \alpha q r_{csp}(\sum_{i=1}^n r_i + r) + r} \quad (4) \\
&= g_1^{\frac{1000 \sum_{i=1}^n w_{u_i}^t}{n}} h_1^{\widetilde{r}} \in G_1
\end{aligned}
$$

## 6.2  Authentication of the Scheme

Theorem 2: According to our proposed scheme, authentication of all participating medical institution is guaranteed.

Proof: During the Group Training and Server Aggregation, each MI uses their own signing private key to generate a signature for the encrypted data. Our scheme is secure because of the proven security of Schnorr signatures in the Forking Lemma. The validity of timestamps prevents reconstruction attacks, and the verification of each MI's signature ensures the authenticity of their identity, preventing free-riding attacks.

## 6.3  Data Privacy

Theorem 3: Our scheme achieves data privacy security by preventing the adversary who obtain ciphertext without the corresponding keys from decrypting the data.

Proof: Firstly, during the training process, MIs encrypt the information every time it is transmitted. Secondly, because MIs must pass a qualification assessment by government officials, honest MIs have Schnorr signature public-private key pair. MIs that are malicious or semi-honest cannot register with the KGC. Based on Theorems 1 and 2, it can be ensured that the ciphertext of transmitted information remains inaccessible to adversaries. Identify applicable funding agency here. If none, delete this text box.

## 7  Performance Evaluation

In this section, we first compare our scheme with the existing schemes in terms of characteristics. Then we analyze the performance of the proposed scheme in terms of computation cost, and make the comparison with FedAvg [22], DP-FedAvg [15] and NGDP-FedAvg [16]. We conduct experiments on a variety of security parameter lengths, with 4096 bits being the maximum length examined.

### 7.1    Evaluation Environment

To evaluate the efficiency of our proposed scheme in an online healthcare diagnosis system, we ran Python experiments on Ubuntu 20.04 and a Tesla V100 32 GB GPU. The VGG19 model is employed as the initial model. The entire experiment is trained for 200 epochs globally, with each client training for three epochs locally. Clients are split into two groups and trained using peer-to-peer federated learning. We demonstrate the efficiency of the proposed scheme on the Chest CT-Scan images Dataset [30] and evaluate its precision and training duration. We also compare it to FedAvg, DP-FedAvg, and NGDP-FedAvg schemes using the Chest CT-Scan images Dataset. In addition to separate folders containing images of normal cells, the dataset contains photos of three different types of chest cancer, such as adenocarcinoma, large cell carcinoma, and squamous cell carcinoma. In the comparative experiment, we set the value of $\zeta$ to 2 to obtain a better balance between aggregation precision and privacy protection for NGDP-FedAvg.

### 7.2    Characteristic Analysis

We compare the characteristics with the three existing schemes, and the results are shown in Table 1.

**Table 1.** Comparison Results

|                     | FedAvg | DP-FedAvg | NGDP-FedAvg | Ours |
|---------------------|--------|-----------|-------------|------|
| Support Offline     | No     | No        | No          | Yes  |
| Model Privacy       | No     | N.A.      | N.A.        | Yes  |
| Verification        | No     | No        | No          | Yes  |
| Support Multi-user  | Yes    | No        | Yes         | Yes  |

N.A. denotes not available.

### 7.3    Accuracy and System Runtime

We compare the accuracy and training time of FedAvg, DP-FedAvg, and NGDP-FedAvg on Chest CT-Scan images dataset. Each algorithm is trained for 200 epochs. Figure 3 that DP-FedAvg and NGDP-FedAvg is unstable during training and frequently fails to produce a model. This is due to the fact that differential privacy prunes model parameters on the client side, and in order to prevent adversaries from obtaining the model, the server prunes the model again and adds noise after aggregation. In deep learning, the pruning parameter can readily lead to iteration instability, making it difficult to obtain a trained model. The precision of our scheme is comparable to that of FedAvg. However, FedAvg does not perform any encryption on the model parameters during the transmission process. Compared to DP-FedAvg and NGDP-FedAvg, our scheme's security is superior due to the distinction between its differential privacy and public key encryption scheme.

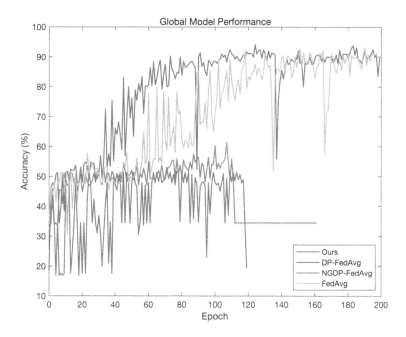

**Fig. 3.** Comparison of accuracy

In contrast, as depicted in Fig. 4 demonstrate ours has a shorter group training time than other schemes. In our experiments, seven clients are divided into two groups. The first group had two clients, while the second had five clients. Both groups are able to attain a more proficiently trained model in less time. This demonstrates that the our scheme is preferable.

## 7.4  Cryptosystem Runtime

Simultaneously, we conduct the performance of BGN homomorphic cryptosystem and Schnorr signature in our scheme. Both MIs and CSP necessitate multiple homomorphic additions using BGN in our proposed scheme. Additionally, CSP necessitates homomorphic multiplication. Each time data represents the mean duration of 100 operations in Table 2. When the security parameter is insufficiently large, the algorithm is vulnerable to attack. However, when the security parameter is set to an excessively high value, the computational cost will increase substantially. In addition, when the security parameter exceeds 7680 bits, the computer is unable to perform the calculation and stack overflow occurs. In order

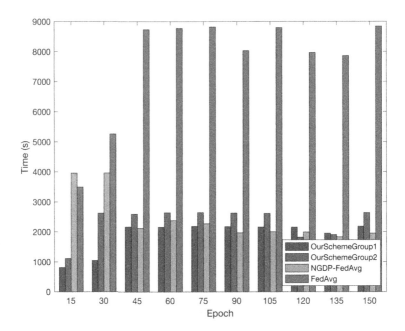

**Fig. 4.** Runtime of the proposed scheme vs NGDP-FedAvg vs FedAvg

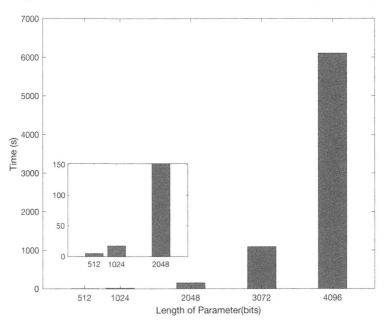

**Fig. 5.** Running time of KeyGen in our scheme

to determine the computation cost of key generation, encryption, and decryption using values between 512 and 4096 bits, we conduct experiments. Figure 5 displays the results of key generation algorithm.

**Table 2.** Performance of Our Scheme

| Security Parameter | 512 | 1024 | 2048 | 3072 | 4096 |
|---|---|---|---|---|---|
| Encryption | 0.002 s | 0.007 s | 0.033 s | 0.087 s | 0.180 s |
| Decryption | 0.055 s | 0.150 s | 0.499 s | 1.077 s | 2.027 s |
| Additive Homomorphic | 0.0002 s | 0.0017 s | 0.00177 s | 0.00198 s | 0.00192 s |
| Multiplicative Homomorphic | 0.072 s | 0.188 s | 0.535 s | 1.099 s | 1.983 s |

As the security parameter increases, the computational cost of encryption, decryption, homomorphic addition, and homomorphic multiplication also increases. Moreover, for each additional bit in the large parameter, the computational time cost increases significantly.

In our experiments, we use the Ed25519 curve for parameter generation in the Schnorr signature scheme. Table 3 presents the computation cost of Schnorr signature in our scheme.

**Table 3.** Performance of signatures in our scheme

| Algorithm | KeyGen | Sign | Verify |
|---|---|---|---|
| Our Scheme | 0.01322 s | 0.00597 s | 0.002703 s |

## 7.5 Computational Cost of Clients Participating and Revoking Analysis

Next, we compare the performance of client participating and revoking. We assume that scheme [23] differs from our scheme only in the absence of peer-to-peer federated learning and group partitioning in the traditional scheme. Therefore, after each client joins or leaves, CSP needs to traverse all clients and adjust accordingly. This time cost is positively correlated with the number of clients. As shown in Fig. 6 and Fig. 7, our scheme has a significant advantage in the client addition and revocation phases. Therefore, for large-scale peer-to-peer federated learning, the proposed algorithm in our scheme is feasible.

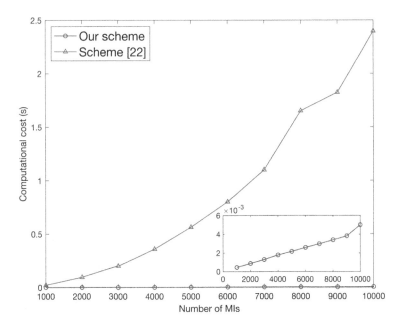

**Fig. 6.** Computational cost for client participating

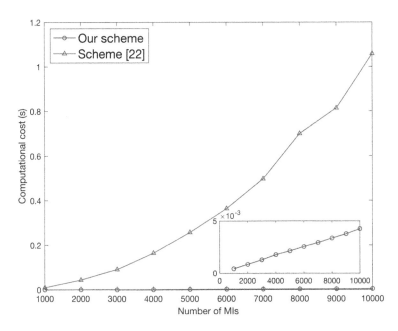

**Fig. 7.** Computational cost for client revoking

# 8 Conclusion

In response to communication and security issues in smart healthcare system, we propose a privacy-preserving authenticated federated learning scheme for smart healthcare system. Experiments and performance evaluations demonstrate that the proposed federated learning scheme enables data owners to participate in federated training efficiently and securely. In addition, extensive experiments have shown that this method facilitates the rapid participation and revocation of a large number of data owners from the training procedure.

# 9 Discussion and Future Work

In the future, our work will focus on how to improve the efficiency of training, while ensuring that our scheme can be applied to more occasions. We will investigate the implementation of privacy evaluation functionality in a real-world setting, and analyze its performance. Furthermore, we will enhance the single-user homomorphic encryption scheme to make it more applicable to real-life applications.

**Acknowledgements.** This work supported in part by the Major Research Plan of Hubei Province under Grant/Award No. 2023BAA027, and the National Natural Science Foundation of China under grants 62072134, U2001205, and the key Research and Development Program of Hubei Province under Grant 2021BEA163. In addition, Jun Tu would like to express gratitude to his classmate Yifan Liu for his support in providing the experimental conditions.

# References

1. Konečný, J., McMahan, H.B., Ramage, D., Richtárik, P.: Federated optimization: distributed machine learning for on-device intelligence. arXiv preprint arXiv:1610.02527 (2016)
2. Konečný, J., McMahan, H.B., Yu, F.X., Richtárik, P., Suresh, A.T., Bacon, D.: Federated learning: strategies for improving communication efficiency. arXiv preprint arXiv:1610.05492 (2016)
3. Bhowmick, A., Duchi, J., Freudiger, J., Kapoor, G., Rogers, R.: Protection against reconstruction and its applications in private federated learning. arXiv preprint arXiv:1812.00984 (2018)
4. Hitaj, B., Ateniese, G., Perez-Cruz, F.: Deep models under the GAN: information leakage from collaborative deep learning. In: Proceedings of the 2017 ACM SIGSAC Conference on Computer and Communications Security, pp. 603–618 (2017)
5. Truex, S., Liu, L., Gursoy, M.E., Yu, L., Wei, W.: Demystifying membership inference attacks in machine learning as a service. IEEE Trans. Serv. Comput. **14**(6), 2073–2089 (2019)
6. Nasr, M., Shokri, R., Houmansadr, A.: Comprehensive privacy analysis of deep learning: passive and active white-box inference attacks against centralized and federated learning. In: 2019 IEEE Symposium on Security and Privacy (SP), pp. 739–753. IEEE (2019)

7. Lin, J., Du, M., Liu, J.: Free-riders in federated learning: attacks and defenses. arXiv preprint arXiv:1911.12560 (2019)
8. Zong, B., et al.: Deep autoencoding gaussian mixture model for unsupervised anomaly detection. In: International Conference on Learning Representations (2018)
9. Aono, Y., Hayashi, T., Wang, L., Moriai, S., et al.: Privacy-preserving deep learning via additively homomorphic encryption. IEEE Trans. Inf. Forensics Secur. **13**(5), 1333–1345 (2017)
10. Zhu, L., Liu, Z., Han, S.: Deep leakage from gradients. In: Advances in Neural Information Processing Systems, vol. 32 (2019)
11. Lian, X., Zhang, C., Zhang, H., Hsieh, C.J., Zhang, W., Liu, J.: Can decentralized algorithms outperform centralized algorithms? A case study for decentralized parallel stochastic gradient descent. In: Advances in Neural Information Processing Systems, vol. 30 (2017)
12. Lu, Y., Huang, X., Zhang, K., Maharjan, S., Zhang, Y.: Communication-efficient federated learning and permissioned blockchain for digital twin edge networks. IEEE Internet Things J. **8**(4), 2276–2288 (2020)
13. Boneh, D., Goh, E.-J., Nissim, K.: Evaluating 2-DNF formulas on ciphertexts. In: Kilian, J. (ed.) TCC 2005. LNCS, vol. 3378, pp. 325–341. Springer, Heidelberg (2005). https://doi.org/10.1007/978-3-540-30576-7_18
14. Schnorr, C.P.: Efficient signature generation by smart cards. J. Cryptol. **4**, 161–174 (1991)
15. McMahan, H.B., Ramage, D., Talwar, K., Zhang, L.: Learning differentially private recurrent language models. arXiv preprint arXiv:1710.06963 (2017)
16. Wang, X., Wang, J., Ma, X., Wen, C.: A differential privacy strategy based on local features of non-gaussian noise in federated learning. Sensors **22**(7), 2424 (2022)
17. Yao, A.C.: Protocols for secure computations. In: 23rd Annual Symposium on Foundations of Computer Science (SFCS 1982), pp. 160–164. IEEE (1982)
18. Yao, A.C.C.: How to generate and exchange secrets. In: 27th Annual Symposium on Foundations of Computer Science (SFCS 1986), pp. 162–167. IEEE (1986)
19. Chang, Y., Zhang, K., Gong, J., Qian, H.: Privacy-preserving federated learning via functional encryption, revisited. IEEE Trans. Inf. Forensics Secur. **18**, 1855–1869 (2023)
20. Melis, L., Song, C., De Cristofaro, E., Shmatikov, V.: Exploiting unintended feature leakage in collaborative learning. In: 2019 IEEE Symposium on Security and Privacy (SP), pp. 691–706. IEEE (2019)
21. Pugh, W.: Skip lists: a probabilistic alternative to balanced trees. Commun. ACM **33**(6), 668–676 (1990)
22. McMahan, B., Moore, E., Ramage, D., Hampson, S., Arcas, B.A.: Communication-efficient learning of deep networks from decentralized data. In: Artificial Intelligence and Statistics, pp. 1273–1282. PMLR (2017)
23. Truex, S., et al.: A hybrid approach to privacy-preserving federated learning. In: Proceedings of the 12th ACM Workshop on Artificial Intelligence and Security, pp. 1–11 (2019)
24. Boneh, D., Boyen, X., Shacham, H.: Short group signatures. In: Franklin, M. (ed.) CRYPTO 2004. LNCS, vol. 3152, pp. 41–55. Springer, Heidelberg (2004). https://doi.org/10.1007/978-3-540-28628-8_3
25. Yang, Q., Liu, Y., Chen, T., Tong, Y.: Federated machine learning: concept and applications. ACM Trans. Intell. Syst. Technol. (TIST) **10**(2), 1–19 (2019)
26. Su, Y., Shen, G., Zhang, M.: A novel privacy-preserving authentication scheme for V2G networks. IEEE Syst. J. **14**(2), 1963–1971 (2019)

27. Shen, G., Fu, Z., Gui, Y., Susilo, W., Zhang, M.: Efficient and privacy-preserving online diagnosis scheme based on federated learning in e-healthcare system. Inf. Sci. 119261 (2023)
28. Wang, F., Zhu, H., Lu, R., Zheng, Y., Li, H.: Achieve efficient and privacy-preserving disease risk assessment over multi-outsourced vertical datasets. IEEE Trans. Dependable Secure Comput. **19**(3), 1492–1504 (2020)
29. Paillier, P.: Public-key cryptosystems based on composite degree residuosity classes. In: Stern, J. (ed.) EUROCRYPT 1999. LNCS, vol. 1592, pp. 223–238. Springer, Heidelberg (1999). https://doi.org/10.1007/3-540-48910-X_16
30. Chest CT-Scan images Dataset. https://www.kaggle.com/datasets/mohamedhanyyy/chest-ctscan-images. Accessed 3 Sept 2023

# A Systematic Method for Constructing ICT Supply Chain Security Requirements

Yinxing Wei[✉] 🆔, Jun Zheng, and Hong Zhong

ZTE Corporation, Nanjing, China
`wei.yinxing@zte.com.cn`

**Abstract.** This paper studies how to construct Information and Communication Technology (ICT) supply chain security requirements from the perspective of ICT supply chain security assurance. Firstly, the security environment of ICT supply chain is established through ICT supply chain relationship, product life cycle stages, security driving factors and security properties. Then it is proposed to derive ICT supply chain security requirements from regulatory requirements and security best practices, each requirement is validated through the Asset-Threat-Objective-Requirement (ATOR) methodology, and 10 categories of 100 items of ICT supply chain security requirements are established in this way. Finally, the application scenarios and usages of ICT supply chain security requirements are described.

**Keywords:** ICT Supply Chain · Security Requirement · Security Assurance · Security Management · Software Bill of Material

## 1 Introduction

Information and Communication Technology (ICT) supply chain refers to a set of linked resources and processes between acquirers, integrators and suppliers, starting from the design of ICT products and services and extending to the development, sourcing, manufacturing, handling and delivery of ICT products and services to the acquirer [1]. The ICT supply chain is a globally distributed complex system with multi-dimensional characteristics such as supplier diversity, product service complexity, and full life cycle coverage. Supply chain compromise can take place at any stage of the supply chain. MITRE pointed out that attackers may manipulate products or product delivery mechanisms to compromise data or systems before the final consumer receives the products [2]. Problems in any part of the ICT supply chain, such as any supplier in the supply chain, any component in the product/service, and any security risk in any stage of the system life cycle, may cause ICT products, systems or services to be insecure, leading to ICT supply chain security risks [3].

The SolarWinds incident has demonstrated to attackers (and defenders) the potential for supply chain attacks. Surveys by the World Economic Forum and Anchore report that between 39% and 62% of organizations have been affected by third-party cyber incidents. According to Mandiant, supply chain compromises were the second most prevalent initial infection vector discovered in 2021. Additionally, they accounted for 17% of intrusion incidents in 2021, compared to less than 1% in 2020 [4].

ICT supply chain faces five challenges from the view of security according to the literature surveys.

- Challenge 1: Complexity

    Components used in ICT are manufactured in countries around the world, creating the complexity of a globally distributed supply chain in people, processes and technologies [5]. The ICT product itself is a complex system. For example, literature [6] shows that there are tens of millions of lines of code in the Optical Line Terminal (OLT) equipment, which the code base contains a large number of open sources and third-party software. It is a challenge to secure such complex ICT products because there exist various security threats at any stage of the product life cycle.

- Challenge 2: Visibility

    The complexity of the ICT supply chain has led many Original Equipment Manufacturers (OEM) to outsource firmware development to third-party suppliers, which introduces risks related to the lack of transparency into suppliers [7]. There are limited industry standards and best practices related to how much visibility a provider expects a supplier to provide into their supply chain processes, and what visibility a provider is prepared to give a customer into its own supply chain processes [8].

- Challenge 3: Integrity

    The statistics in literature [9] shows that 160,741 Common Vulnerabilities and Exposures (CVE) vulnerabilities have been publicly disclosed in the last 10 years, of which 19.2% are rating of Critical and 36.9% are rating of High. In addition to these known vulnerabilities, there may be hidden and undocumented features, zero-day vulnerabilities in the product, which may be exploited by attackers, thereby affecting the integrity of the product. Additionally, components and products may be counterfeit or tainted, affecting the integrity of software and hardware supply chains [8].

- Challenge 4: Workforce Shortage

    It is challenging to hire cybersecurity-trained and skilled resources given the complex, emergent and technological demands of supply chain security [10]. According to (ISC)$^2$ 2022 cybersecurity workforce study, there is a worldwide gap of 3.4 million cybersecurity workers [11]. The cybersecurity workforce shortage play an important risk on supply chain security.

- Challenge 5: Compliance

    The United States issued Executive Order 14028 to improve the Nation's cybersecurity, Sect. 4 of which requires enhancing software supply chain security [12]. The EU NIS2 directive requires member states to regard supply chain security as a national strategy and requires security risk assessment of the critical ICT product supply chain [13]. ICT vendors are challenged by supply chain security compliance risks.

Mitigating the security risks of the ICT supply chain is a complex system engineering. This paper studies how to establish ICT supply chain security requirements from the perspective of improving the overall security assurance level of the ICT supply chain, which addresses the above challenges:

1. ICT supply chain security requirements consider the aspects of personnel, processes and technologies, which the key control points cover the procurement, in-house development and delivery processes for entire product life cycle;
2. The security requirements are used as baselined criteria for supplier, which the visibility of the supply chain is also enhanced;
3. The processes are strictly performed, reducing the probability of introducing vulnerabilities, counterfeiting or tainting components, which will improve the integrity of the supply chain;
4. The ICT supply chain security requirements established in this paper unifies the industry best practices from multiple sources, saving the research and learning cost for suppliers, which mitigates the risks of security workforce shortage;
5. The security requirements incorporate the state-of-the-art regulations and best practices, which reduces the compliance risks for the supply chain.

By these ways, the security risks of the ICT supply chain are mitigated and the trust from regulators and customers is enhanced.

The contributions of this paper are as follows.

- Define a framework for the ICT supply chain security environment;
- Propose a systematic method to establish ICT supply chain security requirements;
- Describe scenarios and usages for ICT supply chain security requirements.

## 2  Related Work

Related work to establish ICT supply chain security requirements are as follows.

- Methodology for establishing ICT product security requirements

  ETSI proposed the Threat Vulnerability Risk Analysis (TVRA) method, which can systematically analyze the assets, vulnerabilities and threats of ICT systems and identify detailed security requirements [14]. GSMA NESAS establishes security requirements for equipment vendor's development and product lifecycle processes by analyzing the assets, threats, risks, and security objectives of network equipment [15].
- ICT Supply chain security environment

  In ETSI, the security environment is described as the security aspects of the environment in which assets are intended to be used [14]. ENISA points out that the means to identify the boundary between the environment and the supply chain, and the means by which the supply chain interacts with the environment are recommended as a starting point to analyze the supply chain security [5].

  ENISA proposes a taxonomy to describe supply chain attacks that considers the four elements of the supply chain (supplier, supplier assets, customer, customer assets), as well as the techniques used by attackers [16]. Miller summarized the supply chain attack framework and attack pattern [17]. Ladisa et al. classify the attack patterns of the open source software supply chain and mapped them to mitigation measures [18]. Okafor et al. propose a four-stage software supply chain attack pattern and analyzed the security properties of a secure supply chain [19].

Stancy pointed out that security, integrity and authenticity are the three elements of software assurance, and proposed that each software supplier has three phases in the supply chain: supplier procurement, product development and testing, product delivery; IT system supply chain is a set of the personnel, process, and technology, each vendor applies practices and controls for software security, integrity, and authenticity in three phases [20, 21]. ISO/IEC 27036-3 provides guidance on ICT supply chain security in the system life cycle process, incorporates information security processes and practices into the system life cycle process in ISO/IEC 15288, and supports the information security controls described in ISO/IEC 27002 [22].

- ICT supply chain security requirements

ISO/IEC 20243-1 defines requirements for technology development and supply chain security for the risks of malicious tainted and counterfeit products in the supply chain [23]. NSA, ODNI, and CISA provide a comprehensive summary of common threat scenarios and mitigations in the product life cycle for customers, suppliers, and developers in the Enduring Security Framework (ESF) [24]. Boyens et al. defines that the cybersecurity risk of the entire supply chain refers to the harm or damage that may be caused by the cybersecurity risk brought by the supplier, its supply chain and its products or services, and defines a set of controls related to the cybersecurity supply chain [25]. GB/T 36637 describes the ICT supply chain security risk management process and defines control measures from a technical and management perspective [3].

- Application of ICT supply chain security requirements

ISO/IEC 20243–2 defines assessment procedures for mitigating malicious tainted and counterfeit products, proposes general requirements for conformance evidence, and characterizes the requirements for process evidence and implementation evidence [26].

In summary, existing studies solve some basic problems in ICT supply chain security, however our contribution in this paper points out some new solutions for the topic and fills some gaps, as shown in Table 1.

**Table 1.** Comparison of related work

| Topics | Related work | Our work |
|---|---|---|
| Methodology | Security requirements are derived through the analysis of assets, threats, vulnerabilities, risks, and objectives [3, 14, 15, 24, 25], which the common characteristics is based on risk analysis. This method is a widely used for security requirements analysis, however it is relatively more complex and time-consuming | Adequately reuse existing best practices and validate results using the Asset-Threat-Objective-Requirement (ATOR) methodology. It follows the principle of "reusing but validation". This method is suitable for relatively mature areas and less resource investment |

*(continued)*

Table 1. (*continued*)

| Topics | Related work | Our work |
|---|---|---|
| Security environment | The factors involved in the security environment, such as attacks, assurance and stages, are identified [14, 16, 17, 19–22]. However a holistic framework is lacked for combining these factors together, and some important factors are not identified | A global view among security drivers, security properties, security stages, and supply chain relationships is established, which the driving factor of regulatory requirements is identified, and security properties are more complete for ICT supply chain security requirements |
| Security requirements | Security requirements are established from different viewpoints, such as procurement, development, and delivery stage [3, 23–25]. However, it is incomplete for end-to-end ICT supply chain security requirements | The security requirements defined in the paper is for end-to-end ICT supply chain, which fully reflect the processes in system life cycle, covering organization, personnel, processes and technologies |
| Security application | Defines the assessment requirements and evidence requirements corresponding to security requirements [26] | Assessment steps and evidence requirements are defined for each requirement, taking into account the risks of product classification and supplier category, which is more cost-effective and practical for implementation |

## 3 ICT Supply Chain Security Environment

The security environment describes the security aspects of the asset's intended use environment, which includes security assumptions, assets, threats, and organizational security policies [14]. In this paper, the focus is the entire ICT supply chain and every stage in the product life cycle, which is constrained by security driving factors and meets certain security properties. These elements constitute the security environment of the ICT supply chain and serve as the basis for deriving the security requirements of the ICT supply chain, as shown in Fig. 1.

### 3.1 Supply Chain Relationship

The supply chain relationship shown in Fig. 1 is defined in [27], which is the basis of ICT supply chain security. Products are transferred from the raw material to customers or final consumers through the supply chain network. An organization in the ICT supply chain is an acquirer relative to the upstream organization and a supplier relative to

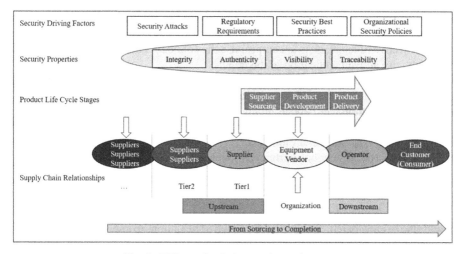

**Fig. 1.** ICT supply chain security environment

the downstream organization. An organizations have complete control over itself, and relatively weak control over upstream and downstream organizations. Any problem in the ICT supply chain will lead to security risks in the ICT supply chain. Therefore, it is necessary for each organization in the supply chain to comply with the baseline ICT supply chain security requirements, as shown in Sect. 4.3 of this paper, in order to improve the overall security assurance level of the supply chain.

### 3.2   Product Life Cycle Stages

Each organization in the supplier relationship shown in Fig. 1, from procurement to completion, needs security considerations in each stags of sourcing, development and delivery [20]. ICT supply chain security needs to be considered in the complete product life cycle, and each stage needs to deploy security control measures, covering people, processes, technologies and organizational elements. The combination of these security control points forms the supply chain security requirements, as shown in 4.3 of this paper.

### 3.3   Security Driving Factors

Among the security driving factors shown in Fig. 1, supply chain security attacks are an important factor. ICT supply chain attacks involve multiple aspects [16–18]:

- The target of attack is commonly important assets, such as ICT internal components, third-party components, and ICT system information.
- The attack methods comprise the security threats, such as information or resource destruction, modification, loss, disclosure and interruption [28], ICT component contamination (including replacement, modification, malware insertion), modification of system data or information (such as documents, checksum).

- The attacker who imposes malicious actions is also called threat agent, such as internal malicious personnel, Advanced Persistent Threat (APT) organization.
- The objective of an attack is to compromise the confidentiality, integrity, availability, authenticity and authentication of the targets.
- The attack time can happen in any stage of the life cycle, such as sourcing, development, delivery, maintenance, etc.
- The attack location can happen in any places, such as third-party component market, logistics, supplier environment, internal Research and Development (R&D) environment, customer environment.
- The attack process may has a life cycle, such as detection, weaponization, delivery, utilization, control, execution and maintenance, which can be mapped to the supply chain product life cycle, [29].

In addition to considering supply chain security attacks, other security driving factors should also be considered: multiple countries have legislations to impose requirements on the supply chain, such as EO14028, NIS2 [12, 13]; the security industry has accumulated a large number of standards and best practices, guiding organizations to carry out security activities; as far as the organization itself is concerned, the organizational security policies constrains its business activities. These driving factors guide the establishment of supply chain security requirements, as shown in Sect. 4 of this paper.

### 3.4  Security Properties

Stacy proposes that software assurance includes three areas in the software supply chain integrity framework: security, authenticity and integrity [20]. However, authenticity and integrity are part of security in a general sense. ISO/IEC 27036-3 aims to solve the problems faced by the supply chain: visibility, transparency and traceability [22]. According to the term defined in literature [1], visibility is also referred to as transparency. In this paper, the security properties of ICT supply chain security are summarized into four aspects: integrity, authenticity, visibility and traceability, which reflect the supply chain security assurance.

Integrity: Integrity is a fundamental security objective, and in the context of supply chains, integrity refers to the development and/or manufacturing process performing its intended function in an uncompromised manner, free from intentional or unintentional manipulation [8]. In the context of security assurance, integrity is the process of sourcing, development, and delivering software that incorporates controls to increase confidence that the software performs as intended by the vendor, and is the collection of processes and controls that protect the security of developed code quality, prevents the inadvertent introduction of vulnerabilities, and helps prevent the intentional insertion of malicious code [20].

Authenticity: Authenticity is the attribute of data originating from its claimed source [30]. In the supply chain, authenticity applies to both the supplier and the product supplied. When working with trusted suppliers according to clearly defined guidelines and standards, the risk of counterfeit products or concerns about the authenticity of suppliers can be minimized [5].

Visibility: Visibility is the nature of openness and accountability throughout the supply chain [1]. Visibility means disclosing the composition and production process of products, enhancing the confidence of customers, and at the same time quickly locating and solving product vulnerabilities. Providing an SBOM, vulnerability disclosure, and providing white-box external audits are examples for achieving visibility.

Traceability: Traceability is the property that allows the activities of an identity, process, or element to be tracked throughout the supply chain [22]. Traceability can be established through version identifiers, Issue ID, barcodes, and internal Requirements Traceability Matrix (RTM).

As shown in Table 1, related literatures have identified some factors involved in the security environment, However a holistic framework is lacked for combining these factors together, and some important factors are not identified. This paper establishes a global view among those factors related to security environments, such as security drivers, security properties, security stages, and supply chain relationships. This paper also identifies some necessary factors for ICT supply chain security. The security environment described in this paper guides the establishment of security requirements in Sect. 4.

## 4   ICT Supply Chain Security Requirements

Security requirements usually include technical requirements and assurance requirements. ICT supply chain security requirements need to consider all stages of the product life cycle, involving organizations, personnel, processes, and technologies [20, 22, 31].

This paper proposes a systematic method to derive ICT supplier security requirements, which firstly establishes the set of requirements from regulatory requirements and security best practices, and then uses the ATOR methodology to validate each requirement.

### 4.1   Establishment Process of Security Requirements

Figure 2 shows the process of establishing ICT supply chain security requirements.

1. Determine the process framework: ICT supply chain security involves the whole life cycle process of the product. ISO/IEC 27036-3 chooses ISO/IEC15288 as the process framework and integrates the ISO/IEC27002 controls [22]. This paper also chooses ISO/IEC 15288 as the process framework, however maps each control of the supplier chain security requirements to the corresponding process of ISO/IEC 15288.
2. Choose candidate topic: This is the key step in establishing security requirements for ICT supply chain. The specific topics to be selected usually depend on the experience of subject-matter-experts. It is also preferable to choose a security standard as a starting point, for example, for the topic of vulnerability management, one of the following specifications can be selected, such as ISO/IEC 29147, ISO/IEC 30111, FIRST service framework, or GSMA NESAS FS.16, and then analyze each of the requirements one by one.
3. Establish a mapping table: This method is based on the fact that there exist multiple similar external requirements for the same topic, with similar content, but there may be some differences, such as the topic of vulnerability management in step 2. For the selected topic, examine each requirement one by one and create a mapping table for the similar requirements.

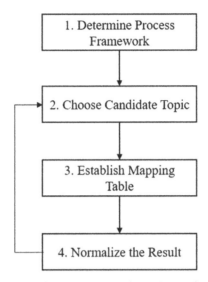

**Fig. 2.** Establishment process of security requirements

4. Normalized the result: Each requirement is usually formulated from a different perspective with a different focus. After the mapping is completed, each set of common and important requirements is summarized as candidate external requirements.
According to our experiences, for each requirement, if more than 2 mapping entries
are found, it can usually be used as a candidate external requirement. If there are other
candidate topics, go to step 2.

Take the Software Bill of Material (SBOM) as an example for illustrating the establishment process of ICT supply chain security requirements. In order to improve product
visibility and traceability, SBOM is a useful tool. Therefore, SBOM is selected as a topic,
and a set of specifications (e.g. regulations, security standards and best practices) are
investigated. As shown in Table 2.

**Table 2.** SBOM Requirements

| Specification | No. | Description |
|---|---|---|
| EO14028 [12] | 4.e.vii | providing a purchaser a Software Bill of Materials (SBOM) for each product directly or by publishing it on a public website |
| EU CRA [32] | I.(2)(1) | identify and document vulnerabilities and components contained in the product, including by drawing up a software bill of materials in a commonly used and machine-readable format covering at the very least the top-level dependencies of the product |

*(continued)*

**Table 2.** (*continued*)

| Specification | No. | Description |
|---|---|---|
| SSDF [33] | PS3.2 | Collect, safeguard, maintain, and share provenance data for all components of each software release (e.g., in a software bill of materials [SBOM]) |
| BSIMM13 [34] | SE3.6 | Create bills of materials for deployed software |

For the candidate topic of SBOM, the corresponding security requirement can be described as: The supplier shall provide the Software Bill of Material (SBOM) of the product.

Some key supplementary information can be stated in the guidance of this requirement, such as the scenarios where SBOM is used, the SBOM standards to be followed, etc.

### 4.2 Validation Process of Security Requirements

For each of the candidate security requirements established in Sect. 4.1, further justification can be provided. Its rationality can be checked on the basis of the following principles: security requirements are based on the results of risk analysis and can effectively reduce the risk of the organization. Some detailed criteria are as follows:

- Do the security requirements mitigate the security risk of one or more elements of confidentiality, integrity, availability of the assets to be protected.
- Whether the security requirements are met: laws and regulations, standards, best practices, customer requirements or top-level management requirements, etc.
- Whether the security requirements are consistent with the supplier's security objectives.
- Whether there are specific cyber attack methods corresponding to the security requirements.

Inspired by the idea of the TVRA method from ETSI [14] and GSMA FS.16 [15], this paper proposes a simplified security requirement analysis method, which is named as ATOR, as shown in Fig. 3, if each requirement can be traced back to security objectives, security threats and assets, then the security requirement is considered as reasonable.

- Environment: refers to the collection of procedures, conditions and objects that affect product development, operation and maintenance [35], such as the build environment;
- Assets: refers to the network products and their components that exist in the process of supplier development and product life cycle, such as products delivered by suppliers, components, documents [15];
- Security threats: refers to the potential cause of an event that may cause harm to the system or organization, and the threat is implemented by a threat agent [14], such as malicious person, APT group;
- Security objectives: refers to confidentiality, integrity, availability, authenticity and accountability [14];

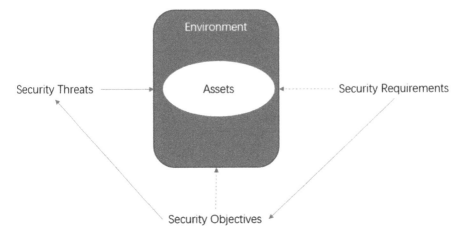

**Fig. 3.** Asset-Threat-Objective-Requirement (ATOR) Methodology

- Security requirements: refers to a requirement that specifies the functional, assurance and strength characteristics of products [36].

Still take the security requirements of SBOM as an example derived in Sect. 4.1, the relationships among the assets, security threats, security objectives, and security requirement for the identified SBOM requirement are shown in Fig. 4.

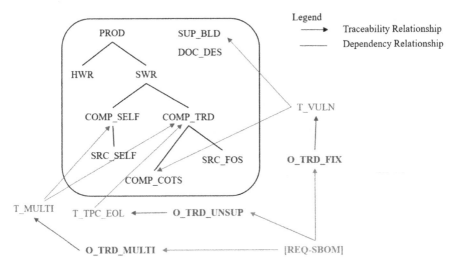

**Fig. 4.** ATOR analysis for the SBOM requirement

The detailed description of the above ATOR analysis is shown in Table 3.

**Table 3.** Description of the ATOR analysis for the SBOM requirement

| Element | Identifier | Description |
|---|---|---|
| Asset (A) | PROD | Product delivered to customer |
| | HWR | Hardware part of the product, which software image is usually installed |
| | SWR | Software part of the product, which is built from software components |
| | COMP_SELF | Self-developed components |
| | SRC_SELF | Self-developed source code |
| | COMP_TRD | Third-party developed components |
| | COMP_COTS | Software package created by the third-party supplier |
| | SRC_FOS | Third-party free open-source component |
| | ENV_BLD | Build environment |
| | DOC_DES | Design document |
| Threat (T) | T_VULN | An attacker compromises a third-party component |
| | T_MULTI | The organization uses multiple versions of the same component, and may not fix all vulnerabilities |
| | T_TPC_EOL | The organization is not aware of the use of unsupported and vulnerable versions, and cannot fix the vulnerabilities in a timely manner, resulting in loss to users |
| Target (O) | O_TRD_FIX | Analyze the impact of vulnerabilities and quickly fix them |
| | O_TRD_MULTI | Identify all versions of the same component |
| | O_TRD_UNSUP | Avoid using expired unsupported and vulnerable versions |
| Requirement (R) | REQ-SBOM | The supplier shall provide the Software Bill of Material (SBOM) of the product |

From the above analysis which is based on ATOR methodology, it can be concluded that the SBOM requirements is justified. This method addresses ICT supply chain security requirements from two different ways, which shows that the security requirement is valid and reasonable. All other requirements can be derived in the similar way.

### 4.3 Summary of the ICT Supply Chain Security Requirements

According to the methodology in Sect. 4.1 and 4.2, the ICT supply chain security requirements are currently established with a total of 10 categories and 100 items of requirements, which the summary is shown in Table 4.

The ICT supply chain security requirements defined in this paper adequately reuse existing best practices, and the ATOR methodology is used to validate the results. It is

**Table 4.** ICT supply chain security requirement category, quantity, key points and mapping to ISO/IEC 15288 process

| Category | Quantity | Key Points | ISO/IEC 15288 Process |
|---|---|---|---|
| Organization and Personnel | 5 | Organization's security policies, personnel roles and responsibilities, skills, training, and code of conduct | Human Resource |
| Environment security | 6 | Endpoint security, R&D and production environment security, access control, and monitoring | Infrastructure Management |
| Technology Management | 23 | Continuous improvement, asset classification, asset protection, configuration item management and control, reproducible build, build parameters, version identification, and version release gating control | Quality Management, Information Management, Configuration Management, and Transition |
| Technology Baseline | 21 | Identification, authentication, authorization, and accounting, key security parameter management, personal and critical data protection, cryptography, and resilience | System Requirement Definition |
| Third-party Component Security | 4 | Sourcing, review, and continuous monitoring of components | Acquisition |
| Security Design and Development | 7 | Security design principles, threat modeling, attack surface analysis, secure coding, and code review | Architecture Definition, Design Definition |
| Security Test | 8 | Security feature test, abuse case test, fuzzy test, and penetration test | Verification, Validation |
| Product manufacturing security | 3 | Authenticity and integrity check of components | Implementation |

*(continued)*

**Table 4.** (*continued*)

| Category | Quantity | Key Points | ISO/IEC 15288 Process |
|---|---|---|---|
| Secure delivery | 14 | End-of-life, SBOM, patch, upgrade, hardening, security documents Example: The supplier shall provide the Software Bill of Material (SBOM) of the product | Transition |
| Security Vulnerability and Incident Management | 9 | Disclosure Policy, Vulnerability Reception, Analysis, Remediation, and Release | Operation, Maintenance |

suitable for relatively mature topics and less resource investment. The security requirements is for end-to-end ICT supply chain, which fully reflect the processes in system life cycle, covering organization, personnel, processes and technologies.

## 5  Application of ICT Supply Chain Security Requirements

In addition to formulating its own security governance system, each organization also needs to convey security requirements to upstream suppliers. There are several scenarios in applying ICT supply chain security requirements:

1. Organization establishes its own baselined supply chain security requirements or uses them for self-assessment;
2. The organization provides the security requirements to upstream suppliers as supplement of the supplier contract;
3. The security requirements are used for supplier security self-assessment or supplier on-site assessment conducted by the downstream organization.

The implementation of ICT supply chain security requirements can follow the Plan-Do-Check-Act (PDCA) methodology:

- Plan (P): The organization specifies the security requirements of the ICT supply chain in the product life cycle based on laws and regulations, security standards, security best practices, and customer security requirements;
- Do (D): The supply chain security requirements are conveyed to the suppliers through supplier security agreements;
- Check (C): Assess whether the supplier's security requirements are implemented and identify the gaps.
- Act (A): Resolve the identified gaps and continuously improve.

Furthermore, due to the inconsistent levels of different products and suppliers, they can be categorized and classified according to the risks of the product and supplier. For example, mature suppliers only need to provide self-assessment reports, while high-risk suppliers need on-site assessment, as shown in Table 5 and Table 6.

**Table 5.** Selection of Security Requirements

| Product Risks | Security Requirements |
| --- | --- |
| Low | Basic Requirements |
| Medium | Basic requirements + medium requirements |
| High | All requirements |

**Table 6.** Selection of Assessment Method

| Supplier risk | Assessment Method |
| --- | --- |
| Low | Self-Assessment |
| Medium | Sampling products |
| High | Onsite Assessment: Process audit and product evaluation |

The security requirements defined in Sect. 4 are independent of specific products, the products provided by supplier only affect the depth and method of the assessment. For example, database component is usually deployed on the core network zone, according to the EU-5G classification [37], this product is classified as a high-risk component, the product will be verified against all requirements according to Table 5. The application of the systematic method introduced in this paper is shown as follows.

1. Establish security requirements

   The security requirements are established before sourcing suppliers. According to the method in Sect. 4, the security requirements for the topic "Security Vulnerability and Incident Management" are established, some of them are excerpted as follows.
   a) A vulnerability disclosure policy shall be developed and published.
   b) Security contact point shall be communicated to the customer and third-party vulnerability disclosures.
   c) A secure channel for receiving vulnerability reports shall be provided.
   d) Vulnerability verification shall be completed within the specified time.
2. Determine assessment criteria

   Each security requirement above shall be assessed according to the criteria established by the acquirer, some of them are shown in Table 7.

   Each security requirement in Table 4 has a detailed description and corresponding assessment criteria.

   The assessment results can one of the following values: Fully Compliant, Largely Compliant, Partially Compliant, Not Compliant and Not Applicable, depending on the degree of conformance.

**Table 7.** Assessment Criteria

| No | Assessment steps | Evidence of organizational level | Evidence of product line or business unit | Assessment results |
|---|---|---|---|---|
| a) | Check whether the vulnerability disclosure policy is established and published | 1) Vulnerability disclosure policy 2) Release record of vulnerability disclosure policy | N/A[a] | |
| b) | Check whether security contact point is communicated to the customers and third-party vulnerability disclosers | Notification record of security contact point | N/A | |
| c) | 1) Check whether secure channels are provided to receive vulnerability reports; 2) Check whether the reported vulnerability is processed within the specified time | 1) The secure channel for receiving vulnerability reports 2) Execution record for reported vulnerability | N/A | |
| d) | Check whether the authenticity of the vulnerability is verified within the specified time, and whether it is a repeated vulnerability report | Specification of vulnerability verification | Vulnerability verification record | |

[a] N/A is the abbreviation of "Not Applicable".

3. Convey security requirements and assessment criteria

Security requirements and assessment criteria are delivered to suppliers in the form of Service-Level Agreement (SLA), which are used as the basis for supplier self-assessment or on-site assessments initiated by the acquirer.

4. Selection and implementation of assessment methods

As mentioned earlier, the selected product is a high-risk component and all requirements need to be checked according to Table 5. According to the organization's policy, the provider is a high-risk supplier, so an on-site assessment of the supplier is carried out, covering process audit and product evaluation according to Table 6.

Finally, the supplier shall resolve the gaps for the discovered issues during the assessment.

## 6   Conclusions and Future Work

In this paper, based on the context of ICT supply chain relationships, the environment of ICT supply chain security is established through attack frameworks, regulatory requirements, industry best practices, security properties, and life cycle stages. A systematical method is proposed to establish security requirements for ICT supply chain based on regulatory requirements and industry best practices, to use ATOR methodology to validate the rationality of each requirement, and finally to come up with security requirements for ICT supply chain. The application scenario and method of supplier security requirements is put forward from the perspective of product and supplier. Some further works include establishment of trust relationship among suppliers, in-depth research on visibility and traceability properties in the context of ICT supply chain security.

## References

1. Boyens, J., Paulsen, C., Bartol, N., Shankles, S.A., Moorthy, R.: Notional supply chain risk management practices for federal information systems. National Institute of Standards and Technology, Gaithersburg, MD (2012). https://doi.org/10.6028/NIST.IR.7622
2. Supply Chain Compromise, Technique T1195 - Enterprise | MITRE ATT&CK®. https://attack.mitre.org/techniques/T1195/. Accessed 10 June 2023
3. TC260: GB/T 36637-2018 Information security technology-Guidelines for the information and communication technology supply chain risk management (in Chinese) (2018)
4. ENISA Threat Landscape 2022. https://www.enisa.europa.eu/publications/enisa-threat-landscape-2022. Accessed 11 May 2023
5. Supply Chain Integrity: An overview of the ICT supply chain risks and challenges, and vision for the way forward (2015). https://www.enisa.europa.eu/publications/sci-2015. Accessed 25 May 2023
6. Authoritative UK Organization Recognizes Code and Build Engineering of Huawei OLT Product MA5800. https://www.huawei.com/en/news/2019/12/huawei-ma5800-code-evaluation-build-engineering-assessment. Accessed 17 Oct 2023
7. Assessment of the Critical Supply Chains Supporting the U.S. ICT Industry | Homeland Security. https://www.dhs.gov/publication/assessment-critical-supply-chains-supporting-us-ict-industry. Accessed 18 May 2023
8. The Open Group: Open Trusted Technology Provider Framework (O-TTPF) (2021)
9. CVE security vulnerability database. Security vulnerabilities, exploits, references and more. https://www.cvedetails.com/index.php. Accessed 18 Oct 2023
10. Ghadge, A., Weiß, M., Caldwell, N.D., Wilding, R.: Managing cyber risk in supply chains: a review and research agenda. Supply Chain Manage.: Int. J. **25**, 223–240 (2020). https://doi.org/10.1108/SCM-10-2018-0357

11. Cybersecurity Workforce Study. https://www.isc2.org/research. Accessed 18 Oct 2023
12. Executive Order on Improving the Nation's Cybersecurity. https://www.whitehouse.gov/bri efing-room/presidential-actions/2021/05/12/executive-order-on-improving-the-nations-cyb ersecurity/. Accessed 19 Apr 2023
13. Directive (EU) 2022/2555 of the European Parliament and of the Council of 14 December 2022 on measures for a high common level of cybersecurity across the Union, amending Regulation (EU) No 910/2014 and Directive (EU) 2018/1972, and repealing Directive (EU) 2016/1148 (NIS 2 Directive). OJ L333, pp. 80–152 (2022). https://eur-lex.europa.eu/eli/dir/ 2022/2555. Accessed 18 Apr 2023
14. ETSI: ETSI TS 102 165-1 V5.2.5 CYBER; Methods and protocols; Part 1: Method and pro forma for Threat, Vulnerability, Risk Analysis (TVRA) (2022)
15. GSMA: FS.16 - Network Equipment Security Assurance Scheme – Development and Lifecycle Security Requirements Version 2.2 (2022)
16. Threat Landscape for Supply Chain Attacks. https://www.enisa.europa.eu/publications/thr eat-landscape-for-supply-chain-attacks. Accessed 18 Apr 2023
17. Miller, J.F.: Supply Chain Attack Framework and Attack Patterns. https://www.mitre.org/ news-insights/publication/supply-chain-attack-framework-and-attack-patterns. Accessed 06 May 2023
18. Ladisa, P., Plate, H., Martinez, M., Barais, O.: Taxonomy of attacks on open-source software supply chains. arXiv preprint arXiv:2204.04008 (2022)
19. Okafor, C., Schorlemmer, T.R., Torres-Arias, S., Davis, J.C.: SoK: analysis of software supply chain security by establishing secure design properties. In: Proceedings of the 2022 ACM Workshop on Software Supply Chain Offensive Research and Ecosystem Defenses, pp. 15–24 (2022). https://doi.org/10.1145/3560835.3564556
20. Stacy, S.: Framework for Software Supply Chain Integrity. https://safecode.org/resource-secure-development-practices/framework-for-software-supply-chain-integrity/. Accessed 18 Apr 2023
21. Stacy, S.: Overview of Software Integrity Controls. https://safecode.org/resource-secure-dev elopment-practices/overview-of-software-integrity-controls/. Accessed 18 Apr 2023
22. ISO/IEC: ISO/IEC 27036-3:2013 Information technology - Security techniques - Information security for supplier relationships - Part 3: Guidelines for information and communication technology supply chain security (2013)
23. ISO/IEC: ISO/IEC 20243-1:2018 Information technology - Open Trusted Technology Provider Standard (O-TTPS) - Mitigating maliciously tainted and counterfeit products - Part 1: Requirements and recommendations (2018)
24. Enduring Security Framework ESF. https://www.nsa.gov/About/Cybersecurity-Collabora tion-Center/Cybersecurity-Partnerships/ESF/. Accessed 19 Apr 2023
25. Boyens, J., Smith, A., Bartol, N., Winkler, K., Holbrook, A., Fallon, M.: Cybersecurity supply chain risk management for systems and organizations. National Institute of Standards and Technology, Gaithersburg, MD (2022). https://doi.org/10.6028/NIST.SP.800-161r1
26. ISO/IEC: ISO/IEC 20243-2:2018 Information technology - Open Trusted Technology Provider Standard (O-TTPS) - Mitigating maliciously tainted and counterfeit products - Part 2: Assessment procedures for the O-TTPS and ISO/IEC 20243-1:2018 (2018)
27. ISO/IEC: ISO/IEC 27036-1:2021 Cybersecurity - Supplier relationships - Part 1: Overview and concepts (2021)
28. ITU-T: X.805: Security architecture for systems providing end-to-end communications (2003)
29. Heinbockel, W.J., Laderman, E.R., Serrao, G.J.: Supply chain attacks and resiliency mitiga-tions. https://www.mitre.org/news-insights/publication/supply-chain-attacks-and-resiliency-mitigations. Accessed 06 May 2023
30. The Minimum Elements for a Software Bill of Materials (SBOM). https://www.ntia.gov/rep ort/2021/minimum-elements-software-bill-materials-sbom. Accessed 22 Apr 2023

31. ISO/IEC: ISO/IEC 15408-1:2022 Evaluation criteria for IT security - Part 1: Introduction and general model (2022)
32. Cyber Resilience Act | Shaping Europe's digital future. https://digital-strategy.ec.europa.eu/en/library/cyber-resilience-act. Accessed 18 Apr 2023
33. Souppaya, M., Scarfone, K., Dodson, D.: Secure software development framework (SSDF) version 1.1: recommendations for mitigating the risk of software vulnerabilities. National Institute of Standards and Technology, Gaithersburg (2022). https://doi.org/10.6028/NIST.SP.800-218
34. BSIMM13 Foundations. https://www.synopsys.com/software-integrity/engage/bsimm-web/bsimm13-foundations. Accessed 14 June 2023
35. NIST: Minimum security requirements for federal information and information systems. National Institute of Standards and Technology, Gaithersburg (2006). https://doi.org/10.6028/NIST.FIPS.200
36. Ross, R., Pillitteri, V., Graubart, R., Bodeau, D., McQuaid, R.: Developing cyber-resilient systems: a systems security engineering approach. National Institute of Standards and Technology, Gaithersburg (2021). https://doi.org/10.6028/NIST.SP.800-160v2r1
37. EU-wide coordinated risk assessment of 5G networks security | Shaping Europe's digital future. https://digital-strategy.ec.europa.eu/en/news/eu-wide-coordinated-risk-assessment-5g-networks-security. Accessed 20 Oct 2023

# Pairing Compression on Some Elliptic Curves with Subgroups of Embedding Degree 6 and Its Applications to Pairing-Based Cryptography

Liang Li[1,2] and Gengran Hu[1(✉)]

[1] School of Cyberspace, Hangzhou Dianzi University, Hangzhou 310018, China
grhu@hdu.edu.cn
[2] Zhejiang Lab, Hangzhou 311121, Zhejiang, China
liangli@zhejianglab.com

**Abstract.** As a subfield of elliptic curve cryptography, pairing-based cryptography has gained significant attention due to its practical and flexible functionality. In pairing-based cryptographic systems, it is necessary to have elliptic curves defined over finite fields with an appropriate embedding degree and non-degenerate bilinear pairing maps. This paper primarily focuses on the pairing maps. When certain conditions are met, it becomes feasible to compress the pairing values simultaneously on specific elliptic curves, achieving a compression ratio of $1/6$. Additionally, in pairing-based cryptography, it is feasible to represent the elliptic curve points only by their x-coordinate or y-coordinate through a compression function. This approach enables saving a significant amount of communication or storage in protocols such as BLS and IBE, thereby enhancing their efficiency.

**Keywords:** elliptic curves · pairing-based cryptography · compression

## 1 Introduction

For an elliptic curve $E$ over a finite field $\mathbb{F}_q$, the elliptic curve discrete logarithm problem (ECDLP) is solving the equation $[m]P = P'$ with a solution $m$ for known points $P, P' \in E(\mathbb{F}_q)$. There are some researches on MOV and FR-reduction, such as [1,2]. These attacks reduce ECDLP in $\langle G \rangle \subset E(\mathbb{F}_q)$ to DLP in a subgroup of $\mathbb{F}_{q^k}^*$ for $k$ to be the embedding degree. MOV-reduction reduces ECDLP to DLP by utilizing the Weil pairing and FR-reduction through the Tate pairing. There also exist some other pairings, including the Eta pairing [3], the Ate pairing [4], and their generalizations [5]. Pairings are used in cryptographic

This work was supported by the Scientific Research Fund of Zhejiang Provincial Education Department (No. Y201942341), the National Natural Science Foundation of China (No. 61602143), and the Postdoctoral Research Project of Zhejiang Province (No. ZJ2022115).

J. Shao et al. (Eds.): EISA 2023, CCIS 2004, pp. 77–91, 2024.
https://doi.org/10.1007/978-981-99-9614-8_5

applications widely such as identity-based encryption [6], one-round 3-party key agreement protocols [7], and short signature schemes [8].

Pairing-based cryptography is a cryptographic framework that utilizes bilinear pairings on elliptic curve groups to provide advanced security features and enable new cryptographic functionalities. It extends the capabilities of traditional public-key cryptography by leveraging the mathematical properties of bilinear maps. In pairing-based cryptography, the central component is the bilinear pairing function, which takes as input two elements from elliptic curve groups and produces a result in a different group. This pairing function exhibits useful properties, such as bilinearity, non-degeneracy, and computationally hard problems, which form the basis for various cryptographic protocols. Pairing computation, the most time-consuming operation in pairing-based cryptographic systems, is still relatively expensive compared to ECC operations. Therefore, developing new techniques and methods to optimize the efficiency of pairing-based cryptography has become a significant research topic.

Identity-Based Encryption (IBE) scheme allows encryption and decryption operations based on user identities rather than traditional public keys. It enables more efficient key management and secure communication in large-scale systems. The Boneh-Franklin IBE scheme [9] is a well-known and widely-used construction in the field of cryptography. The pairing-based short signature schemes, such as the BLS signature scheme [8], provide compact signatures with efficient verification. They are useful for scenarios with limited resources and bandwidth constraints. Pairing-based cryptography has witnessed significant advancements in recent years, with developing research focused on enhancing security, efficiency, and expanding its applications [10–12].

## 1.1  Related Work

Generally speaking, pairing includes two points defined as $P \in E(\mathbb{F}_q)$, $Q \in E(\mathbb{F}_{q^k})$ on a curve with $k$ to be the embedding degree. Some researchers found $Q$ can be chosen from a smaller field. Barreto, Lynn and Scott [13] showed that if $k$ is even, $Q$ can be set as a point on $E'(\mathbb{F}_{q^{k/2}})$, where $E'$ is a quadratic twist curve of $E$. Barreto and Naehrig [14] worked on curves with sextic twists and embedding degree $k = 12$, showing that $Q$ can be set as a point on $E'(\mathbb{F}_{q^{k/6}})$, where $E'$ is a sextic twist curve of $E$. Scott and Barreto [15] found how to compute and implicitly exponentiate the compressed pairings by using laddering algorithms. The compression ratio in their work is $1/2$ for characteristic $p > 3$ and $1/3$ for characteristic $p = 3$. Barreto and Naehrig [14] got the compression ratio of $1/6$ when the embedding degree is 12. They also suggested that prime pairs $(p, n)$ could define an extension of XTR (see [16]). In addition, there are other compression techniques available [17,18]. These techniques provide alternative approaches to compressing data and offer additional options for improving efficiency in cryptographic protocols.

## 1.2   Contributions

In this paper, the pairing compression on some elliptic curves is discussed. Drawing inspiration from the method proposed by Barreto and Naehrig, we generalize pairing compression on one single elliptic curve to several elliptic curves and present how to compress the pairing values of some elliptic curves when there exists at least one elliptic curve satisfied the fixed conditions. By leveraging the compression properties of elliptic curve points, we apply them to improve the efficiency of protocols such as BLS signature and IBE. This involves utilizing point compression techniques on elliptic curves to enhance the performance of these protocols.

This paper is organized as follows. In Sect. 2, we give the preliminaries of Tate pairing, embedding degree and compressed pairing. Section 3 describes the detailed process of pairing compression. And in Sect. 4, the applications to pairing-based cryptography is proposed, such as BLS signature scheme and IBE scheme. We draw the conclusion in Sect. 5.

## 2   Preliminaries

Let $E/K$ be an elliptic curve. The divisor group of $E$ is an abelian group generated by the points on $E$,

$$\mathrm{Div}(E) = \{ \sum_{P \in E} m_P \langle P \rangle \mid m_P \in \mathbb{Z}, \text{ there are finitely}$$

$$\text{many } P \in E \text{ with } m_P \neq 0\}.$$

A divisor is an element $\Delta = \sum_{P \in E} m_P \langle P \rangle \in \mathrm{Div}(E)$. The degree of the divisor $\Delta$ is the sum $\deg \Delta = \sum_{P \in E} m_P$. The divisor of a non-zero function $f \in K(E)$ is $\mathrm{div}(f) = \sum_{P \in E} \mathrm{ord}_P(f) \langle P \rangle$. A divisor $\Delta$ is called principal if $\Delta = \mathrm{div}(f)$ for some function $f$. The support of a divisor $D = \sum_{P \in E} m_P \langle P \rangle$ is the set of points $P \in E$ for which $m_P \neq 0$. If $\mathrm{supp}(\Delta) \cap \mathrm{supp}(\mathrm{div}(f)) = \emptyset$, define $f(\Delta) := \prod_P f(P)^{m_P}$. A divisor $\Delta$ is principal if and only if $\deg \Delta = 0$ and $\sum_{P \in E} m_P P = \mathcal{O}$ ([19], Corollary 3.3.5). Two divisors $\Delta_1, \Delta_2$ are equivalent, $\Delta_1 \sim \Delta_2$ if $\Delta_1 - \Delta_2$ is a principal divisor.

For prime number $r$, $\#E(\mathbb{F}_q) = q+1-t$ is divisible by $r$. An $r$-order subgroup of $E(\mathbb{F}_q)$ has embedding degree $k$, implying that $k$ is the minimum positive number satisfying $r \mid q^k - 1$. For $P \in E(\mathbb{F}_{q^k})[r]$, $Q \in E(\mathbb{F}_{q^k})$, let $f_{m,P}$ be a rational function in $\mathbb{F}_{q^k}(E)$ such that $\mathrm{div}(f_{m,P}) = m\langle P \rangle - \langle [m]P \rangle - (m-1)\langle \mathcal{O} \rangle$ for any $m \in \mathbb{N}^*$. Let $\mathcal{D}_Q$ be a divisor such that $\mathcal{D}_Q \sim \langle Q \rangle - \langle \mathcal{O} \rangle$ and $\mathcal{D}_Q$'s support is disjoint from $\mathrm{div}(f_{r,P})$'s where $\mathrm{div}(f_{r,P}) = r\langle P \rangle - r\langle \mathcal{O} \rangle$. Let $\mu_r$ be a subgroup of $\mathbb{F}_{q^k}^*$ generated by the $r$-th root of unity. Then the $r$-th Tate pairing [20] is a map

$$\tau_r : E(\mathbb{F}_{q^k})[r] \times E(\mathbb{F}_{q^k})/rE(\mathbb{F}_{q^k}) \to \mu_r,$$

where $\tau_r(P, Q) = f_{r,P}(\mathcal{D}_Q)^{(q^k-1)/r}$. Compared with the Weil pairing, the Tate pairing is bilinear and non-degenerate, and it has wide applications in both theoretical and cryptographic fields.

When $r \mid \#E(\mathbb{F}_q)$, since $E(\mathbb{F}_q)[r] \subseteq E(\mathbb{F}_{q^k})[r]$, the Tate pairing can be represented as:

$$\tau_r : E(\mathbb{F}_q)[r] \times E(\mathbb{F}_{q^k})/rE(\mathbb{F}_{q^k}) \rightarrow \mu_r.$$

We use the example in [15] to give the definition of compressed pairings. In the case that the embedding degree is $k = 2$ for a subgroup of prime order $n$, every element in $\mathbb{F}_{q^2}$ has the form of $x + iy$, with $x, y \in \mathbb{F}_q$, and $i^2 = \delta \in \mathbb{F}_q$ is a quadratic non-residue. Then

$$(x + iy)^{q-1} = (x + iy)^q/(x + iy) = (x - iy)/(x + iy).$$

Here $a + ib = (x + iy)^{q-1}$ satisfying:

$$a^2 - \delta b^2 = 1,$$

with $a^2 - \delta b^2$ to be the norm of $a + ib$. So $(a + ib)^{-1} = (a - ib)$.

More generally, each element in $\mathbb{F}_{q^2}$ with order dividing $q + 1$ has the above property. By the definition of Tate pairing, we know $\tau_n(P, Q) = z^{(q^2-1)/n}$ where $z = f_{n,P}(\mathcal{D}_Q)$. Since the embedding degree is 2, $n \mid q + 1$. Let $x + iy = z^{(q+1)/2}$, then

$$\tau_n(P, Q) = a + ib$$
$$\Rightarrow a - ib = (a + ib)^{-1} = \tau_n(P, Q)^{-1} = \tau_n(P, -Q).$$

Thus $\mathbb{F}_q$-trace $\mathrm{tr}(\tau_n(P, Q)) \equiv \tau_n(P, Q) + \tau_n(P, Q)^q = (a + ib) + (a + ib)^q = (a + ib) + (a - ib) = 2a$. Since there is no imaginary part, $\mathrm{tr}(\tau_n(P, Q)) = \mathrm{tr}(\tau_n(P, -Q))$. Here we give the definition of the compressed Tate pairing as $\varepsilon(P, Q) \triangleq \mathrm{tr}(\tau_n(P, \overline{Q}))$, where $\overline{Q} \in \{Q, -Q\}$.

## 3  Pairing Compression

Barreto and Naehrig [14] worked on elliptic curves with sextic twists and embedding degree $k$ to be 12, and presented the pairing compression by the traces of the pairing values. In this section, we will use this method to handle a more general case and give the pairing compression on some elliptic curves simultaneously with subgroups of embedding degree 6.

Now we consider that $char(\mathbb{F}_q) \neq 2, 3$, or the case $E(\mathbb{F}_{q^2}) : y^2 = x^3 + b$. Suppose $n$ is the prime order of the subgroup and $k$ is the embedding degree.

**Lemma 1.** *Let $q$ be a power of an odd prime. When $q \equiv 1 \pmod{k}$ and $(k, w) = 1$, $x^k - \xi^w$ is irreducible over $\mathbb{F}_q[x]$ for any primitive element $\xi \in \mathbb{F}_q^*$.*

*Proof.* If $x^k - \xi^w$ is reducible, then there is an irreducible polynomial $f(x)$ in $\mathbb{F}_q[x]$ and $f(x)|x^k - \xi^w$. Let $\beta$ be a root of $f(x)$ and $0 < c = \deg f(x) < k$, then $\beta^{q^c-1} = 1$. And $\beta^k = \xi^w \in \mathbb{F}_q$, then $\beta^{q^c-1} = \xi^{\frac{w(q^c-1)}{k}} = \xi^{\frac{q-1}{k} \cdot cw} \neq 1$ for $c < k$ which yields a contradiction.

Let
$$S = \{n \mid E(\mathbb{F}_{q^2}) \text{ has a subgroup of prime}$$
$$\text{order } n, \text{with embedding degree } 6\}. \tag{1}$$

That is, $\forall\, n \in S$, $k < 6$, $n \nmid q^{2k} - 1$ and $n \mid q^{12} - 1$. We assume $S \neq \emptyset$.

For $\mathrm{char}(\mathbb{F}_q) \neq 3$, we know $6 \mid q^2 - 1$. Choose a primitive element $\xi \in \mathbb{F}_{q^2}^*$ and $w$ satifying $(q^2 - 1, w) = 1$, by Lemma 1, $\mathbb{F}_{q^{12}} \cong \mathbb{F}_{q^2}[x]/(x^6 - \xi^w)$. As $(q^2 - 1, q^2 - 2) = 1$ and $q^2 - 2 \equiv 5 \pmod{6}$, we have $w \equiv 1$ or $5 \pmod 6$. Let $z \in \mathbb{F}_{q^{12}}$ be a root of $x^6 - \xi^w$, then $z^6 = \xi^w$. Define a twist curve $E' : y^2 = x^3 + \frac{b}{\xi^w}$.

For given $s$, the numbers of rational points of $y^2 = x^3 + \frac{b}{\xi^{s+6l}}$ over $\mathbb{F}_{q^2}$ are the same for every $l \in \mathbb{N}$. We call $\eta$ *effective* on $E(\mathbb{F}_{q^2})$ if $\eta \in \mathbb{F}_{q^2}$ and for every integer $s$, the numbers of $\mathbb{F}_{q^2}$-rational points of $E_1 : y^2 = x^3 + \frac{b}{\eta^s}$ and $E_2 : y^2 = x^3 + \frac{b}{\eta^{s+2}}$ are different.

**Lemma 2.** *If there exists $\eta$ effective on $E(\mathbb{F}_{q^2})$, then any primitive element $\xi \in \mathbb{F}_{q^2}^*$ is effective on $E(\mathbb{F}_{q^2})$.*

*Proof.* We only need to prove the cases of $\eta = \xi^t$, $t \equiv 2$ or $4 \pmod 6$. Then the numbers of $\mathbb{F}_{q^2}$-rational points of these elliptic curves $\{y^2 = x^3 + \frac{b}{\xi^s} \mid s = 0, 2, 4\}$ are different, so as the corresponding twist curves.

**Theorem 1** ([21] **Theorem 1**). *Let $E/\mathbb{F}_q$ be an elliptic curve. Let $l$ be a prime number satisfying $l \mid \#E(\mathbb{F}_q)$ and $l \nmid q - 1$. Then $E(\mathbb{F}_{q^k})$ contains $l^2$ points with order $l$ if and only if $l \mid q^k - 1$.*

**Proposition 1.** *By the above notations, for every $n \in S$, $\xi$ is effective on $E(\mathbb{F}_{q^2})$ if and only if there exists $w$ s.t. $n \mid \#E'(\mathbb{F}_{q^2})$.*

*Proof.* Necessity: We know that $w \equiv 1$ or $5 \pmod 6$. Let $E_1 : y^2 = x^3 + \frac{b}{\xi}$ and $E_2 : y^2 = x^3 + \frac{b}{\xi^5}$. For $s = 1$ or $2$, $n_s = \#E_s(\mathbb{F}_{q^2})$ and $t_s$ is the Frobenius trace. Let $N$ to be $\#E(\mathbb{F}_{q^2})$ and $T$ to be the corresponding Frobenius trace, clearly, $n \mid N$. Since $\xi$ is a quadratic non-residue in $\mathbb{F}_{q^6}$, so $E_1$ is a twisted curve of $E$ over $\mathbb{F}_{q^6}$. By Weil theory, $\#E(\mathbb{F}_{q^6}) = q^6 + 1 - (T^3 - 3Tq^2)$ and $\#E_1(\mathbb{F}_{q^6}) = q^6 + 1 - (t_1^3 - 3t_1q^2)$, then we have $t_1^3 - 3t_1q^2 = 3Tq^2 - T^3$. As $\xi$ is effective, we have $t_1^2 - t_1T + T^2 = 3q^2$. Similarly, there is the same result for $E_2$. Then $t_1 + t_2 = T$ and $t_1t_2 = T^2 - 3q^2$. We have
$$n_1 n_3 = (q^2 + 1 - t_1)(q^2 + 1 - t_2)$$
$$= (q^2 + 1)^2 - (q^2 + 1)T + T^2 - 3q^2$$
$$= (q^4 - q^2 + 1) - T(q^2 + 1 - T).$$

Since $n \mid N$ and $n \mid q^4 - q^2 + 1$, for $\forall n \in S$, $n \mid (n_1 n_3)$, so $n \mid n_1$ or $n \mid n_3$.

Sufficiency: For $\forall s \in \mathbb{Z}$, define a map $\dot{E} : y^2 = x^3 + \frac{b}{\xi^s} \to \ddot{E} : y^2 = x^3 + \frac{b}{\xi^{s\pm2}}$, $(x, y) \mapsto (\xi^{\mp\frac{2}{3}}x, \xi^{\mp1}y)$. For $n \in S$, if $n \mid \#\dot{E}(\mathbb{F}_{q^2})$, by Theorem 1, $\#\dot{E}(\mathbb{F}_{q^2})[n] = n$. Since $\xi^{\frac{2}{3}} \in \mathbb{F}_{q^6} \setminus \mathbb{F}_{q^2}$, then $\#\dot{E}(\mathbb{F}_{q^2}) \neq \#\ddot{E}(\mathbb{F}_{q^2})$. By the above notations, we have $T \neq -t_1$ and $T \neq -t_2$. As $S \neq \emptyset$ and there exists $w \equiv 1$ or $5 \pmod 6$ such that $n \mid \#E'(\mathbb{F}_{q^2})$, then $t_1 \neq t_2$.

In the following, we define three sets of elliptic curves,

$$\Gamma_1 = \{\widetilde{E} \mid \widetilde{E} : y^2 = x^3 + \frac{b}{\xi^{1+6l}}, \ \forall \, l \in \mathbb{Z}\}, \tag{2}$$

$$\Gamma_2 = \{\widetilde{E} \mid \widetilde{E} : y^2 = x^3 + \frac{b}{\xi^{5+6l}}, \ \forall \, l \in \mathbb{Z}\}, \tag{3}$$

and

$$\Gamma = \{\widetilde{E} \mid \widetilde{E} : y^2 = x^3 + c, \ \forall \, c \in \mathbb{F}_{q^2}^*\}. \tag{4}$$

Moreover, let

$$S_1 = \{n \in S \mid n \mid \#E_1(\mathbb{F}_{q^2}), \ \forall \, E_1 \in \Gamma_1\}, \tag{5}$$

$$S_2 = \{n \in S \mid n \mid \#E_2(\mathbb{F}_{q^2}), \ \forall \, E_2 \in \Gamma_2\}, \tag{6}$$

By the above proof, we know $S = S_1 \cup S_2$. Choosing $n \in S$, if $n \in S_i$, then $E' \in \Gamma_i$ where $i \in \{1, 2\}$.

Next, we assume $\xi$ is effective. For every $j \in \mathbb{Z}$, denote the elliptic curve by $E_j' : y^2 = x^3 + \frac{b}{z^{6(1-j)}}$, the injective map by

$$\psi : E'(\mathbb{F}_{q^2}) \longrightarrow E_j'(\mathbb{F}_{q^{12}})$$
$$(x, y) \longmapsto (z^{2j} x, z^{3j} y),$$

and the isomorphic map by

$$f : E_j'(\mathbb{F}_{q^{12}}) \longrightarrow E(\mathbb{F}_{q^{12}})$$
$$(x, y) \longmapsto (z^{2(1-j)} x, z^{3(1-j)} y).$$

The inverse map $g = f^{-1} : E(\mathbb{F}_{q^{12}}) \to E_j'(\mathbb{F}_{q^{12}})$ is $(x', y') \mapsto (\frac{x'}{z^{2(1-j)}}, \frac{y'}{z^{3(1-j)}})$. Let $\phi$ be $q$-Frobenius map with $\phi(x, y) = (x^q, y^q)$. We know $\phi^2$ is the Frobenius endomorphism on $E$. For every positive even $c \mid 12$, we define the trace map by

$$\mathrm{tr}_{\mathbb{F}_{q^c}} : E(\mathbb{F}_{q^{12}}) \longrightarrow E(\mathbb{F}_{q^c})$$
$$P \longmapsto \sum_{i=0}^{\frac{12}{c}-1} \phi^{ic}(P).$$

Obviously, $E_1'$ is the elliptic curve $E$.

The following result is paralleled to Lemma 3 in [14].

**Lemma 3.** *Suppose $Q \in E(\mathbb{F}_{q^{12}})[n]$. Then $\mathrm{tr}_{\mathbb{F}_{q^6}}(Q) = 0$ if and only if $\phi^2(Q) = [q^2]Q$.*

*Proof.* We know $n \mid q^{12} - 1$, so $n \mid q^6 + 1$. If $\phi^2(Q) = [q^2]Q$, $\mathrm{tr}_{\mathbb{F}_{q^6}}(Q) = Q + \phi^6(Q) = [1 + q^6]Q = 0$. On the other hand, we know $Q$ is in the 2-dimensional space over $\mathbb{Z}_n$ for $Q \in E(\mathbb{F}_{q^{12}})[n]$, and the Frobenius endomorphism $\phi^2$ has two eigenspaces in $E(\mathbb{F}_{q^{12}})[n]$, which are 1 and $q^2$ (By Hasse Theorem, we know the eigenvalues of $\phi^2$ are not $-1$ or $q^{10}$). Then $Q = Q_1 + Q_2$, where $\phi(Q_1) = Q_1$ and $\phi^2(Q_2) = [q^2]Q_2$. Since $\mathrm{tr}_{\mathbb{F}_{q^6}}(Q) = [2]Q_1 = 0$, we have $Q_1 = 0$.

**Lemma 4.** *We define $l_t$ from $E_1 : y^2 = x^3 + b$ to $E_2 : y^2 = x^3 + t^6 b$ by $(x, y) \mapsto (t^2 x, t^3 y)$. Then $l_t(Q_1 + Q_2) = l_t(Q_1) + l_t(Q_2)$ for any points $Q_1, Q_2 \in E_1$, i.e. $l_t$ is an isogeny.*

*Proof.* We can check this result directly by the additive rule in the elliptic curve.

**Lemma 5.** *Let $Q \in E'_j(\mathbb{F}_{q^{12}})[n]$. If $\mathrm{tr}_{\mathbb{F}_{q^6}}(f(Q)) = 0$, then $\phi^2(Q) = [q^2]l_{z^{(j-1)(q^2-1)}}(Q)$.*

*Proof.* We know $f(Q) \in E(\mathbb{F}_{q^{12}})[n]$ and $f = l_{z^{1-j}}$, then

$$\mathrm{tr}_{\mathbb{F}_{q^6}}(f(Q)) = 0 \stackrel{\text{Lemma3}}{\Longrightarrow} \phi^2 f(Q) = [q^2]f(Q)$$
$$\stackrel{\text{Lemma4}}{\Longrightarrow} l_{z^{(1-j)q^2}}\phi^2(Q) = f([q^2]Q)$$
$$\Longrightarrow \phi^2(Q) = [q^2]l_{z^{(j-1)(q^2-1)}}(Q).$$

Similarly, $\phi^{2u}(Q) = [q^{2u}]l_{z^{(j-1)(q^{2u}-1)}}(Q)$ for any $u \in \mathbb{N}^*$.

**Lemma 6.** *Suppose $Q' = (x, y) \in E'(\mathbb{F}_{q^2})$ and $Q = \psi(Q')$. Then $\mathrm{tr}_{\mathbb{F}_{q^6}}(f(Q)) = 0$.*

*Proof.* Since $x, y \in \mathbb{F}_{q^2}$, $x = x^{q^2}$ and $y = y^{q^2}$. Simultaneously, $z^{q^6 - 1} = (z^{6 \cdot \frac{q^2-1}{2}})^{\frac{q^4 + q^2 + 1}{3}} = -1$. It is easy to prove $z^2 x = z^{2q^6} x^{q^6}$ and $z^3 y = -z^{3q^6} y^{q^6}$.

**Lemma 7.** $\#E'(\mathbb{F}_{q^2})[n] = n$.

*Proof.* By Theorem 1, since $n$ is prime and $n \nmid q^2 - 1$, thus $E'[n] \not\subseteq E'(\mathbb{F}_{q^2})$, then $\#E'(\mathbb{F}_{q^2})[n] = n$.

Suppose $Q' = (x, y) \in E'(\mathbb{F}_{q^2})[n]$, then $Q = \psi(Q') = (z^{2j} x, z^{3j} y)$ in $E'_j(\mathbb{F}_{q^{12}})$. For $\mathrm{char}(\mathbb{F}_q) \neq 2$ or 3, we know $3 \mid q^2 - 1$. Denote by $\zeta_3$ the 3-rd root of unity in $\mathbb{F}_{q^2}$, that is $\zeta_3 = \xi^{\frac{q^2-1}{3}}$. We have

$$\phi^2(Q) = (\zeta_3^{jw} z^{2j} x, (-1)^j z^{3j} y),$$
$$\phi^4(Q) = (\zeta_3^{2jw} z^{2j} x, z^{3j} y),$$
$$\phi^6(Q) = (z^{2j} x, (-1)^j z^{3j} y),$$
$$\phi^8(Q) = (\zeta_3^{jw} z^{2j} x, z^{3j} y),$$
$$\phi^{10}(Q) = (\zeta_3^{2jw} z^{2j} x, (-1)^j z^{3j} y).$$

It is easy to check $\phi^{2u}(Q)$ is on $E'_j$ for any $u \in \mathbb{N}^*$. When $j \equiv 0 \pmod 3$, $Q = \phi^4(Q) = \phi^8(Q)$ (Simultaneously, $\phi^2(Q) = \phi^6(Q) = \phi^{10}(Q)$). When $j \equiv 1, 2 \pmod 3$, the coordinates of points $Q, \phi^4(Q)$, and $\phi^8(Q)$ are precisely $(x(Q), y(Q))$, $(\zeta_3 x(Q), y(Q))$, and $(\zeta_3^2 x(Q), y(Q))$ respectively with y-coordinate of $y(Q)$. By Lemma 5, we have

$$\phi^2(Q) = [q^2]g^{q^2-1}(Q)$$
$$= [q^2](\zeta_3^{(j-1)w} z^{2j} x, (-1)^{j-1} z^{3j} y),$$

$$\phi^4(Q) = [q^4]g^{q^4-1}(Q)$$
$$= [q^4](\zeta_3^{(2j-2)w} z^{2j} x, z^{3j} y),$$

$$\phi^6(Q) = [q^6]g^{q^6-1}(Q)$$
$$= [q^6](z^{2j} x, (-1)^{j-1} z^{3j} y),$$

$$\phi^8(Q) = [q^8]g^{q^8-1}(Q)$$
$$= [q^8](\zeta_3^{(j-1)w} z^{2j} x, z^{3j} y),$$

$$\phi^{10}(Q) = [q^{10}]g^{q^{10}-1}(Q)$$
$$= [q^{10}](\zeta_3^{(2j-2)w} z^{2j} x, (-1)^{j-1} z^{3j} y).$$

When $j \equiv 1 \pmod 3$,

$$\phi^4(Q) = [q^4]Q.$$
$$\phi^8(Q) = [q^8]Q.$$

When $j \equiv 2 \pmod 3$,

$$\phi^4(Q) = [q^8]Q.$$
$$\phi^8(Q) = [q^4]Q.$$

Let $tr_{\mathbb{F}_{q^c}} : \mathbb{F}_{q^{12}} \to \mathbb{F}_{q^c}$ by $x \mapsto \sum_{i=1}^{\frac{12}{c}} x^{q^{ic}}$ be the trace map of finite field.

Let $Q'_1 = (\zeta_3 x, y)$ and $Q'_2 = (\zeta_3^2 x, y)$. Let $PS_+ = \{Q', Q'_1, Q'_2\}$ and $PS_- = \{-Q', -Q'_1, -Q'_2\}$. When $n' \mid \#E'_j(\mathbb{F}_{q^2})$ and the $n'$-order subgroup has embedding degree 6, fix any point $P \in E'_j(\mathbb{F}_{q^2})[n']$, $tr_{\mathbb{F}_{q^4}}(\tau_{n'}(P, \psi(\overline{Q})))$ has the same value for every fixed $\overline{Q} \in PS_+$, that is $\tau_{n'}(P, \psi(Q')) + \tau_{n'}(P, \psi(Q'))^{q^4} + \tau_{n'}(P, \psi(Q'))^{q^8}$. Thus the choice of the cube root of x-coordinate is irrelevant to the computation of the compressed pairing $tr_{\mathbb{F}_{q^4}}(\tau_{n'}(P, \psi(\overline{Q})))$, whose length is

1/3 of the length of $\tau_{n'}(P, \psi(Q'))$. Similarly, the compressed pairing of $\mathbb{F}_{q^4}$-trace also has a same value for every point in $PS_-$.

The image of $n'$-th Tate pairing is $n'$-th root of unity $\mu_{n'} \in \mathbb{F}_{q^{12}}$, then $\mathrm{tr}_{\mathbb{F}_{q^4}}(\mu_{n'}^{-1}) = \mathrm{tr}_{\mathbb{F}_{q^4}}(\mu_{n'})^{q^2}$. Since $\mathrm{tr}_{\mathbb{F}_{q^2}}(\mu_{n'}) = \mathrm{tr}_{\mathbb{F}_{q^4}}(\mu_{n'}) + \mathrm{tr}_{\mathbb{F}_{q^4}}(\mu_{n'})^{q^2}$, the compressed pairing of $\mathbb{F}_{q^2}$-trace has the same value whose length is 1/6 of the length of $\tau_{n'}(P, \psi(Q'))$ for every point in $PS_+ \cup PS_-$. By the Tate pairing on $E'_j$, the $\mathbb{F}_{q^2}$-trace of pairing values give the compression ratio of 1/6. As a result, it is meaningful to define the compressed pairing $\varepsilon(P, Q) \equiv \mathrm{tr}_{\mathbb{F}_{q^2}}(\tau_{n'}(P, \psi(\overline{Q})))$ for $\forall \, \overline{Q} \in PS_+ \cup PS_-$.

The next lemma gives the $E'_j$ with 1/6-compression ratio.

**Lemma 8.** (i) *When* $j \equiv 1 \pmod 6$, $\forall \, n' \in \{n \prod_{a \in A} a : \forall \, A \in 2^{S \setminus \{n\}} \setminus \{\emptyset\}\} \cup \{n\}$, $n' \mid \#E'_j(\mathbb{F}_{q^2})$ *and the* $n'$-*order subgroup has embedding degree* 6.
(ii) *When* $j \equiv 2 \pmod 6$, *if* $S_{3-i} \neq \emptyset$, $\forall \, n' \in \{\prod_{a \in A} a : \forall \, A \in 2^{S_{3-i}} \setminus \{\emptyset\}\}$, $n' \mid \#E'_j(\mathbb{F}_{q^2})$ *and the* $n'$-*order subgroup has embedding degree* 6.

In (i) of the above lemma, the Tate pairing on $E'_j$ can be reduced to

$$\tau_{n'} : E'_j(\mathbb{F}_{q^2})[n'] \times E'_j(\mathbb{F}_{q^{12}})/n'E'_j(\mathbb{F}_{q^{12}}) \to \mathbb{F}^*_{q^{12}}.$$

For (ii), $E'_j[n] \subseteq E'_j(\mathbb{F}_{q^{12}})$ and $E'_j[n'] \subseteq E'_j(\mathbb{F}_{q^{12}})$. Since $(n, n') = 1$, there exist integers $a$, $b$ satisfying $an + bn' = 1$ by Euclidian algorithm. Define the group morphisms:

$$E'_j[n] \times E'_j[n'] \to E'_j[nn'] : (P, T) \mapsto P + T,$$
$$E'_j[nn'] \to E'_j[n] \times E'_j[n'] : P \mapsto (bn'P, anP).$$

We have $E'_j[nn'] \cong E'_j[n] \times E'_j[n']$. So $E'_j[nn'] \subseteq E'_j(\mathbb{F}_{q^{12}})$, The image of $Q$ is zero in $E'_j(\mathbb{F}_{q^{12}})/n'E'_j(\mathbb{F}_{q^{12}})$. Then we consider the $nn'$-th Tate pairing:

$$\tau_{nn'} : E'_j(\mathbb{F}_{q^2})[n'] \times E'_j(\mathbb{F}_{q^{12}})/nn'E'_j(\mathbb{F}_{q^{12}}) \to \mathbb{F}^*_{q^{12}},$$

where $E'_j(\mathbb{F}_{q^2})[n'] \subseteq E'_j(\mathbb{F}_{q^{12}})[nn']$.

To sum up, we define the map $\psi : E'(\mathbb{F}_{q^2}) \to E'_j(\mathbb{F}_{q^{12}})$ for every $j$. When $n' \mid \#E'_j(\mathbb{F}_{q^2})$, the pairing computation uses the first pairing arguments $P \in E'_j(\mathbb{F}_{q^2})[n']$, and the second argument $Q \in E'_j(\mathbb{F}_{q^{12}})$ as the image $\psi(Q')$ of a point $Q' \in E'(\mathbb{F}_{q^2})[n]$. This way works only with $E'_j(\mathbb{F}_{q^2})$ and $E'(\mathbb{F}_{q^2})$ for non-pairing operations. When computing pairings, the points on $E'(\mathbb{F}_{q^2})$ are map to $E'_j(\mathbb{F}_{q^{12}})$. By this method, the compressed value is in $\mathbb{F}_{q^2}$ and its compression ratio is 1/6.

**Theorem 2.** *Let* $S, \Gamma_1, \Gamma_2, \Gamma, S_1, S_2$ *are defined by* (1)–(6). *Let* $E(\mathbb{F}_{q^2}) : y^2 = x^3 + b$ (char$(\mathbb{F}_q) \neq 2, 3$) *be an elliptic curve, who has a subgroup of prime order* $n$ *with embedding degree* 6. *If there is a primitive element* $\xi$ *that is effective on* $E(\mathbb{F}_{q^2})$. *When* $S_i \neq \emptyset$ ($i = 1$ *or* 2), $\forall \, m \in S$, *the elliptic curve* $\tilde{E}(\mathbb{F}_{q^2})$ *with subgroup of order* $m$ *has compression ratio of* 1/6, *where* $\tilde{E} \in \Gamma \setminus \Gamma_i$.

*Proof.* First, $\xi^w$ is a generator of $\mathbb{F}_{q^2}^*$. Second, for $\forall\ m \in S$ and $j \equiv 3 \pmod 6$, $E_j'(\mathbb{F}_{q^2})$ has no subgroup of order $m$. Then it is easy to check by the above compression process.

If $S_1$ and $S_2$ are non-empty sets, and for every $n$ in $S$, the elliptic curve $\widetilde{E}(\mathbb{F}_{q^2})$ with a subgroup of order $n$ exhibits a compression ratio of $1/6$, where $\widetilde{E} \in \Gamma$. According to Lemma 8, both types of elliptic curves possess the aforementioned compression property.

# 4    Applications to Pairing-Based Cryptography

For the elliptic curves with an embedding degree of 6 introduced above, by utilizing a compression function, it is possible to represent it only by the x-coordinate or y-coordinate of the elliptic curve points. This method is quite similar to the example of embedding degree 2. By doing so, it becomes possible to save a certain amount of communication or storage in many cryptographic protocols, thereby improving the efficiency of the protocols. In particular, when representing the point using the y-coordinate, the six points corresponding to $\pm y$ values can be compressed into a single point using the compression function. This leads to an additional saving of 1 bit in terms of overhead.

## 4.1    BLS Short Signatures

Several discrete logarithm-based classical signature schemes, including the DSA, are variations of the ElGamal signature [22]. In these schemes, signatures consist of a pair of integers modulo $n$, where $n$ is the group order. BLS short signature is a digital signature scheme proposed by in [8]. It is a cryptographic signature scheme based on bilinear pairing operations on elliptic curve groups.

In the BLS short signature scheme, a signature is represented by a single group element, making it more compact and efficient compared to traditional signature schemes that require multiple elements. The security of this scheme relies on the computational Diffie-Hellman problem's hardness in the underlying elliptic curve group.

### BLS Short Signature Scheme

1. **Key Generation**: Choose an elliptic curve group with a generator point $G$ and prime order $q$. Then randomly generate a private key $sk \in [1, q-1]$. Finally, compute the corresponding public key $pk$ as $pk = sk \cdot G$.
2. **Signing**: To sign a message $m$, compute the message's hash as $H(m)$. Then calculate the signature as $sig = H(m) \cdot sk$.
3. **Verification**: Given a signature $sig$ and the public key $pk$, compute the message's hash as $H(m)$. Then verify the signature by checking the equation $e(H(m), G) \overset{?}{=} e(sig, pk)$, where $e(\cdot, \cdot)$ represents the bilinear pairing operation.

The BLS short signature scheme leverages the bilinear pairing operation on elliptic curves to compress the signature into a single group element and verifies its correctness using the verification equation. This provides the advantages of efficiency and compactness for BLS short signatures. Various cryptographic applications uses BLS short signature, such as threshold signatures, identity-based cryptography, and blockchain technology. Their compactness and efficiency make them suitable for resource-constrained environments and scenarios where signature size and verification speed are important factors.

The signature, denoted as sig, is a point on the elliptic curve. Using our approach, sig only needs to select either the x-coordinate or the y-coordinate. If the x-coordinate is chosen as the signature, the verifier can obtain two points, $Q$ and $-Q$. Choosing either one, the verification equation

$$\varepsilon(\mathrm{pk}, h(m)) = \varepsilon(G, \pm Q)$$

holds. On the other hand, if the y-coordinate is selected as the signature, regardless of the sign, the verifier can obtain six points, $Q_i$, where $i = 1, \cdots, 6$. Choosing any one of these points, the verification equation

$$\varepsilon(\mathrm{pk}, h(m)) = \varepsilon(G, Q_i)$$

holds.

Therefore, by utilizing the compression function, the length of the signature can be further halved. If the y-coordinate is chosen as the signature, an additional 1 bit can be saved by eliminating the need for a sign bit. However, this optimization method for BLS signatures also has a drawback. Due to the non-bilinearity of the mapping $\varepsilon$, it is not possible to achieve multi-party signature optimization. Instead, this method can only be applied to aggregated signature optimization.

## 4.2  Identity-Based Encryption

Identity-based encryption (IBE) is a cryptographic technique that allows encryption and decryption operations according to users' identities rather than traditional public keys. In traditional public-key encryption, a user's public key origins from a complex and time-consuming certificate management infrastructure. However, in IBE, a user's identity, such as an email address, serves as its public key. In contrast to traditional encryptions, IBE have several advantages. First, it simplifies the key management process by eliminating the need for a centralized certificate authority. Users can generate their private keys directly based on their identities. This makes key distribution and management more efficient and scalable, especially in large-scale systems.

The Boneh-Franklin identity-based encryption (IBE) scheme is a well-known and widely-used construction in the field of cryptography. It was proposed by Dan Boneh and Matt Franklin in [9]. This scheme provides a practical and efficient solution for identity-based encryption, offering several desirable properties.

In the Boneh-Franklin IBE scheme, the setup involves a trusted authority called the Private Key Generator (PKG) that generates and distributes private keys to users according to their identities. The PKG selects a master secret key and generates the corresponding public parameters. These parameters include a bilinear pairing function on elliptic curves, a generator point, and other necessary elements. To encrypt a message for a specific recipient in the Boneh-Franklin IBE scheme, the sender uses the recipient's identity and the public parameters to generate an encryption key. The encryption process involves applying the bilinear pairing function and the recipient's identity to produce the encryption key. The message is then encrypted using this key. When a recipient wants to decrypt a ciphertext, they request their private key from the PKG, providing their identity as proof of authorization. The PKG uses the master secret key to generate the recipient's private key, which is securely sent to the recipient. The recipient can use its private key to do the decryption.

The security of the IBE scheme relies on the hardness of certain mathematical problems, such as the computational Diffie-Hellman problem in the underlying elliptic curve group. The scheme ensures that only the intended recipient, with the correct private key derived from their identity, can decrypt the ciphertext and recover the original message. Careful selection of parameters and appropriate security assumptions are essential for achieving data confidentiality and data integrity. IBE has various applications in secure communication and access control. It can be used for secure email systems, where users can encrypt and decrypt messages using their email addresses as their public keys. IBE can also used for secure communication systems, access control mechanisms, and secure data sharing in various settings. Its efficiency, simplicity, and practicality have made it an important contribution to the field of cryptography.

**Boneh-Franklin Identity-Based Encryption (IBE) Scheme**

1. **Setup**: The Private Key Generator (PKG) selects a randomly secret integer $(t)$ and generates public parameters, including an elliptic curve group, a generator point $(P)$, and other necessary elements. Then the PKG publishes the public parameters $T = tP$. Suppose $H_1$ and $H_2$ are two hash functions.
2. **Key Extraction**: For a user with identity $(ID)$, the PKG computes the private key $(sk_{ID})$ by applying the hash function $H_1$ to the identity and combining it with the master secret key: $sk_{ID} = tH_1(ID)$.
3. **Encryption**: To perform the encryption of message $M$ for a recipient with identity $ID$, the sender obtains the recipient's hashing the identity $H_1(ID)$. Then the sender randomly selects a value $(r)$ and obtains the ciphertext as $C = M \oplus H_2(e(H_1(ID), T)^r)$ and $R = rP$, where $e(\cdot, \cdot)$ represents the bilinear pairing operation.
4. **Decryption**: On receiving the ciphertext $(R, C)$, the recipient applies the private key to obtain the message: $M = C \oplus H_2(e(sk_{ID}, R))$, where $e(sk_{ID}, R)$ is computed using the bilinear pairing operation.

Similar to the optimization of the aforementioned signatures, we can also compress the ciphertext using our method. The first part of the ciphertext is a point R on the elliptic curve, and we can select one of its coordinates as a substitute. If we specify that the x-coordinate is chosen as part of the ciphertext, the decryptor can obtain two points R and −R, based on that coordinate. By selecting either point, decryption is possible due to the equation

$$\varepsilon(H_1(ID), rT) = \varepsilon(sk_{ID}, \pm R).$$

On the other hand, if we specify that the y-coordinate is chosen as part of the ciphertext, regardless of the sign, the decryptor can obtain six points $R_i$, where $i = 1, \cdots, 6$, based on that coordinate. By selecting any one of these points, decryption is possible due to the equation

$$\varepsilon(H_1(ID), rT) = \varepsilon(sk_{ID}, R_i).$$

By utilizing this compression method, the IBE scheme requires modifications to both the encryption and decryption steps. In the encryption step, the ciphertext is represented as $(R_x, C)$ or $(|R_y|, C)$, where $R_x$ and $R_y$ are the x-coordinate and y-coordinate of R, respectively, and $C = M \oplus H_2(\varepsilon(H_1(ID), rT))$. In the decryption step, the decryptor uses the first value (coordinate) of the ciphertext to compute any point $R_i$ and obtain the corresponding plaintext $M = C \oplus H_2(\varepsilon(sk_{ID}, R_i))$.

## 5   Conclusion

In this paper, we primarily investigate elliptic Curves with subgroups of embedding degree 6. Our focus lies on pairing maps and their applications. When there is an elliptic curve satisfying suitable conditions, we can simultaneously compress the pairing values on some other elliptic curves with compression ratio of 1/6. Furthermore, in terms of practical applications, we introduce a compression function that allows representation of compressed values solely using the x-coordinate or y-coordinate of the elliptic curve points. This compression technique enables significant savings in communication and storage requirements for various protocols, including BLS signature and IBE, ultimately enhancing their efficiency. But there is a limitation in the optimization of BLS signatures. Specifically, due to the non-bilinearity of the mapping $\varepsilon$, multi-party signature optimization cannot be achieved through this approach. The future research work is to further improve the compression rate and the efficiency of pairing-based cryptographic protocol.

## References

1. Harasawa, R., Shikata, J., Suzuki, J., Imai, H.: Comparing the MOV and FR reductions in elliptic curve cryptography. In: Stern, J. (ed.) EUROCRYPT 1999. LNCS, vol. 1592, pp. 190–205. Springer, Heidelberg (1999). https://doi.org/10.1007/3-540-48910-X_14

2. Kanayama, N., Kobayashi, T., Saito, T., Uchiyama, S.: Remarks on elliptic curve discrete logarithm problems. IEICE Trans. Fundam. **E83-A**(1), 17–23 (2000)
3. Barreto, P.S.L.M., Galbraith, S., O'hEigeartaigh, C., Scott, M.: Efficient pairing computation on supersingular abelian varieties. Des. Codes Cryptogr. **42**, 239–271 (2007)
4. Hess, F., Smart, N., Vercauteren, F.: The Eta pairing revisited. IEEE Trans. Inf. Theory **52**, 4595–4602 (2006)
5. Hess, F.: Pairing lattices. In: Galbraith, S.D., Paterson, K.G. (eds.) Pairing 2008. LNCS, vol. 5209, pp. 18–38. Springer, Heidelberg (2008). https://doi.org/10.1007/978-3-540-85538-5_2
6. Boneh, D., Boyen, X., Shacham, H.: Short group signatures. In: Franklin, M. (ed.) CRYPTO 2004. LNCS, vol. 3152, pp. 41–55. Springer, Heidelberg (2004). https://doi.org/10.1007/978-3-540-28628-8_3
7. Joux, A.: A one round protocol for tripartite Diffie-Hellman. In: Bosma, W. (ed.) ANTS 2000. LNCS, vol. 1838, pp. 385–393. Springer, Heidelberg (2000). https://doi.org/10.1007/10722028_23
8. Boneh, D., Lynn, B., Shacham, H.: Short signatures from the weil pairing. In: Boyd, C. (ed.) ASIACRYPT 2001. LNCS, vol. 2248, pp. 514–532. Springer, Heidelberg (2001). https://doi.org/10.1007/3-540-45682-1_30
9. Boneh, D., Franklin, M.: Identity-based encryption from the weil pairing. In: Kilian, J. (ed.) CRYPTO 2001. LNCS, vol. 2139, pp. 213–229. Springer, Heidelberg (2001). https://doi.org/10.1007/3-540-44647-8_13
10. Morales-Sandoval, M., Gonzalez-Compean, J.L., Diaz-Perez, A., et al.: A pairing-based cryptographic approach for data security in the cloud. Int. J. Inf. Secur. **17**, 441–461 (2018)
11. Miret, J.M., Sadornil, D., Tena, J.G.: Pairing-based cryptography on elliptic curves. Math. Comput. Sci. **12**, 309–318 (2018)
12. Venema, M., Alpár, G., Hoepman, J.H.: Systematizing core properties of pairing-based attribute-based encryption to uncover remaining challenges in enforcing access control in practice. Des. Codes Cryptogr. **91**, 165–220 (2023)
13. Barreto, P.S.L.M., Lynn, B., Scott, M.: On the selection of pairing-friendly groups. In: Matsui, M., Zuccherato, R.J. (eds.) SAC 2003. LNCS, vol. 3006, pp. 17–25. Springer, Heidelberg (2004). https://doi.org/10.1007/978-3-540-24654-1_2
14. Barreto, P.S.L.M., Naehrig, M.: Pairing-friendly elliptic curves of prime order. In: Preneel, B., Tavares, S. (eds.) SAC 2005. LNCS, vol. 3897, pp. 319–331. Springer, Heidelberg (2006). https://doi.org/10.1007/11693383_22
15. Scott, M., Barreto, P.S.L.M.: Compressed pairings. In: Franklin, M. (ed.) CRYPTO 2004. LNCS, vol. 3152, pp. 140–156. Springer, Heidelberg (2004). https://doi.org/10.1007/978-3-540-28628-8_9
16. Lenstra, A.K., Verheul, E.R.: The XTR public key system. In: Bellare, M. (ed.) CRYPTO 2000. LNCS, vol. 1880, pp. 1–19. Springer, Heidelberg (2000). https://doi.org/10.1007/3-540-44598-6_1
17. Kumar, V., Singh, G., Singh, I.: A review on geo-location-based authentication with various lossless compression techniques. In: Shukla, A., Murthy, B.K., Hasteer, N., Van Belle, J.P. (eds.) Computational Intelligence. LNEE, vol. 968, pp. 365–374. Springer, Singapore (2023). https://doi.org/10.1007/978-981-19-7346-8_31
18. Guodong, Y., Min, L., Mingfa, W.: Double image encryption algorithm based on compressive sensing and elliptic curve. Alex. Eng. J. **61**(9), 6785–6795 (2022)
19. Silverman, J.H.: The Arithmetic of Elliptic Curves. Graduate Texts in Mathematics, vol. 106. Springer, New York (1986). https://doi.org/10.1007/978-1-4757-1920-8

20. Frey, G., Rück, H.G.: A remark concerning m-divisibility and the discrete logarithm in the divisor class group of curves. Math. Comp. **62**, 865–874 (1994)
21. Balasubramanian, R., Koblitz, N.: The improbability that an elliptic curve has subexponential discrete log problem under the Menezes-Okamoto-Vanstone algorithm. J. Cryptology. **11**, 141–145 (1998)
22. ElGamal, T.: A public key cryptosystem and a signature scheme based on discrete logarithms. IEEE Trans. Inf. Theory **31**, 469–472 (1985)

# Enhancing Chinese Named Entity Recognition with Disentangled Expert Knowledge

Hongkai Wang[1], Jun Feng[1], Yidan Wang[1(✉)], Sichen Pan[1], Shuai Zhao[1], and Yi Xue[2]

[1] State Grid Zhejiang Electric Power Corporation Information and Telecommunication Branch, Hangzhou, China
{wang_hongkai,fengjun,pan_sichen,zhao_shuai}@zj.sgcc.com.cn,
demi0901@126.com
[2] Nanjing Duotuo Intelligent Technology Limited Liability Company, Nanjing, China

**Abstract.** Chinese Named Entity Recognition (NER) requires model identify entity boundaries in the sentence *i.e.*, entity segmentation, and meanwhile assign entities to pre-defined categories, *i.e.*, entity classification. Current NER tasks follows sequence tagging scheme and assign the characters to different labels by considering both segmentation position and entity categories. In such a scheme, the characters in the same entity will be regarded as different classes in the training process according to different positions. In fact, the knowledge of entity segmentation is shared across different entity categories, while entity category knowledge is relatively independent of entity segmentation. Such labeling scheme will lead to the entanglement of these two objectives, hindering the effective knowledge acquisition by the models. To address the entanglement issue and comprehensively extract useful knowledge of two objectives, we propose a novel framework that disentangle the original NER labels into two additional training labels for entity segmentation and entity classification respectively. Then we introduce two dedicated expert models to effectively extract specific knowledge from the disentangled labels. Afterwards, their predictions will be integrated into the original model as auxiliary knowledge, further enhancing the primary NER model learning process. We conduct experiments on three publicly available datasets to demonstrate the effectiveness of our proposed method.

**Keywords:** Chinese Named Entity Recognition · Bidirectional Encoder Representations from Transformers · Information Extraction

## 1 Introduction

The primary objective of Named Entity Recognition (NER) is to identify and extract specific entity names from text while categorizing these entities into predefined classes, such as individuals, locations, or organizations. NER serves

J. Shao et al. (Eds.): EISA 2023, CCIS 2004, pp. 92–106, 2024.
https://doi.org/10.1007/978-981-99-9614-8_6

as a foundational task within the realm of natural language processing (NLP), forming the bedrock for a multitude of downstream NLP applications, including information extraction, question answering, and so on.

In recent years, Chinese Named Entity Recognition has garnered increasing attention, with numerous studies extensively exploring this field and achieving noteworthy success. Nevertheless, Chinese NER is inherently intricate, primarily owing to the absence of distinct word boundaries and the intricacy of named entities themselves. The core target of Chinese NER encompass two distinct objectives: entity segmentation, which involves identifying the boundaries of entities within sentences, and entity classification, where each recognized entity is assigned to a predefined category.

Currently, the NER task is carried out using a sequence labeling method that assigns labels to individual characters. In such a scheme, characters belonging to the same entity category receive different class labels based on their positions within the entity. For instance, in the widely adopted BIOES tagging scheme, given an entity of category $X$, its characters will be tagged as four different class labels depending on their position: "B-$X$", "I-$X$", "E-$X$", "S-$X$". Unfortunately, this labeling approach leads to the objective entanglement of entity segmentation and entity classification and does not facilitate effective knowledge acquisition for the model with regard to the two types of knowledge.

In fact, the knowledge related to entity segmentation is applicable across various entity categories, while the objective of entity classification is relatively independent of entity segmentation. However, in the conventional sequence labeling paradigm, these two objectives are entangled together, obstructing the efficient knowledge extraction from distinct class labels. On one hand, the available training data for each annotated is relatively reduced by splitting to various subclasses. On the other hand, the presence of similar class labels in the training will lead to confusion within the model learning process, thereby hindering the acquisition of specific knowledge.

To address the issue of objective entanglement and facilitate comprehensively knowledge learning of both objectives, we present a novel framework that disentangle the NER objective into two distinct sub-objectives: entity segmentation and entity classification. Within this framework, the original labels are disentangled to generate specific labels for each objective respectively. Subsequently, we introduce two dedicated expert models, each focused on capturing the intricacies of either entity segmentation or entity classification. These expert models are trained using the disentangled labels to effectively extract task-specific knowledge. Then their prediction results will be incorporated into the original model's training process as auxiliary knowledge to assist the model learning.

In summary, this paper introduces a novel method for Chinese Named Entity Recognition, addressing the challenge of objective entanglement by breaking down the original NER task into two distinct sub-objectives: entity segmentation and entity classification. By creating dedicated expert models and integrating their knowledge into the primary model framework, our aim is to more effectively leverage the unique knowledge relevant to each specific objective. We conduct experiments based on three publicly available datasets and the extensive experimental results have demonstrated the effectiveness of our approach.

## 2   Related Work

### 2.1   Named Entity Recognition

Named Entity Recognition (NER) is a long standing task in Natural Language Processing that aims to identify and classify named entities (*e.g.,* names of persons, organizations, locations, dates) in text. Over decades, several research works have been conducted to improve the accuracy and efficiency of NER systems.

One area of research focuses on applying various machine learning approaches for NER. Early works have explored the use of traditional models like Hidden Markov Models (HMMs) and Conditional Random Fields (CRFs) to capture the sequential dependencies between words and labels [7]. Deep learning techniques such as Recurrent Neural Networks (RNNs) [16,23], Convolutional Neural Networks (CNNs) [11], and Transformer models have also been employed to achieve state-of-the-art performance in NER [29].

Another research direction involves exploring different features and representations to enhance NER performance. Some studies have investigated the use of linguistic features like part-of-speech tags [8], morphological information [5], and syntactic structures to provide contextual information and improve entity recognition [2,18]. Word embeddings, such as Word2Vec [28] and GloVe [26], have been utilized to capture semantic relationships between words and improve NER accuracy [15,21].

Domain adaptation [3,22] and transfer learning [6] have also been researched to address NER challenges in different domains or with limited labeled data. Techniques such as domain adaptation algorithms, distant supervision [12,13], and active learning [14,31] have been explored to adapt pre-trained models or leverage external knowledge for improved entity recognition.

Moreover, there have been efforts to address specific challenges in NER, such as handling ambiguous entities [20], multi-lingual [19] and cross-lingual [30] NER, and incorporating context and discourse information. Researchers have proposed various strategies to address these challenges, including incorporating external knowledge sources [24], leveraging multi-task learning [1], and utilizing contextualized word representations like ELMo, BERT, and GPT.

Overall, research works on NER have made significant progress in developing more accurate and robust models by leveraging different machine learning techniques, exploring various features and representations, addressing domain adaptation and transfer learning, and tackling specific challenges in NER.

### 2.2   Chinese Named Entity Recognition

Chinese characters are ideographic, which makes character-level representations crucial for Chinese NER. Recent studies have investigated the use of character embeddings [35] and sub-character information [34] (*e.g.,* radicals, character components) to capture the fine-grained semantic information encoded in Chinese characters. Researchers have explored two distinct approaches in addressing this task: character-based and word-based methods. The character-based approach is particularly effective for handling the challenges posed by the Chinese language's lack of explicit word boundaries, while the word-based approach leverages linguistic information to recognize entities based on word units. Researchers continue to explore and innovate within these approaches to improve Chinese NER system performance for diverse applications.

The character-based approach to Chinese NER involves treating individual characters as the basic units of analysis. This approach is well-suited for handling the absence of clear word boundaries in Chinese text and has gained significant attention in recent years. For example, Pend *et al.* [25] proposed a character-based approach that jointly trains character embeddings and NER models, demonstrating the importance of contextual information in informal social media text. Chiu *et al.* [4] combined bidirectional LSTM and Convolutional Neural Networks (CNN) to achieve character-level NER. It has been widely adopted for its robust performance on Chinese NER tasks.

In the word-based approach, Chinese text is segmented into words or tokens, and NER is performed at the word level. This approach leverages linguistic structures and word boundaries to recognize entities. For instance, Ma *et al.* [17] introduced an end-to-end word-based sequence labeling approach for NER, incorporating bidirectional LSTM, CNN, and Conditional Random Fields (CRF). It has become a cornerstone in Chinese NER research.

# 3    Methods

In this section, we will introduce the framework of our proposed method and how to integrate it with an arbitrary NER model. The framework of our method is composed of three parts: Contextual Representation Generation (CRG), which is used to generate contextual representations for each character in the text sentences, Disentangled Expert Knowledge Learning (DEKL), which is used to extract specific knowledge for entity segmentation and classification respectively, and Knowledge Enhancement (KE), which aims to enhance the input features with the extracted knowledge.

## 3.1    Contextual Representation Generation

As the recognition of entities in the text corpus is highly related to its contextual information, we firstly encode each character in the sentence with an contextual encoder to get its representation. This step can be implemented by various powerful pretrained language models, such as ELMo [27] and BERT [10]. Here, we exploit BERT [10] as our contextual encoder and the framework is shown in Fig. 1. The input layer of BERT is mainly responsible for word embedding operations on original text. The model uses the [CLS] tag to process the beginning of each sentence, which is a reserved tag of BERT and can be ignored.

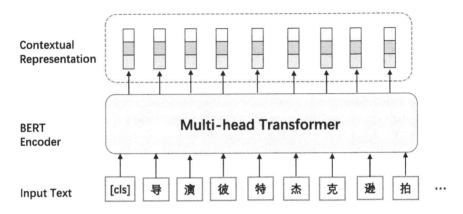

**Fig. 1.** The illustration of contextual representation generation process with language model BERT.

The BERT input vector is composed of three parts: token embeddings, which represents the vector representation of each character in the sentence, segment embeddings, which records the sentence representation, and position embeddings, which records the position information of the current word.

After sending the input texts into BERT model, it uses a bidirectional Transformer [32] encoder to generate word vectors can fully integrate the contextual information around the words. The key component of Transformer is self-attention mechanism, which is formulated as:

$$\text{Attention}(Q, K, V) = \text{softmax}\left(\frac{QK^T}{\sqrt{d_k}}\right) V, \tag{1}$$

where $d_k$ represents the dimension of representation vectors, and $Q, K, V$ is different transformed matrices from the same matrix. Transformer introduces multi-head attention mechanism to obtain multiple feature representations through multiple heads and concatenate them together to generate more powerful representations.

Given a sentence with character sequence $[c_1, c_2, \ldots, c_n]$ ($n$ is the sequence length), we send them into BERT and obtain their contextual embedding sequence $\mathbf{E} = [\mathbf{e}_1, \mathbf{e}_2, \ldots, \mathbf{e}_n]$.

### 3.2   Disentangled Expert Knowledge Learning

To fully learn the knowledge of word segmentation and entity classification, we disentangle the original learning objective of NER task as two sub-objectives and exploit two experts to learn each specific knowledge. We firstly disentangle the training labels for each objective from the original annotation labels. We merge the labels belonging to the same entity category as the category-specific label $l^c$, and merge the labels with the same location in the words as the segmentation-

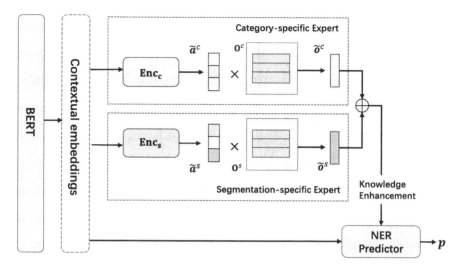

**Fig. 2.** The knowledge extraction process of two objective-specific experts.

specific label $l^s$. Then we exploit the label to train two networks to learn the knowledge (Fig. 2).

We exploit two encoders as the experts to learn entity classification knowledge and segmentation knowledge.

$$\mathbf{a^c} = \text{Enc}_c(\mathbf{E}), \tag{2}$$

$$\mathbf{a^s} = \text{Enc}_s(\mathbf{E}), \tag{3}$$

where $\mathbf{E}$ is the contextual embeddings from BERT. Here we set both $\text{Enc}_c$ and $\text{Enc}_s$ as two-layer Multi-Layer Perceptrons (MLP) and leave other fancy operations as future work.

After obtaining the predicted probabilities of each knowledge, we can enhance the input features of NER models with their predictions. For each expert, we define a set of learnable vectors and each vector corresponds to one category, denoted as $\mathbf{O}^s = [\mathbf{o}_1^s, \mathbf{o}_2^s, \ldots, \mathbf{o}_n^s]$ and $\mathbf{O}^c = [\mathbf{o}_1^c, \mathbf{o}_2^c, \ldots, \mathbf{o}_n^c]$. These learnable vectors can be regarded as the knowledge to be incorporated into contextual embeddings together with the probability scores. We firstly normalize the predicted probability scores with softmax function and multiply them with the learned vectors as attention scores:

$$\tilde{\mathbf{o}}^s = \sum_i \tilde{\mathbf{a}}_i^s \mathbf{o}_i^s, \quad \tilde{\mathbf{a}}^s = \text{Softmax}(\mathbf{a^s}), \tag{4}$$

$$\tilde{\mathbf{o}}^c = \sum_i \tilde{\mathbf{a}}_i^c \mathbf{o}_i^c, \quad \tilde{\mathbf{a}}^c = \text{Softmax}(\mathbf{a^c}). \tag{5}$$

The attended features $\tilde{\mathbf{o}}^s$ and $\tilde{\mathbf{o}}^c$ will be incorporated into the contextual features to enhance NER models learning process. While prediction scores $\mathbf{a^c}$ and $\mathbf{a^s}$ will be regarded as output logits to participate in the training process of two experts. The details is introduced in Sect. 3.5.

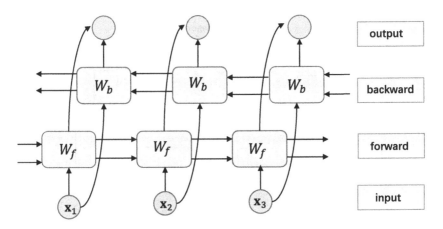

**Fig. 3.** The structure of Bi-LSTM.

### 3.3 Knowledge Enhancement

The original input features of models is the encoded contextual embeddings $\mathbf{E} = [\mathbf{e}_1, \mathbf{e}_2, \ldots, \mathbf{e}_n]$. We concatenate the attended embeddings with the contextual features for each token:

$$\mathbf{x} = [\tilde{\mathbf{o}}^\mathbf{s}; \tilde{\mathbf{o}}^\mathbf{c}; \mathbf{e}], \tag{6}$$

wherein, $[\cdot;\cdot]$ represents concatenate operation. Then we send the integrated features to an arbitrary NER model to get the final predictions.

### 3.4 NER Prediction

Here we mainly introduce three popular predictors and compare their performance in our experiments.

**MLPs.** One simple prediction operation is to send the contextual embeddings into Multi-Layer Perceptrons (MLPs) to make classification directly. A Multi-layer Perceptron (MLP) is a feed-forward neural network its multiple layers that consists of interconnected nodes, or neurons.

$$\mathbf{y} = \text{MLP}(\mathbf{x}). \tag{7}$$

The output score is the prediction logits of all the annotated categories.

**Bi-LSTM.** Bidirectional Long Short-Term Memory (Bi-LSTM) is a type of Recurrent Neural Network (RNN) architecture used in machine learning and natural language processing tasks, particularly for sequence modeling and sequence-to-sequence tasks. It is an extension of the traditional Long Short-Term Memory (LSTM) network that processes input sequences in both forward and backward directions, enabling it to capture contextual information from both past and future time steps.

Bi-LSTMs maintain two separate hidden states: one for processing the sequence from left to right (*i.e.*, forward) and another for processing the sequence from right to left (*i.e.*, backward). By combining the information from both directions, Bi-LSTMs excel at capturing long-range dependencies and contextual information within sequences.

The structure of Bi-LSTM is shown in Fig. 3. To take the advantage of the sequence modeling power of this structure, we can get the final predictions by sending the features into Bi-LSTM model followed by a classification layer:

$$\mathbf{y} = \text{FC}\left(\text{Bi-LSTM}(\mathbf{x})\right). \tag{8}$$

The output score is the prediction logits of all the annotated categories.

**CRF.** Conditional Random Fields (CRFs) are a kind of classical probabilistic graphical models used in machine learning, specifically in the field of structured prediction. They have found extensive application in various natural language processing (NLP) tasks, including part-of-speech tagging, named entity recognition, and syntactic parsing, as well as in computer vision and speech recognition.

CRFs are designed to model the conditional probability distribution of a set of unobserved random variables, typically structured data, given a set of observed random variables. They are a type of discriminative model, which means they model the posterior probabilities directly, making them well-suited for tasks where the output has a clear, structured relationship with the input. Hence, CRFs are particularly useful for sequence labeling tasks and have been widely used in NER task. CRFs can capture dependencies between adjacent words and exploit contextual information to make accurate predictions. The basic formulation of a linear-chain CRF for sequence labeling tasks involves defining the conditional probability of a sequence of labels given a sequence of observations.

For an input $\mathbf{x}$, we can get the output prediction scores $P$ of MLP or Bi-LSTM, we can seed them into a CRF encoder, the computation involves the emission scores generated by the MLP or Bi-LSTM and transition scores. The calculation formula is depicted as:

$$S(\mathbf{x}, \mathbf{y}) = \sum_{i=1}^{n} P_{i,y_i} + \sum_{i=1}^{n} A_{y_i, y_{i+1}}, \tag{9}$$

where $A$ is the transition matrix and $A_{y_i, y_{i+1}}$ is the score of transitioning from label $y_i$ to label $y_{i+1}$.

During training, the maximum likelihood of the probability of correct sequences in the training are maximized. The final output tag sequence is decided based on the maximum score given by:

$$\mathbf{y}^* = \text{argmax}_{y' \in y} S(\mathbf{x}, y'). \tag{10}$$

### 3.5  Model Training

Our training objective is composed of three parts: the training loss of NER model, the training loss for two experts: entity segmentation and entity classification. For the training loss for entity segmentation and entity classification is formulated as cross entropy loss:

$$\mathcal{L}_{e1} = \frac{1}{N_B} \sum \log \tilde{\mathbf{a}}^s, \tag{11}$$

$$\mathcal{L}_{e2} = \frac{1}{N_B} \sum \log \tilde{\mathbf{a}}^c, \tag{12}$$

where $\tilde{\mathbf{a}}^s$ and $\tilde{\mathbf{a}}^c$ are the predicted probabilities of two expert encoders according to Eq. (4) and Eq. (5). The training labels are the disentangled labels $l^c$ and $l^s$ from the original labels.

Then the total training loss of our model is a multi-task training loss:

$$\mathcal{L}_{total} = \lambda_{NER}\ \mathcal{L}_{NER} + \lambda_{e1}\ \mathcal{L}_{e1} + \lambda_{e2}\ \mathcal{L}_{e2}, \tag{13}$$

where $\mathcal{L}_{NER}$ is the training loss for NER model and $\lambda_*$ is the weight assigned for each task training loss.

**Adaptive Weights.** We formulate the method as multiple task learning in the training process, we can observe that the weights assigned to each task loss strongly affect the model performance. Unfortunately, tuning these weights manually is very time-consuming. Inspired by one relevant work [9], we apply an adaptive weighting strategy by considering the homoscedastic uncertainty of each task:

$$\mathcal{L}_{total} = \sum_{i \in \mathcal{R}} (\mathcal{L}_i/\sigma_i^2 + \log \sigma_i), \tag{14}$$

where $\mathcal{R} = \{NER, e1, e2\}$ is the set of task loss, $\sigma_i$ is the learnable parameter to control the weight of each task.

## 4  Experiments

In this section, we will introduce the evaluation settings of our experiments. We evaluate our methods based on three public datasets and discuss the effectiveness of our proposed method through the experimental results.

### 4.1  Dataset

We conduct our experiments based on three public datasets, and we display the data statistics about number of categories, training and test samples for each dataset in Table 1.

**Table 1.** Data statistics for three public datasets.

| Dataset | Train | Test | Categories |
|---------|-------|------|------------|
| ClueNER | 10,748 | 1,343 | 10 |
| ResumeNER | 3,821 | 477 | 8 |
| MusicNER | 16,982 | 4,338 | 15 |

**Table 2.** Performance Comparison on ClueNER dataset.

| Methods | | F1 Score(%) | Precision(%) | Recall(%) |
|---------|--|-------------|--------------|-----------|
| MLP | Baseline | 76.14 | 73.65 | 78.80 |
| | **DEK(Ours)** | **77.86** | **76.12** | **79.68** |
| MLP+CRF | Baseline | 77.63 | 76.94 | 79.03 |
| | **DEK(Ours)** | **78.47** | **77.45** | **79.52** |
| Bi-LSTM+CRF | Baseline | 77.39 | 75.43 | 79.45 |
| | **DEK(Ours)** | **78.70** | **77.16** | **80.30** |

**ClueNER** is based on Tsinghua University's open source text classification data set THUCTC. It meticulously selected a subset of data and divided the entities into 10 fine-grained named entity categories [33]. ClueNER is a relatively challenging Chinese NER dataset as it reserves more detailed annotations, which is consistent with real-world scenarios.

**ResumeNER** is based on a resume data set collected by Sina Finance, which includes resumes of executives of companies listed on the Chinese stock market. 1027 resume abstracts were randomly selected, and 8 named entities were manually labeled using the YEDDA system.

**MusicNER** is a public dataset which is designed for tasks related to music and comprises 21,352 samples with 15 entity categories.

### 4.2 Evaluation Metrics

Following previous studies [36], we mainly compare methods on three metrics: Precision, Recall and F1 Score. Precision represents the fraction of correctly recognized entities instances among all the predicted entities. The higher precision score represents the stronger recognition ability of NER model.

$$\text{Precision} = \frac{TP}{TP + FP},\tag{15}$$

where TP means True Positives and FP means False Positives.

Recall represents the proportion of correctly recognized entities to the total number of annotated entities. The higher the recall score represents the stronger the model coverage ability.

**Table 3.** Performance Comparison on ResumeNER dataset.

| Methods | | F1 Score(%) | Precision(%) | Recall(%) |
|---|---|---|---|---|
| MLP | Baseline | 89.93 | 84.32 | **96.34** |
| | **DEK(Ours)** | **95.10** | **94.81** | 95.40 |
| MLP+CRF | Baseline | 94.65 | 93.86 | **96.25** |
| | **DEK(Ours)** | **95.16** | **94.33** | 96.01 |
| Bi-LSTM+CRF | Baseline | 95.13 | 94.38 | 95.88 |
| | **DEK(Ours)** | **95.60** | **95.19** | **96.01** |

**Table 4.** Performance Comparison on MusicNER dataset.

| Method | | F1 Score(%) | Precision(%) | Recall(%) |
|---|---|---|---|---|
| MLP | Baseline | 88.90 | 86.83 | **91.07** |
| | **DEK(Ours)** | **89.56** | **89.03** | 90.10 |
| MLP+CRF | Baseline | 89.81 | 88.73 | **90.91** |
| | **DEK(Ours)** | **89.94** | **89.98** | 89.90 |
| Bi-LSTM+CRF | Baseline | 89.58 | 88.74 | 90.43 |
| | **DEK(Ours)** | **89.86** | **89.12** | **90.71** |

$$\text{Recall} = \frac{TP}{TP + FN}, \tag{16}$$

wherein, TP means True Positives and FN means False Negatives.

F1 Score is the harmonic mean of Recall and Precision, which is used to comprehensively evaluate the performance of the NER algorithm.

$$F1 = \frac{2 \times \text{Precision} \times \text{Recall}}{\text{Precision} + \text{Recall}}. \tag{17}$$

### 4.3 Implementation Details

For fair comparison, we set the same batch size and learning rate for all the methods on the same dataset. We set batch size as 64 on ClueNER dataset, 32 on ResumeNER and MusicNER dataset. We apply Adam Optimizer for model training, with an initial learning rate of 0.00003 and a decay rate of 0.01. We integrate our method with different popular methods to show it effectiveness.

### 4.4 Model Comparison

We integrate our method into three different popular NER models and report their performance on three datasets as shown in Table 2, 3 and 4. In the following, we will discuss the performance based on these three datasets.

**Table 5.** Performance Comparison on Fine-Grained Categories on ClueNER dataset.

| Category | Method | F1 Score(%) | Precision(%) | Recall(%) |
|---|---|---|---|---|
| game | Baseline | 81.78 | 79.93 | 83.72 |
| | **DEK(Ours)** | **84.74** | **81.30** | **88.47** |
| government | Baseline | 77.43 | 74.53 | 80.56 |
| | **DEK(Ours)** | **79.31** | **74.64** | **84.61** |
| book | Baseline | 78.54 | 79.86 | 77.27 |
| | **DEK(Ours)** | **79.87** | **79.88** | **79.88** |
| company | Baseline | 77.88 | 74.16 | **82.01** |
| | **DEK(Ours)** | **78.97** | **77.21** | 80.68 |
| movie | Baseline | 78.09 | 75.00 | **80.56** |
| | **DEK(Ours)** | **80.66** | **81.20** | 80.13 |
| name | Baseline | **86.22** | 83.77 | **88.81** |
| | **DEK(Ours)** | 84.28 | **84.67** | 87.95 |
| oganization | Baseline | 75.00 | 70.50 | 80.10 |
| | **DEK(Ours)** | **80.64** | **79.05** | **82.28** |
| position | Baseline | 78.88 | 76.40 | **81.52** |
| | **DEK(Ours)** | **79.32** | **78.07** | 80.60 |
| scene | Baseline | 63.33 | 63.03 | 63.63 |
| | **DEK(Ours)** | **68.42** | **68.42** | **68.42** |
| address | Baseline | **59.74** | **57.93** | **61.66** |
| | **DEK(Ours)** | 58.77 | 57.07 | 60.59 |

**Performance on ClueNER.** From Table 2, we can observe that our method improve baseline model performance on all the metrics. Specifically, our method have obtained 2.47% and 1.73% absolute improvement on Precision based on MLP and Bi-LSTM+CRF respectively. We can observe that the main improvement of our method is on the metric Precision, which verifies that the recognition ability of NER models are significantly improved by equipping with our two expert knowledge.

**Performance on ResumeNER.** From Table 3, we can see that our method mainly improve baseline model performance on F1 Score and Precision. Specifically, our method integrated with MLP have obtained 5.17% and 10.49% absolute improvement on F1 Score and Precision respectively, compared to baseline performance. We can see that the baseline method MLP performs much worse than other methods on ResumeNER dataset, which maybe is owing to that the sentence length in ResumeNER dataset is longer that two other datasets, the simple fully connection layers of MLP is not powerful enough to extract useful information from long sequence data. While by equipping with our method, it is able to achieve the performance comparable to the other two baseline models.

**Performance on MusicNER.** From Table 4, we can see that the improvement of our method are also mainly on F1 Score and Precision. Specifically, our method have obtained 0.66% and 2.20% absolute improvement on F1 Score and Precision based on model MLP respectively. Benefiting from our entity segmentation and classification expert knowledge, our method endow NER models more powerful recognition ability which is verified by the main improvement on Precision in all the datasets.

### 4.5   Performance on Fine-Grained Category

We also show the performance on each fine-grained category on ClueNER dataset. We take the MLP method as an example and the results are shown in Table 5. From the table, we can see that by equipping with our expert knowledge, the evaluation scores of most categories have been improved significantly. For example, the category "game" obtains 2.96% absolute improvement on F1 Score and 4.75% absolute improvement on Recall. We can conclude that our method can help model distinguish the similar categories better, like "government", "company" and "organization", thereby boost their performance. The category-specific knowledge can help NER model learn the crucial knowledge among these fine-grained categories.

## 5   Conclusion

In this paper, we focus on Chinese Named Entity Recognition task which involves two task objectives: entity segmentation and entity classification. To fully extract the hidden knowledge of these two objectives from the annotation data, we proposed a model-agnostic method by disentangling the annotation labels into two additional labels for different objectives. Then we utilize the disentangled labels to train the corresponding expert predictors respectively and enhance the final features of NER models with the expert predictions. We conduct experiments on three public datasets to verify the effectiveness of our method. In future work, we will explore more powerful knowledge extraction approach for two objective-specific expert, like introducing prompt tuning to make use of large pretrained language model. Besides, we will also study on more reasonable integration operation of two knowledge like devising reasonable confidence estimation network.

**Acknowledgments.** This work was supported by the Science and Technology Project of State Grid Zhejiang Electric Power Co., Ltd. (Project number: B311XT220007).

## References

1. Wang, D., Fan, H., Liu, J.: Learning with joint cross-document information via multi-task learning for named entity recognition. Inf. Sci. **579**, 454–467 (2021)
2. Jimeno, A., Jimenez-Ruiz, E., Lee, V., Gaudan, S., Berlanga, R., Rebholz-Schuhmann, D.: Assessment of disease named entity recognition on a corpus of annotated sentences. BMC Bioinform. (2008)

3. Cabrera-Diego, L.A., Moreno, J.G., Doucet, A.: Using a frustratingly easy domain and tagset adaptation for creating slavic named entity recognition systems. In: Proceedings of the 8th Workshop on Balto-Slavic Natural Language Processing (2021)

4. Chiu, J.P., Nichols, E.: Named entity recognition with bidirectional LSTM-CNNs. Trans. Assoc. Comput. Linguist. **4**, 357–370 (2016)

5. Cucerzan, S., Yarowsky, D.: Language independent named entity recognition combining morphological and contextual evidence. In: Empirical Methods in Natural Language Processing (1999)

6. Dniken, P.V., Cieliebak, M.: Transfer learning and sentence level features for named entity recognition on tweets. In: Workshop on Noisy User-Generated Text (2017)

7. Feng, Y., Sun, L., Zhang, J.: Early results for Chinese named entity recognition using conditional random fields model, hmm and maximum entropy. In: Natural Language Processing and Knowledge Engineering, IEEE NLP-KE 2005. Proceedings of 2005 IEEE International Conference on (2005)

8. Jin, G., Chen, X.: The fourth international Chinese language processing bakeoff: Chinese word segmentation, named entity recognition and Chinese POS tagging. In: Proceedings of the Sixth SIGHAN Workshop on Chinese Language Processing (2008)

9. Kendall, A., Gal, Y., Cipolla, R.: Multi-task learning using uncertainty to weigh losses for scene geometry and semantics. In: Proceedings of the IEEE Conference on Computer Vision and Pattern Recognition, pp. 7482–7491 (2018)

10. Kenton, J.D.M.W.C., Toutanova, L.K.: Bert: pre-training of deep bidirectional transformers for language understanding. In: Proceedings of NAACL-HLT, vol. 1, p. 2 (2019)

11. Khalifa, M., Shaalan, K.: Character convolutions for Arabic named entity recognition with long short-term memory networks. Comput. Speech Lang. **58**(Nov), 335–346 (2019)

12. Lee, S.H., Song, Y.K., Kim, H.S.: Named entity recognition using distant supervision and active bagging. J. KIISE **43**(2), 269–274 (2016)

13. Lee, S., Song, Y., Choi, M., Kim, H.: Bagging-based active learning model for named entity recognition with distant supervision. In: International Conference on Big Data & Smart Computing (2016)

14. Lin, Y., Chengjie, S., Xiaolong, W., Xuan, W.: Combining self learning and active learning for Chinese named entity recognition. J. Softw. **5**(5), 530–537 (2010)

15. Luo, J., Jianqiang, D.U., Nie, B., Xiong, W., Jia, H.E., Yang, Y.: TCM named entity recognition based on character vector with bidirectional LSTM-CRF. In: International Conference on eHealth, Telemedicine, and Social Medicine (2019)

16. Lyu, C., Chen, B., Ren, Y., Ji, D.: Long short-term memory RNN for biomedical named entity recognition. BMC Bioinform. **18**(1), 462 (2017)

17. Ma, X., Hovy, E.: End-to-end sequence labeling via bi-directional LSTM-CNNs-CRF. arXiv preprint arXiv:1603.01354 (2016)

18. Mesfar, S.: Named entity recognition for Arabic using syntactic grammars. In: International Conference on Applications of Natural Language to Information Systems (2007)

19. Mukherjee, S., Awadallah, A.H.: Tinymbert: multi-stage distillation framework for massive multi-lingual NER. CoRR abs/2004.05686 (2020)

20. Neves Oliveira, B.S., et al.: HELD: Hierarchical entity-label disambiguation in named entity recognition task using deep learning. Intell. Data Anal. **26**(3), 637–657 (2022)

21. Ning, G., Bai, Y.: Biomedical named entity recognition based on glove-BLSTM-CRF model. J. Comput. Methods Sci. Eng. **3**, 1–9 (2020)
22. Nozza, D., Manchanda, P., Fersini, E., Palmonari, M., Messina, E.: Learningtoadapt with word embeddings: domain adaptation of named entity recognition systems. Inf. Process. Manag. **58**(3), 102537 (2021)
23. Ouyang, E., Li, Y., Jin, L., Li, Z., Zhang, X.: Exploring N-gram character presentation in bidirectional RNN-CRF for Chinese clinical named entity recognition. In: CCKS: China Conference on Knowledge Graph and Semantic Computing 2017 (2017)
24. Patra, R., Saha, S.K.: Utilizing external corpora through kernel function: application in biomedical named entity recognition. Prog. Artif. Intell **9**(3), 209–219 (2020)
25. Peng, N., Dredze, M.: Named entity recognition for Chinese social media with jointly trained embeddings. In: Proceedings of the 2015 Conference on Empirical Methods in Natural Language Processing, pp. 548–554 (2015)
26. Pennington, J., Socher, R., Manning, C.D.: Glove: global vectors for word representation. In: Empirical Methods in Natural Language Processing (EMNLP), pp. 1532–1543 (2014). http://www.aclweb.org/anthology/D14-1162
27. Peters, M.E., et al.: Deep contextualized word representations. In: Proceedings of the 2018 Conference of the North American Chapter of the Association for Computational Linguistics: Human Language Technologies, Volume 1 (Long Papers), pp. 2227–2237 (2018)
28. Rong, X.: word2vec parameter learning explained (2016)
29. Rouhou, A.C., Dhiaf, M., Kessentini, Y., Ben Salem, S.: Transformer-based approach for joint handwriting and named entity recognition in historical document. Pattern Recognit. Lett. **155**, 128–134 (2022)
30. Steinberger, R., Pouliquen, B.: Cross-lingual named entity recognition. Lingvisticae Investigationes **30**(1), 135–162 (2007)
31. Tran, V.C., Nguyen, N.T., Fujita, H., Hoang, D.T., Hwang, D.: A combination of active learning and self-learning for named entity recognition on twitter using conditional random fields. Knowl.-Based Syst. **132**(15), 179–187 (2017)
32. Vaswani, A., et al.: Attention is all you need. In: Advances in Neural Information Processing Systems, vol. 30 (2017)
33. Xu, L., et al.: Cluener 2020: fine-grained named entity recognition dataset and benchmark for Chinese. arXiv preprint arXiv:2001.04351 (2020)
34. Yin, M., Mou, C., Xiong, K., Ren, J.: Chinese clinical named entity recognition with radical-level feature and self-attention mechanism. J. Biomed. Inform. **98**, 103289 (2019)
35. Yu, K., Kurohashi, S., Liu, H., Nakazawa, T.: Chinese word segmentation and named entity recognition by character tagging. In: Proceedings of the Fifth SIGHAN Workshop on Chinese Language Processing, pp. 146–149 (2006)
36. Zhang, Y., Yang, J.: Chinese NER using lattice LSTM. arXiv preprint arXiv:1805.02023 (2018)

# Deep Neural Network Model
# over Encrypted Data

Weixun Li[1], Guanghui Sun[1], Yajun Wang[1], Long Yuan[2], Minghui Gao[3,4], Yan Dong[4], and Chen Wang[4(✉)]

[1] State Grid Hebei Electric Power Co., Ltd., Shijiazhuang 050000, Hebei, China
[2] NARI Group Corporation (State Grid Electronic Power Research Institute), Nanjing 210061, China
[3] Beijing Kedong Electric Power Control System Co., Ltd., Beijing 100192, China
[4] Software College, Northeastern University, Shenyang 110169, China
1193328465@qq.com

**Abstract.** Deep Neural Networks (DNN) model training usually requires a large amount of data as the foundation, so that the model can learn effective features and rules. However, these data often contain sensitive information of users. This paper designs a DNN Classification Model for Ciphertext Data (DNN-CMED), which consists of three-party entities, including two servers and one client. The auxiliary server assists the model training server in completing the computation of the nonlinear layer of the DNN model, and the two servers interact with each other to complete the task of classifying the ciphertext data. The communication protocols of DNN-CMED are designed, including secure linear computation protocol and secure nonlinear computation protocol. The classification process of DNN-CMED is given based on the above protocol. Through safety analysis and experiments, it shows that the models have better security and practicality. The results show that this model has better results in terms of accuracy, time and communication overhead, and on the MNIST test set.

**Keywords:** Deep Neural Network · Encrypted Data · Homomorphic Encryption

## 1 Introduction

Deep Learning Based on Deep Neural Network Models [1] has attracted much attention as a key technology of Artificial Intelligence (AI) and has become the mainstream of current AI research. These results are widely used in computer vision, natural language processing, medical image analysis and other complex data fields. Deep learning plays an important role in many application areas with its excellent accuracy. In medical image analysis, deep learning can be used to classify medical images [2] in order to assist doctors in determining diseases, and it can also be used for medical image segmentation [3] in order to more accurately identify the target area.

© The Author(s), under exclusive license to Springer Nature Singapore Pte Ltd. 2024
J. Shao et al. (Eds.): EISA 2023, CCIS 2004, pp. 107–117, 2024.
https://doi.org/10.1007/978-981-99-9614-8_7

The success of deep learning is closely tied to the amount of data available for training, so business giants that are able to collect user data on a large scale have been the beneficiaries of getting bigger. However, data is often collected from users, whose data may contain sensitive or private information. Therefore, due to privacy concerns, users may be unwilling or unable to provide data, e.g., in healthcare systems, patients may be unwilling to share their data with third-party service providers [4,5], and data privacy limits the further development of deep learning.

To address the problem of data privacy, the literature [6] provides a detailed description of privacy-preserving techniques in machine learning. The research in this paper focuses on the problem that homomorphic encryption cannot participate in the nonlinear layer computation in DNN model ciphertext classification. However, Federated learning and homomorphic encryption have some shortcomings and limitations: 1)When the server collects enough gradients, it is likely to deduce the sensitive information of the participants through the shared gradients. 2) Homomorphic encryption only supports addition and multiplication operations; 3) Local devices with limited resources bear the cost of ciphertext computation.

Traditional federated learning frameworks and homomorphic encryption still suffer from privacy leakage, therefore, in this paper, we propose a DNN classification model for ciphertext data, which is used to solve the problems and limitations of some existing methods, comparing with the existing work, this paper makes the following contributions:

- DNN classification model for ciphertext data. A DNN classification model for ciphertext data is designed. In this model, the arithmetic process of DNN model is analyzed, from which linear and nonlinear operations are extracted. Then, encrypts data using fully homomorphic encryption technology. Communication protocols corresponding to the basic operations are designed, including: secure linear computation protocol and secure nonlinear computation protocol.
- A DNN Classification Model for Ciphertext Data (DNN-CMED) is constructed based on linear and nonlinear communication protocols. The client uploads ciphertext data and goes offline without the need to participate in subsequent calculation processes. DNN-CMED consists of three-party entities, and the security of DNN-CMED is analyzed.
- Finally, the performance of DNN-CMED is analyzed by testing using experimental data. The results show that this model gives better results in terms of accuracy, time and communication overhead.

## 2    Related Work

In recent years, Privacy-Preserving Deep Learning (PPDL) has been widely studied, which is a deep learning method that combines deep learning techniques and privacy-preserving strategies. Its main purpose is to utilize deep learning models for efficient data mining and classification while protecting data privacy. In order to realize privacy-preserving deep learning, many scholars have carried out a lot of research work, scholars proposed privacy-preserving federated learning [7,8] and privacy-preserving deep learning based on homomorphic encryption [9,10]. Andrew et al. [11] proposed a method that applies Bayesian differential privacy to distributed deep learning in order to protect the privacy of user's data, and this method can improve the model's generalization capability while guaranteeing data privacy. Phong et al. [12] proposed a privacy-preserving deep learning method using Additively Homomorphic Encryption, (AHE), which protects data privacy by directly performing forward propagation and back propagation of neural networks over the ciphertext domain.

For privacy-preserving deep learning with homomorphic encryption, Gilad-Bachrach et al. [13] proposed the CryptoNets solution in 2016, which applies the Fully Homomorphic Encryption to convolutional neural networks. The prediction uses a simplified neural network and replaces the ReLU activation function with a squared function of lower multiplicative depth, which achieves a high classification accuracy but is only applicable to small neural networks. In 2018, a PPDL framework-Gazelle that combines HE with Yao's Garbled Circuit (GC) was proposed by Juvekar et al. [14]. This framework allows classification without leaking the input data to the server at the user side, while protecting the privacy of the model in the server. They used Single Instruction Multiple Data (SIMD) to improve the encryption speed of HE, proposed algorithms to accelerate the process of convolution and vector matrix multiplication, and Gazelle can also switch protocols between HE and GC, successfully combining secret sharing and HE.

For privacy-preserving machine learning, Almutairi et al. [15] utilized homomorphic encryption technology to solve the data privacy problem under outsourcing, designed an updatable distance matrix, and utilized the properties of matrix computation to calculate ciphertext. Hyeong et al. [16] proposed a security protocol that supports comparison operations, first encrypting plaintext data using the Paillier cryptosystem, and then replacing plaintext operations with ciphertext security protocols. Although using the Paillier algorithm can ensure semantic security, the computational cost is too high. Chen et al. [17] designed a smart meter data aggregation scheme based on Paillier encryption to protect user privacy information. This scheme introduces a trusted third-party key generation center to generate legitimate public keys for users and store them in the server for verifying their legitimate identities. Angela et al. [18] solved the division problem in ciphertext operations. In homomorphic encryption, direct division of two ciphertext data is not allowed, but one ciphertext data can be divided by a constant, which represents the total data and does not leak critical information even if exposed.

In summary, there have been a number of research results on classification algorithms for privacy-preserving mechine learning, as shown in Table 1. But most of them ignore the problem that homomorphic encryption cannot participate in the nonlinear layer computation in DNN model ciphertext classification.

**Table 1.** Comparison of Privacy-Preserving Machine Learning. Here ✓ means that the property is satisfied whereas x means it is not.

| Proposed Approach | Training | Evaluation | Method |
|---|---|---|---|
| *Mo* [7] | ✓ | x | TEE |
| *Froelicher* [8] | ✓ | ✓ | multi-key FHE |
| *Marcano* [9] | ✓ | x | FHE |
| *Falcetta* [10] | ✓ | x | HE |
| *Triastcyn* [11] | x | ✓ | HE |
| *Moriai* [12] | x | ✓ | AHE |
| *Dowlin* [13] | x | ✓ | FHE |
| *Juvekar* [14] | x | ✓ | HE |
| *Almutairi* [15] | x | ✓ | HE |
| *Hyeong* [16] | x | ✓ | Paillier |
| *Chen* [17] | x | ✓ | Paillier |
| *Angela* [18] | x | ✓ | FHE |

# 3    DNN Classification Model for Ciphertext Data

## 3.1    General Framework of the Model

DNN Classification Model for Ciphertext Data (DNN-CMED) includes three-party entities, Model Training Server (MTS), Auxiliary Server (AS), and Client (C), as shown in Fig. 1, where the shaded area indicates the ciphertext data, ciphertext result, and ciphertext computation. C is the categorized data owner and needs to complete the categorization without leaking the categorized data; MTS is the server involved in the model training, which owns the DNN categorization model and is responsible for responding to C's categorization request and the computation of the linear layer in the DNN model; AS is a trusted third-party server, which is responsible for generating the key and assisting MTS to carry out computation in the nonlinear layer of the DNN model.

The general framework of the model is shown in Fig. 1.

The classification process of DNN-CMED is as follows:

Step 1. The AS generates a different key pair for each client it interacts with, and C uses the key distributed by the AS to encrypt the categorized data and send it to the MTS.

Step 2. MTS responds to the classification request and performs linear computation on the ciphertext classification data through the linear layer of DNN model and sends the linear computation result to AS.

Step 3. The AS utilizes the linear results to assist the MTS in the nonlinear layer computation of the DNN model. The classification task is accomplished through the interaction between MTS and AS.

Step 4. The AS sends the ciphertext classification result to C, and C decrypts it to get the final plaintext result.

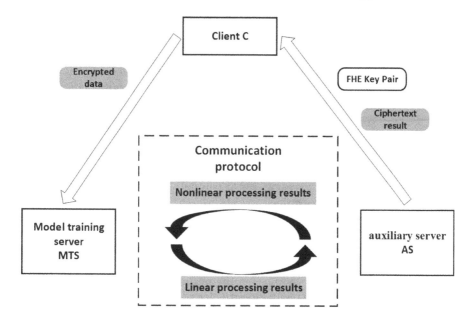

**Fig. 1.** DNN classification model for ciphertext data.

## 3.2   Communication Protocols

The communication protocols of DNN-CMED include the Secure Linear Function Protocol and the Secure Nonlinear Function Protocol. The secure linear function protocol implements linear computations, such as the fully connected layer and convolutional layer of DNN models, while the secure nonlinear function protocol implements nonlinear computations, such as the activation function ReLU function and Softmax output function of DNN models.

**Secure Linear Function Protocol.** The Secure Linear Function (SLF) protocol utilizes the additive homomorphism and multiplicative homomorphism properties of the FHE to compute the linear layer function in the DNN model for the homomorphic encrypted ciphertext, returning a linearly computed value of the ciphertext. In the secure linear function protocol, the main purpose is to compute the linear function W*I+B, where I is the categorized data, W is the weight of its mapping to the next layer of neurons, and B is the bias of the neurons, because the DNN model constructed in this section has a fully-connected layer, so the fully-connected layer with the bias parameter B is considered.

**Secure Nonlinear Function Protocol.** Secure Nonlinear Function Protocol (SNF), can safely compute the nonlinear layer functions of DNN model. In Secure Nonlinear Function Protocol, the activation function is separated from the DNN model and kept uniformly by the AS side.

SNF() is computed in the AS side, the input is the output of the previous layer of computation, and the AS side outputs the nonlinear result of the computation, the specific process is as follows: the AS side receives the result of the previous layer of computation, decrypts and decodes it, and then selects the activation function to compute a nonlinear layer of activation function on its plaintext, and then encodes and encrypts the result of the computation.

### 3.3  Classification Process

The classification process of DNN-CMED model can be specifically categorized into four processes: data encryption, linear computation, nonlinear computation and classification result processing.

Data encryption: party C encodes and encrypts all categorized data to prevent privacy leakage. party C first receives the key pair from AS. party C uses the public key to homomorphically encrypt the categorized data. Linear computation: MTS has a DNN classification model M. The model M is connected by the weighted sum of the neurons, so the output value of the neurons of the previous layer in the model M is the input value of the neurons of the next layer, and calculating the weighted sum of the neurons is the linear computation part of the model M. Assuming that the input is $I_i$, the weight of the jth neuron is $W_{i,j}$ and the bias is $B_i$, the weighted sum of the output is shown in Eq. (1) below:

$$Z_j = \sum_i I_i * W_{i,j} + B_i \tag{1}$$

The operational expression for the convolutional layer is shown in Eq. (2) below:

$$Z_{i,j} = \sum_x \sum_y I_{i+x,j+y} * W_{m,n} + B \tag{2}$$

Nonlinear computation: In DNN models, the activation function is generally a nonlinear function. The ciphertext result of the linear computation in the previous layer is sent to the activation function for computation, therefore, the AS needs to first decrypt the ciphertext result, then put the plaintext result into the activation function for computation, and then encrypt the computed result and return it to the MTS.

Classification result processing: the MTS produces the final output as a probability value of belonging to each class, in determining the class of the unknown input data, it is necessary to normalize the output values of the last layer into a probability distribution so that the value of each output node is between 0 and 1, and the sum of the values of all the nodes is 1. Therefore, after the final layer of the output of the MTS, the encrypted output of the final layer is sent to the AS and then finally run a SoftMax function to compute a better form of the result. Finally the encrypted result is returned to C which decrypts it using the key to get the final plaintext result. Therefore, according to the above

DNN model classification process, the interaction process among the ciphertext data-oriented DNN model client, model training server, and auxiliary server is constructed. The specific process is as follows:

Step 1. First, the auxiliary server generates different encryption keys for different clients and distributes fully homomorphic encryption key pairs to the clients.

Step 2. The client uses this key to encrypt the data to be classified and sends the encrypted data to the model training server.

Step 3. The model training server invokes the SLF() protocol to do a linear function homomorphism operation on the encrypted data from the client to calculate the weighted sum of the ciphertext data; then, the model training server sends the calculated linear result to the auxiliary server.

Step 4. The auxiliary server decrypts with the key and calls the SNF() protocol to complete the calculation of the nonlinear function, the activation function. The computation is then encrypted and returned to the model training server. The model training server and the auxiliary server interact until the last layer of the model.

Step 5. Finally, the auxiliary server runs a Softmax function to compute the better readable form. This is returned to the client, which decrypts it using the previous decryption key to get the final classification result.

## 3.4   Security Analysis

In this subsection the security of the communication protocol and DNN-CMED is analyzed under the model training server as a semi-honest server and the auxiliary server as a trusted third-party server, both the model training server and the client are semi-honest participants that honestly follow the protocol execution and allow inferences from the data obtained during the protocol execution. Their input data is private and can only be known by individuals.

**Theorem 1.** *Our secure protocols designed are secure in a semi-honest model.*

*Proof.* In Secure Linear Function Protocol, the model training server has view $VS = (E(I), E(Zk))$. Since the model training server has no decryption key, the model training server cannot extract the plaintext I and Zk from $E(I)$, $E(Zk)$, which guarantees the privacy of the data I and the computation result Zk; this protocol is computed only at the model training server side. Therefore, this paper's secure linear function protocol is secure under semi-honesty.

In Secure Nonlinear Computing Protocol, the view of the auxiliary server is $VS = (E(Z(k)), Zk, A)$. The auxiliary server only gets the encrypted intermediate result $E(Zk)$ calculated by the DNN model, and will not be given the data inputs, and therefore will not get the real data information.

In DNN-CMED, first invoke the secure linear function protocol to compute the linear values of the encrypted classification samples inputted by the user, the secure linear function protocol is secure under the semi-honest model, and the auxiliary server sends the computed linear ciphertext result to the client to ensure that it only knows the decrypted plaintext linear computation result, but not other information. The model training server does not have the FHE private key to decrypt the ciphertext, so the process is secure. The auxiliary server receives the intermediate results of the ciphertext, decrypts them, and then calls the secure nonlinear function protocol to compute the linear computation results inputted by the server. The secure nonlinear function protocol is safe under the semi-honest model, and the auxiliary server only has the computation results of the activation layer at that time, and does not know the model parameters of the DNN model, which ensures the safety of the model training server model.

# 4    Experiments

## 4.1    Experimental Setup

The relevant environment information used in this experiment, including: hardware environment, software environment, etc. is shown in Table 2.

**Table 2.** Experimental environment.

| Hardware | CPU | Intel(R) Xeon(R) W-2123 CPU @ 3.60 GHz |
| | RAM | 16 GB |
| Software | Operating System | Ubuntu 15.5.0 build-14665864 |
| | Programming Language | Python, C++ |
| | Encryption Tool | OpenSSL library |
| | Deep Learning Environment | TensorFlow |

For homomorphic encryption schemes homomorphic encryption for secure matrix operations was implemented using the CKKS scheme from the SEAL library. In this experiment, we set the security level to 128 bits, the number of polynomial modes to 2048, the plaintext modes to 20 bits, and the noise standard deviation to 4.

## 4.2    Analysis of Experimental Results

**Communication Overhead.** Successful batch prediction of handwritten digits on MNIST test set in encrypted state. This model has good results in terms of accuracy, time and communication overhead, which can reach about 76% on the MNIST test set, with an average latency of roughly 224.7 milliseconds and an average communication overhead of 106.09 KB. Table 3 shows that comparison of the communication overhead of the proposed schemes with that of the Secure DNN model (SDNNM) with one cloud.

**Table 3.** Efficiency tests for the MNIST test set.

| Model | Accuracy | Average delay time (S) | Average communication overhead (KB) |
|---|---|---|---|
| DNN-CMED | 76.4% | 224.7 ms | 106.09 KB |
| SDNNM | 76.8% | 279.3 ms | 119.93 KB |

In the communication overhead, as shown in Fig. 2, for a batch of 64 MNIST images, the client sends encrypted data to the server consuming approximately 0.74 MB, the communication of computation results between the model training server and the auxiliary server consumes roughly 5.34 MB, and the auxiliary server sends classification results to the client consuming roughly 0.18 MB. The communication overhead is mainly generated by the interactive computation process between the model training server and the auxiliary server. The total bandwidth between the client, the model training server and the auxiliary server is about 7.5 MB in one classification.

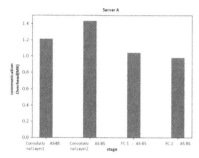
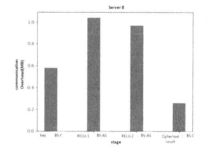

(a) The communication overhead of training server.

(b) The communication overhead of auxiliary server.

**Fig. 2.** Communication overhead at each stage of the DNN-CMED model.

**Computation Overhead.** Figure 3 shows the change in running time of the five-layer DNN model plaintext classification, and ciphertext DNN-CMED model classification when the number of categorized data $n$ varies, as can be seen from Fig. 3, its running time grows linearly with $n$. The running time of ciphertext classification ranges from 14 s to 67 s for 64–320 MNIST data, which is within the acceptable range.

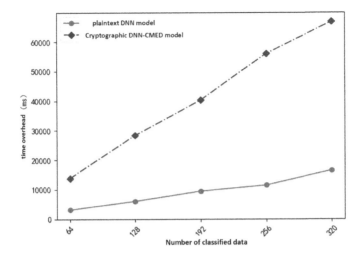

**Fig. 3.** Time overhead of DNN-CMED model vs. plaintext.

## 5    Conclusion

In this paper, we design a DNN classification model for ciphertext data based on the FHE scheme. The problem that fully homomorphic encrypted data cannot be operated in the activation layer of DNN model is solved. The model consists of a client and two servers, protects the user's data privacy by fully homomorphic encryption algorithm, designs a communication protocol for the basic operations, and solves the limitation problem in homomorphism through the communication protocol. It is proved experimentally that the model realizes the ciphertext data classification with guaranteed classification accuracy.

**Acknowledgements.** This work was supported in part by the National Natural Science Foundation of China under Grant Nos. 62372069 and 62173101, in part by the Fundamental Research Funds for the Central Universities under Grant N2017012.

## References

1. Zhao, S., Li, Y., Fu, T., Li, K.: Deep Learning. People's Posts and Telecommunications Press, Beijing (2017)
2. Raj, R.J.S., Shobana, S.J., Pustokhina, I.V., Pustokhin, D.A., Gupta, D., Shankar, K.J.I.A.: Optimal feature selection-based medical image classification using deep learning model in internet of medical things. IEEE Access **8**, 58006–58017 (2020)
3. Fu, Y., Lei, Y., Wang, T., Curran, W.J., Liu, T., Yang, X.: A review of deep learning based methods for medical image multi-organ segmentation. Phys. Med. **85**, 107–122 (2021)

4. Goyal, S., Sharma, N., Bhushan, B., Shankar, A., Sagayam, M.: IoT enabled technology in secured healthcare: applications, challenges and future directions. In: Hassanien, A.E., Khamparia, A., Gupta, D., Shankar, K., Slowik, A. (eds.) Cognitive Internet of Medical Things for Smart Healthcare. SSDC, vol. 311, pp. 25–48. Springer, Cham (2021). https://doi.org/10.1007/978-3-030-55833-8_2
5. Li, D., Liao, X., Xiang, T., et al.: Privacy-preserving self-serviced medical diagnosis scheme based on secure multi-party computation. Comput. Secur. **90**, 101701 (2020)
6. Liu, J., Meng, X.: A review of privacy protection research in machine learning. Comput. Res. Dev. **57**(2), 346–362 (2020)
7. Mo, F., Haddadi, H., Katevas, K., et al.: PPFL: privacy-preserving federated learning with trusted execution environments. In: Proceedings of the 19th Annual International Conference on Mobile Systems, Applications, and Services, pp. 94–108(2021)
8. Froelicher, D., Troncoso-Pastoriza, J.R., Pyrgelis, A., et al.: Scalable privacy-preserving distributed learning. arXiv preprint arXiv:2005.09532 (2020)
9. Marcano, N.J.H., Moller, M., Hansen, S., et al.: On fully homomorphic encryption for privacy-preserving deep learning. In: 2019 IEEE Globecom Workshops, pp. 1–6. IEEE (2019)
10. Falcetta, A., Roveri, M.: Privacy-preserving deep learning with homomorphic encryption: an introduction. IEEE Comput. Intell. Mag. **17**(3), 14–25 (2022)
11. Triastcyn, A., Faltings, B.: Federated learning with bayesian differential privacy. In: 2019 IEEE International Conference on Big Data (Big Data), Los Angeles, CA, USA, 2019, pp. 2587–2596 (2019)
12. Moriai, S.: Privacy-preserving deep learning via additively homomorphic encryption. In: 2019 IEEE 26th Symposium on Computer Arithmetic (ARITH), Kyoto, Japan, pp. 198–198 (2019)
13. Dowlin, N., Gilad-Bachrach, R., Laine, K., et al.: CryptoNets: applying neural networks to encrypted data with high throughput and accuracy. IEEE (2016)
14. Juvekar, C., Vaikuntanathan, V., Chandrakasan, A.: GAZELLE: a low latency framework for secure neural network inference. In: 27th USENIX Security Symposium, pp. 1651–1669 (2018)
15. Almutairi, N., Coenen, F., Dures, K.: K-means clustering using homomorphic encryption and an updatable distance matrix: secure third party data clustering with limited data owner interaction. In: Bellatreche, L., Chakravarthy, S. (eds.) DaWaK 2017. LNCS, vol. 10440, pp. 274–285. Springer, Cham (2017). https://doi.org/10.1007/978-3-319-64283-3_20
16. Hyeong, K., Jae, C.: A privacy-preserving k-means clustering algorithm using secure comparison protocol and density-based center point selection. In: 11th International Conference on Cloud Computing (CLOUD). IEEE (2018)
17. Chen, Y., Martínez-Ortega, J.F., Pedro, C., et al.: A homomorphic-based multiple data aggregation scheme for smart grid. IEEE Sensors J. **19**(10), 3921–3929 (2019)
18. Angela, J., Armknecht, F.: Unsupervised machine learning on encrypted data. In: International Conference on Selected Areas in Cryptography, pp. 453–478. Springer, Heidelberg (2018). https://doi.org/10.1007/978-3-030-10970-7_21

# Toward the Tradeoffs Between Privacy, Fairness and Utility in Federated Learning

Kangkang Sun[1], Xiaojin Zhang[2], Xi Lin[1], Gaolei Li[1], Jing Wang[1], and Jianhua Li[1(✉)]

[1] Shanghai Key Laboratory of Integrated Administration Technologies for Information Security, School of Electronic Information and Electrical Engineering, Shanghai Jiao Tong University, Shanghai, China
{szpsunkk,linxi234,gaolei_li,wangjing08,lijh888}@sjtu.edu.cn
[2] School of Computer Science and Technology, Huazhong University of Science and Technology, Wuhan, China
xiaojinzhang@hust.edu.cn

**Abstract.** Federated Learning (FL) is a novel privacy-protection distributed machine learning paradigm that guarantees user privacy and prevents the risk of data leakage due to the advantage of the client's local training. Researchers have struggled to design fair FL systems that ensure fairness of results. However, the interplay between fairness and privacy has been less studied. Increasing the fairness of FL systems can have an impact on user privacy, while an increase in user privacy can affect fairness. In this work, on the client side, we use the fairness metrics, such as *Demographic Parity* (DemP), *Equalized Odds* (EOs), and *Disparate Impact* (DI), to construct the local fair model. To protect the privacy of the client model, we propose a privacy-protection fairness FL method. The results show that the accuracy of the fair model with privacy increases because privacy breaks the constraints of the fairness metrics. In our experiments, we conclude the relationship between privacy, fairness and utility, and there is a tradeoff between these.

**Keywords:** Fair and Private Federated Learning · Differential Privacy · Privacy Protection

## 1 Introduction

Federated learning (FL) [MMR+17, KMA+21] is a novel distributed machine learning approach that guarantees user privacy by ensuring that user data does not leave the local area. However, FL has been plagued by two ethical issues: privacy and fairness [CZZ+23]. So far, most of the research has considered these two issues separately, but the existence of some kind of intrinsic equilibrium between the two remains unexplored. For example, privacy can come at the expense of model accuracy, however, for different groups of people training privacy results in different accuracies, with disadvantaged groups often suffering a greater cost in the training process. On the other hand, in order to ensure the fairness of the model and eliminate the bias in the training data or model [ABD+18, BHJ+21], the client needs to share more data with the server, which seriously increases the user privacy risk. Therefore, it is an open issue to investigate the intrinsic connection between fairness and privacy in FL and to break the distress caused by its tradeoffs.

J. Shao et al. (Eds.): EISA 2023, CCIS 2004, pp. 118–132, 2024.
https://doi.org/10.1007/978-981-99-9614-8_8

**Privacy Destroys Fairness.** The first observation is that the decrease in accuracy due to deep DP models has a disproportionately negative impact on underrepresented subgroups [BPS19]. DP-SGD enhances model "bias" in different distributions that need to be learned. Subsequently, in the study [PMK+20], the impact of DP on fairness in three real-world tasks involving sensitive public data. There are significant differences in the model outputs when stronger privacy protections are implemented or when the population is small. Many works [TFVH21, EGLC22] have attempted to find reasons why privacy destroys fairness.

**Fairness Increases Privacy Risk.** The client's dataset is usually unbalanced and biased. This bias is gradually amplified during the machine learning process. For example, when a model is trained for accuracy, the model's predictions will correlate with gender, age, skin, and race in a certain demographic group [ZVRG17, BHJ+21, Cho17].

Privacy and fairness are two important concepts in FL, and violating either one is unacceptable. Therefore, this paper explores the intrinsic relationship between privacy and fairness in FL and designs a privacy protection method for fair federated learning, to improve the model learning performance while ensuring the privacy and fairness constraint.

*Relationship of Fairness and Privacy.* We attempt to explore the relationship between fairness and privacy in FL. Intuitively, there is some intrinsic connection between fairness and privacy, and some balance between fairness, privacy, and utility.

- *Fairness:* We consider three fairness metrics, including Demographic Parity (DemP), Equalized Odds (EO) and Disparate Impact (DI). Comparing the research [PMK+20], we design the optimization function to be more complex, taking into account privacy and fairness constraints.
- *Privacy:* In this paper, we consider privacy-protection methods for fair Federated Learning based differential privacy.

Our contributions can be summarized as follows:

- A privacy-protection fairness FL method is proposed, in order to protect the model privacy of the client while sharing model parameters. Our proposed method is mainly divided into two parts: fairness training and privacy-protection training. Specifically, the client first trains a fairness proxy model and then trains a privacy-protection model based on that proxy model.
- In this paper, We experimentally obtained that the increase in privacy destroys the fairness of the model but appropriately increases the accuracy of the model. In order to improve the accuracy of the model and to ensure the fairness of the model, we designed private fair Algorithms 2.
- We demonstrate the superiority of our proposed method and algorithms based on *Adult* datasets comparing popular benchmark *FedAvg* algorithms. Experiments prove that our algorithm can effectively guarantee model privacy in fair FL.

## 2    Related Work

### 2.1    Fairness of FL

Fairness of FL is defined in two ways: client fairness [LSBS19, MBS20, YLL+20, KKM+20] and algorithmic fairness [HPS16, KLRS17]. Algorithmic fairness has been extensively studied in traditional centralized machine learning through debiasing methods [KMA+21]. However, due to the fact that in FL, the server does not have access to client-side local data, it is already difficult to estimate the global data distribution simply by debiasing either server-side or client-side [MMR+17]. Much research has focused on client fairness in FL, such as in augmenting client data aspect [HEKL+21, JOK+18], in the client data distribution aspect [DLC+20, WKNL20]. From a model perspective, training a separate fairness model for each client is an open problem.

### 2.2    Privacy of FL

Many recent studies have focused on FL privacy risks [GMS+23, LGR23a, SLS+23, BWD+22]. A diversity of privacy-protection techniques have been proposed to discourage the risk of privacy leakage for users, including cryptographic techniques and the perturbation approach [CZZ+23]. Cryptographic approaches allow computation on encrypted data and provide strict privacy guarantees. However, they are computationally expensive compared to non-encryption methods [XBJ21]. This computational overhead seriously affects the machine learning training process, especially with a large number of parameters in the model. Therefore, the current state-of-the-art privacy-protection methods are perturbation-based, such as the DP mechanism [GKN17, WLD+20, WKL+21, SMS22]. The shuffler model is proposed to amplify the privacy of LDP's poor performance in comparison with the central DP mechanisms [RSL+08, EFM+19, CSU+19, BBGN20, GGK+21, GDD+21]. Most research based on Shuffler's model has focused on the study of tradeoffs between privacy, utility, and communication [CCKS22, GDD+21, LLF+23, ZXW+22, BBGN19]. However, there is very little research on the privacy protection of fair federated learning.

### 2.3    Fairness and Privacy of FL

Recently, some work [CZZ+23, PMK+20] has led to inconsistent reductions in accuracy due to private mechanisms for classification [FMST20] and generation tasks [GODC22]. Because of the tension between fairness and privacy, researchers often need to make trade-offs between the two perceptions [BPS19, EGLC22, TFVH21]. The trade-off may be to increase privacy preservation at the expense of fairness, i.e., by adopting a loose notion of fairness rather than a precise one or vice versa [BHJ+21, Cho17] (Table 1).

## 3    Preliminaries

### 3.1    Fairness in FL

We consider the following fairness metrics, including DemP, EO and DI. DemP denotes the same probability of getting a chance under some sensitive attribute. EO is a subset

**Table 1.** Private and Fair Federated Learning

| References | Privacy Metrics | Fairness Metrics | Techniques | | Trade-off type |
|---|---|---|---|---|---|
| | | | Privacy | Fairness | |
| [LZMV19] | $\epsilon$-DP | EOs & DemP | Class conditional noise | Fairness constraints | I |
| [JKM+19] | $(\epsilon, \delta)$-DP | EOs | Exponential mechanism & Laplace noise | Fairness constraints | / |
| [LGR23b] | $(\epsilon, \delta)$-DP | EOs & DemP | DP-SGDA | ERMI regularizer | II |
| [TFVH21] | $(\alpha, \epsilon_p)$-Renyi DP | EOs, AP & DemP | DP-SGD | Fairness constraints | II |
| [KGK+18] | / | EA | MPC | Fairness constraints | II |
| [DGK+22] | / | EOs | Proxy attribute | Post-processing | II |
| [WGN+20] | / | DemP | Noisy attribute | Fairness constraints | II |
| [AKM20] | / | EOs | Noisy attribute | Post-processing | II |
| **Our Method** | $(\epsilon, \delta)$-DP | EOs, DemP, DI | Gaussian Noise | Fairness constraints | II |

I: Trade fairness for privacy. II: Trade privacy for fairness.
EOs: Equalized Odds. DemP: Demographic Parity. AP: Accuracy Parity. EA: Equal Accuracy.
DI: Disparate Impact.

of DP, defined as the probability of getting a chance on a given aspect is the same for different sensitive attributes. Let $X, Y$ be the sensitive attribute and the true label, respectively. For example, $Y = 1$ often represents the condition of being able to apply for a loan, and $Y = 0$ is the condition of not meeting the loan. Thus, on the opportunity to apply for a loan, the output has the same probability for each person (characteristic), and then this is EO fairness.

**Definition 1 (Demographic Parity (DemP))** [HPS16]. *We say that a predictor $f$ satisfies demographic parity with respect to attribute $A$, instance space $X$ and output space $Y$, if the output of the prediction $f(X)$ is independent of the sensitive attribute $\mathcal{A}$. For $\forall a \in A$ and $p \in \{0, 1\}$:*

$$\mathbf{P}[f(X) = p \mid \mathcal{A} = a] = \mathbf{P}[f(X) = p] \tag{1}$$

*Given $p \in \{0, 1\}$, for $\forall a \in A$:*

$$\mathbb{E}[f(X) \mid \mathcal{A} = a] = \mathbb{E}[f(X)] \tag{2}$$

*However, the left and right terms of the above equality are often not the same. Then, the loss $l_{DemP}$ of DemP can be defined as follows:*

$$l_{DemP} = \mathbb{E}[f(X) \mid \mathcal{A} = a] - \mathbb{E}[f(X)] \tag{3}$$

**Definition 2 (Equalized Odds (EO))** [HPS16]. *We say that a predictor $f$ satisfies equalized odds with respect to attribute $A$, instance space $X$ and output space $Y$, if the output of the prediction $f(X)$ is independent of the sensitive attribute $\mathcal{A}$ with the label $\mathcal{Y}$. For $\forall a \in \mathcal{A}$ and $p \in \{0, 1\}$:*

$$\mathbf{P}[f(X) = p \mid \mathcal{A} = a, Y = y] = \mathbf{P}[f(X) = p \mid Y = y] \tag{4}$$

*Given $p \in \{0, 1\}$, for $\forall a \in A, y \in Y$:*

$$\mathbb{E}[f(X) \mid \mathcal{A} = a, Y = y] = \mathbb{E}[f(X) \mid Y = y] \tag{5}$$

*Then, the loss $l_{EO}$ of EO can be defined as follows:*

$$l_{EO} = \mathbb{E}[f(X) \mid \mathcal{A} = a, Y = y] - \mathbb{E}[f(X) \mid Y = y] \tag{6}$$

*Remark 1* A binary predictor $f$, satisfying the demographic parity, is a special instance of equalized odds.

**Definition 3 (Disparate Impact (DI))** [PMK+20]. *We say that a predictor $f$ satisfies disparate impact with respect to attribute $\mathcal{A}$, if the output of the prediction $f(X)$ is independent of the sensitive attribute $\mathcal{A}$ with a similar proportion of the different groups. For $a \in \{0,1\}$, we have:*

$$\min \left( \frac{\mathbf{P}(f(x) > 0 \mid a = 1)}{\mathbf{P}(f(x) > 0 \mid a = 0)}, \frac{\mathbf{P}(f(x) > 0 \mid a = 0)}{\mathbf{P}(f(x) > 0 \mid a = 1)} \right) = 1 \tag{7}$$

*For $i \in [0, n]$ and $i$ is a positive integer:*

$$\min \left( \frac{\mathbf{P}(f(x) > 0 \mid a = i+1)}{\mathbf{P}(f(x) > 0 \mid a = i)}, \frac{\mathbf{P}(f(x) > 0 \mid a = 0)}{\mathbf{P}(f(x) > 0 \mid a = n)} \right)_{i=0}^{n} = 1 \tag{8}$$

Then, the loss $l_{DI}$ of DI can be defined as follows:

$$l_{DI} = \min \left( \frac{\mathbf{P}(f(x) > 0 \mid a = i+1)}{\mathbf{P}(f(x) > 0 \mid a = i)}, \frac{\mathbf{P}(f(x) > 0 \mid a = 0)}{\mathbf{P}(f(x) > 0 \mid a = n)} \right)_{i=0}^{n} - 1 \tag{9}$$

### 3.2   Privacy in FL

The local dataset of clients contains sensitive data, which requires protecting the sensitive attributes while training. Differential Privacy (DP) is a privacy protection technique designed to safeguard individual data while allowing data analysis and mining [DR+14]. Local Differential Privacy (LDP) is deployed on clients to protect the attributes of the local dataset, in order to make sure that any algorithm built on this dataset is differentially private. The $\epsilon$- differentially private mechanism $\mathcal{M}$ is defined as follows:

**Definition 4 (Local Differential Privacy (LDP))** [DR+14]. *A randomize algorithm $\mathcal{M} : X \rightarrow Y$ satisfies $(\epsilon, \delta)$-LDP with respect to a input set $X$ and a noise output set $Y$, if $\forall x, x' \in X$ and $\forall y \in Y$ hold:*

$$\mathbf{P}[\mathcal{M}(x) = y] \leq e^{\epsilon} \mathbf{P}[\mathcal{M}(x') = y] + \delta \tag{10}$$

**Definition 5 (Gaussian Mechanism** ([DR+14])**).** *Assume that a deterministic function $f : \mathcal{M}X \rightarrow Y$ with $\Delta_2(f)$ sensitivity, then for $\forall \delta \in (0,1)$, random noise follows a normal distribution $\mathcal{N}(0, \sigma^2)$, the mechanism $\mathcal{M}(d) = f(d) + \mathcal{N}(0, \sigma^2)$ is $(\epsilon, \delta)$-DP, where*

$$\epsilon \geq \frac{\sqrt{2 \ln(1.25/\delta)}}{\frac{\sigma}{\Delta_2 f}}, \quad \Delta_2(f) = \max_{d, d' \in \mathcal{D}} \|f(d) - f(d')\|_2 \tag{11}$$

### 3.3 Problem Formulation

There is a set of $n$ clients in the FL system, where $m \in n$ clients are selected to participate in the FL training process. The clients have its own local dataset $\mathcal{D}_i = \{d_1, ..., d_n\}$.
Let $\mathcal{D} = \bigcup_{i=1}^{n} \mathcal{D}_i$ denote the entire dataset and $f(\theta_i, d_i)$ as the loss function of client
$i$, where the parameter $\theta \in \Theta$ is the model parameter. There are $m \in n$ clients
The clients are connected to an untrusted server in order to solve the ERM problem
$F_i(\theta, \mathcal{D}_i) = \frac{1}{b} \sum_{j=1}^{b} f(\theta, d_{ij})$, where local estimated loss function dependent on the
local dataset $\mathcal{D}_i$, and $b$ is the local batch size. We give the ERM problem [KMA+21] in
FL, as follows:

$$\arg\min_{\theta \in \mathcal{C}} \left( F(\theta) := \frac{1}{m} \sum_{i=1}^{m} F_i(\theta) \right),$$

$$s.t. \quad l_{DemP} < \mu_{DemP}, \tag{12}$$
$$l_{EO} < \mu_{EO},$$
$$l_{DI} < \mu_{DI},$$

where the $l_{DemP}, l_{EO}, l_{DI}$ are the loss constraint of DemP, EO and DI, respectively.
We use the Lagrangian multiplier [PMK+20] to transform the ERM problem (12) into
a Min-Max problem, as follows:

$$F(\theta, \lambda, l) = \arg\min_{\theta_i \in \Theta} \max_{\lambda_{ij} \in \Lambda} \frac{1}{m} \sum_{i=1}^{m} \left\{ \frac{1}{b} \sum_{j=1}^{b} f_i(\theta_i + d_{ij}) + \lambda_{ij} l_k \right\},$$

$$k \in \{DemP, EO, DI\}, \tag{13}$$

where the parameter $\lambda \in \Lambda$ is the Lagrangian multiplier. In this fairness stage, the
purpose is to train the proxy model under the fairness matrixes, which is to solve the
optimization problem (13). For the optimization problem (13), there is the Lagrangian dual-
ity between the following two functions:

$$\begin{aligned} \min_{\theta \in \Theta} \quad &\max_{\lambda \in \Lambda} F(\theta, \lambda, l), \\ \max_{\lambda \in \Lambda} \quad &\min_{\theta \in \Theta} F(\theta, \lambda, l). \end{aligned} \tag{14}$$

In order to solve the above dual optimization problem (14), many works assume the
function $F$ is Liptches and convex and obtain a $\nu$-*approximate saddle point* of Lan-
grangian, with a pair $(\widehat{\theta}, \widehat{\lambda})$, where

$$\begin{aligned} F(\widehat{\theta}, \widehat{\lambda}, l) \leq F(\theta, \widehat{\lambda}, l) + \nu \quad \text{for all} \quad \theta \in \Theta, \\ F(\widehat{\theta}, \widehat{\lambda}, l) \geq F(\widehat{\theta}, \lambda, l) - \nu \quad \text{for all} \quad \lambda \in \Lambda. \end{aligned} \tag{15}$$

Therefore we can get the Max-Min and the Min-Max dual problems are equivalent
in the ERM problem (12). In order to search for the optimal value $(\theta^*, \lambda^*)$ (or *Nash
Equilibrium* in game [JKM+19]) of the problem (12), many works study the fairness
model by many approaches, such as the Zero-Game [JKM+19, MOS20], Distribution-
ally Robust Optimization (DRO) [WGN+20], and Soft Group Assignments [WGN+20].

In this paper, the fair model is optimized by the DRO method through a Lagrangian dual multiplier in clients, and the model parameters are then transmitted to the server for model aggregation through privacy-protection.

# 4 Method

In this section, we design privacy protection for fair federated learning based on differential privacy. In Sect. 4.1, the fair model in the FL system is obtained by the Algorithm 1, where the fair model of each client can be optimized under constraints of *DemP*, *EO* and *DI*. In Sect. 4.2, we design a privacy protection Algorithm 2 for the fair model optimized in Sect. 4.1.

## 4.1 Fairness Predictor (Model) in Client

Firstly, the clients train their own personalized fairness predictor, and we designed an Algorithm 1 to train the fair model on each client. In the Algorithm 1 line 5 and line 7, the optimal values $(\theta^*, \lambda^*)$ are derived from the partial differential expression of the ERM problem (12). Secondly, each $\theta_i$ and $\lambda_i$ update their own information according to the partial differential expression in Algorithm 1 line 6 and line 8. Finally, after time $T_1$ rounds, the fair model of the client $i$ is output.

## 4.2 Privacy Protection Method in Fair FL

In this section, we design a privacy-protection fairness FL framework to protect the privacy and fairness of sensitive datasets in clients. As the above section, there is a trade-off between privacy, fairness and accuracy in the FL system. In this paper, we designed a privacy-protection algorithm, named FedLDP Algorithm 2, based on the FedAvg algorithm.

**FedLDP:** In the algorithm, we design to add differential privacy preservation to the fairness model training process in Algorithm 2. The algorithm, while reducing privacy consumption, can effectively improve the training accuracy of the model. Moreover, the algorithm does not guarantee that the intermediate entities are trustworthy, so the shuffler model is hijacked or attacked without any impact on user privacy.

---

**Algorithm 1.** `Fair-SGD` for client

---

**Input:** Local loss function $f(\cdot)$, train dataset $\mathcal{D}_i$, learning rate $\eta$, batch size $B$
1: Initialize: $f_i(\theta_i) \leftarrow$ random, $\lambda_i \leftarrow$ max value
2: **for** Each client $i \in \mathcal{N}$ **do**
3:   **for** $t \in T_1$ **do**
4:     Take a random batch size $B$ and $j \in B$
5:     For $\theta_i$: $\mathbf{g}_t(x_j) \leftarrow \nabla_{\theta_{(i,t)}} f_i(\cdot)$
6:     $\theta_{(i,t+1)} \leftarrow \theta_{(i,t)} - \eta_t \mathbf{g}_t(x_j)$
7:     For $\lambda_i$, $\mathbf{g}'_t(x_j) \leftarrow \nabla_{\lambda_{(i,t)}} f_i(\cdot)$
8:     $\lambda_{(i,t+1)} \leftarrow \lambda_{(i,t)} + \eta \mathbf{g}'_t(x_j)$
9:   **end for**
10: **end for**
**Output:** Fair model $f_i(\theta_i)$

---

**Algorithm 2.** `FedLDP`

---

**Input:** Selected clients $m$, the local dataset $\mathcal{D}_i$ of client $i$, Maximum $L_2$ norm bound $C$, local privacy budget $\varepsilon_l$
1: Initial the local model and download the global gradients from the server
2: **for** $i \in m$ in parallel **do**
3:   `Fairness stage` in Algorithm (1)
4:   $\mathbf{g}_t(x_j) \leftarrow \nabla_{\theta_{(i,t)}} f_i(\cdot)$
5:   $\overline{\mathbf{g}}_t(x_j) \leftarrow \mathbf{g}_t(x_j) / \max\left(1, \frac{\|\mathbf{g}_t(x_j)\|_2}{C}\right)$
6:   $\tilde{\mathbf{g}}_t(x_j) \leftarrow \frac{1}{B}\left(\sum_i \overline{\mathbf{g}}_t(x_j) + \mathcal{N}\left(0, \sigma^2 C^2 \mathbf{I}\right)\right)$
7:   $\theta_{(i,t+1)} \leftarrow \theta_{(i,t)} - \eta_t \tilde{\mathbf{g}}_t(x_j)$
8: **end for**
9:   **Server**
10: **Aggregate:** $\overline{\mathbf{g}}_t \leftarrow \frac{1}{\mathcal{N}_t} \sum_{i \in \mathcal{N}_t} \boldsymbol{w}_t(d_{ij})$
11: **Gradient Descent:** $\theta_{t+1}^G \leftarrow \theta_t^G + \mathbf{g}_t$

---

## 5 Experiments

### 5.1 Dataset and Experimental Settings

In order to test the performance proposed in this paper, we use the *Adult* [PG20], which is extracted from the U.S. Census dataset database, which contains 48,842 records, with 23.93% of the annual income greater than $50k and 76.07% of the annual income less than $50k, and has been divided into 32,561 training data and 16,281 test data. The class variable of this dataset is whether the annual income is more than $50k or not, and the attribute variables include 14 categories of important information such as age, type of work, education, occupation, etc., of which 8 categories belong to the category discrete variables and the other 6 categories belong to the numerical continuous variables. This dataset is a categorical dataset that is used to predict whether or not annual income exceeds $50k. We choose race as the sensitive attribute, including white person and black person.

## 5.2   Experimental Hyperparameter Settings

In the experiment, each client applied three (100×100) fully connected layers.

**Machines.** The experiment was run on an ubuntu 2022.04 system with an intel i9 12900K CPU, GeForce RTX 3090 Ti GPU, and pytorch 1.12.0, torchversion 0.13.0, python 3.8.13.

**Software.** We implement all code in PyTorch and the fair_learn tool.

## 5.3   Performance Comparison Results

In the experiment, we compared the test accuracy between different algorithms. In the FL system, we tested both cases of fairness training without noise, and fairness training with noise, shown in Fig. 1(a) and (b). In Fig. 1 (a), the test accuracy of the white person is the same as the black person without noise in the client training process, while the fair client model with noise increases discrimination against different races in Fig. 1(b).

Table 2 and Table 3 represent the test accuracy of differential clients in the FL system without noise and with noise, respectively. It can see from the table, that adding privacy improves the test accuracy for clients. The increase in privacy affects fairness because the increase in noise facilitates the optimizer to solve the global objective optimum while weakening the limitations of the fairness metrics, i.e., the constraints function $\lambda_{ij}l_k$.

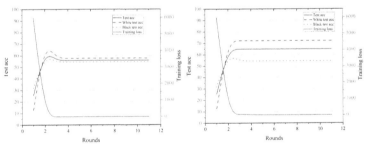

(a) Fairness predictor with no privacy (b) Fairness predictor with privacy ($\mathcal{N}(0, 1)$)

**Fig. 1.** The average test accuracy of the fair stage training process in FL settings with 5 clients on *Adult* dataset. (*a*) and (*b*) are the training results with no privacy and privacy ($\mathcal{N}(0, 1)$), respectively. (*a*) is shown that the test accuracy of sensitive data *black* and *white* are approximately the same for both. With the addition of noise privacy, test accuracy improves but fairness decreases, shown in (*b*).

**Table 2.** The fair stage training process in FL settings with 5 clients (no privacy) on *Adult* dataset.

|       | Client 1 | Client 2 | Client 3 | Client 4 | Client 5 |
|-------|----------|----------|----------|----------|----------|
| Black | 32.20 %  | 69.42 %  | 68.80%   | 68.96%   | 33.36 %  |
| White | 12.26%   | 88.39 %  | 87.20%   | 87.05%   | 13.85 %  |

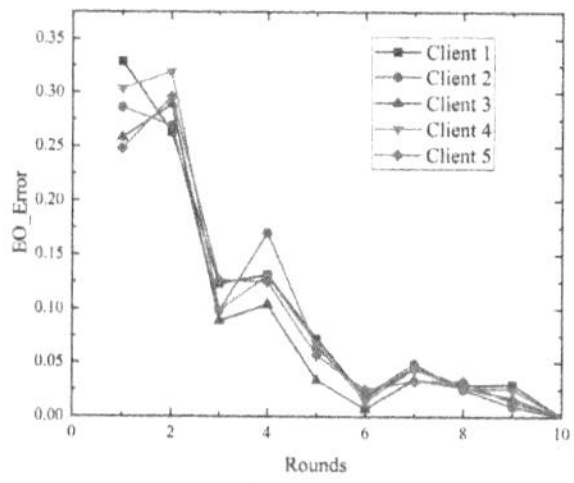

(*a*) EO error without privacy

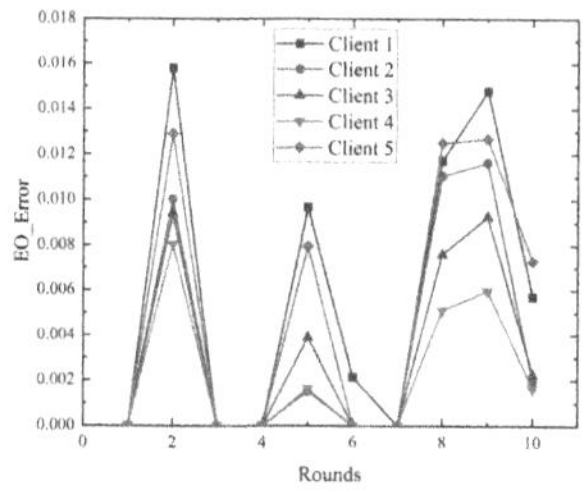

(*b*) EO error with privacy

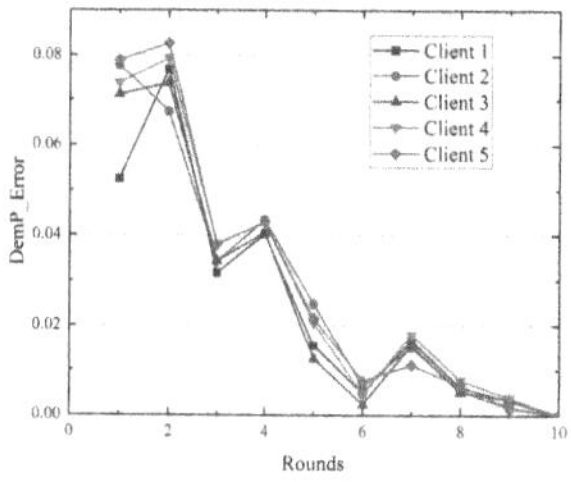

(*c*) DemP error without privacy

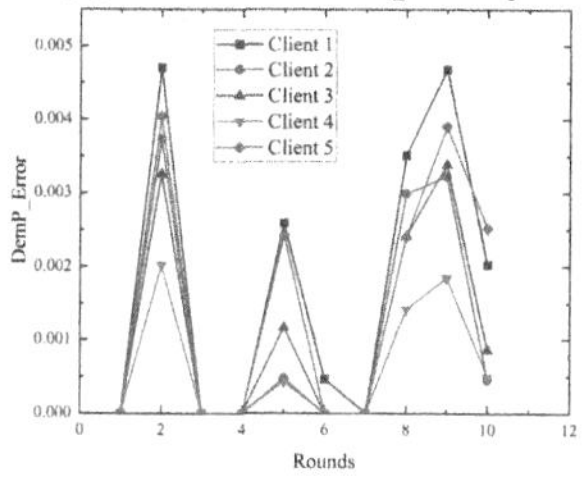

(*d*) Demp error with privacy

**Fig. 2.** The EO and DemP error comparison of different clients with privacy and no privacy on *Adult* dataset

**Table 3.** The fair stage training process in FL settings with 5 clients (privacy $\mathcal{N}(0,1)$) on *Adult* dataset.

|       | Client 1 | Client 2 | Client 3 | Client 4 | Client 5 |
|-------|----------|----------|----------|----------|----------|
| Black | 66.63 %  | 73.75 %  | 68.96 %  | 69.41 %  | 67.79 %  |
| White | 86.11 %  | 85.70 %  | 87.05%   | 88.39%   | 87.73 %  |

### 5.4  Analysis of Privacy and Fairness

In this section, we analyse the influence of privacy and fairness on the client model. We analyse the fairness metrics of *EO Error* and *DemP Error* to evaluate the error of the training fairness model by adding the privacy ($\sigma = 1$). Figure 2(*a*)–(*d*) show the *EO Error* and *DemP Error* of different algorithms when each client trains the local fairness model and adds privacy noise. From Fig. 2(*a*) and (*c*), the *EO Error* and *DemP Error* without privacy converge to zero. It can be shown that the client-trained model is fair in both *Demographic Parity* and *Equalized Odds*. However, when privacy is added during federated learning training, the *EO* $l_{EO}$ and *Demp* $l_{Demp}$ loss of the model does not converge, which indicates that adding privacy to the model training process affects the fairness of the model.

In Fig. 3, it is shown the fairness metrics in the client model with privacy and without privacy. In particular, client-side prediction performance is significantly increased by adding noise to the accuracy metric. One of the reasons for this is probably because, with the addition of privacy, the optimizer can jump out of the local optimum in finding the optimal solution.

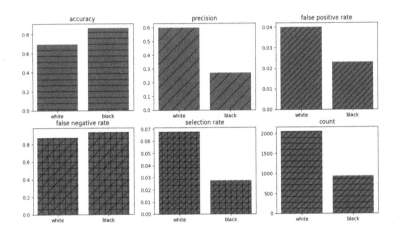

(*a*) Fair model of client 1 without privacy

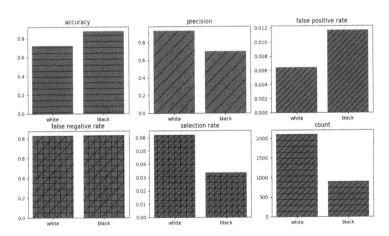

(*b*) Fair model of client 1 with privacy ($\mathcal{N}(0, 1)$)

**Fig. 3.** The fairness matrics of clients on *Adult* dataset

# 6 Conclusion

In this paper, we research the relationship between fairness and privacy in the FL system. Through the experiment, we found that there is a trade-off between privacy, fairness and accuracy in the FL system. In this paper, we construct the fairness model in clients under the fair metrics constraints, such as *Demographic Parity* (DemP) and *Equqlized Odds* (EOs). In order to protect the fair model privacy, we design a privacy-protecting fairness FL method and we give a private fair algorithm *FedLDP*). In our experiments, we conclude that by adding privacy we can appropriately increase the accuracy of the model while at the same time destroying its fairness.

**Acknowledgment.** This work was supported in part by the National Natural Science Foundation of China under Grant U20B2048, 62202302.

# References

[ABD+18] Agarwal, A., Beygelzimer, A., Dudík, M., Langford, J., Wallach, H.: A reductions approach to fair classification. In: International Conference on Machine Learning, pp. 60–69. PMLR (2018)

[AKM20] Awasthi, P., Kleindessner, M., Morgenstern, J.: Equalized odds postprocessing under imperfect group information. In: International Conference on Artificial Intelligence and Statistics, pp. 1770–1780. PMLR (2020)

[BBGN19] Balle, B., Bell, J., Gascón, A., Nissim, K.: The privacy blanket of the shuffle model. In: Boldyreva, A., Micciancio, D. (eds.) CRYPTO 2019. LNCS, vol. 11693, pp. 638–667. Springer, Cham (2019). https://doi.org/10.1007/978-3-030-26951-7_22

[BBGN20] Balle, B., Bell, J., Gascón, A., Nissim, K.: Private summation in the multi-message shuffle model. In: Proceedings of the 2020 ACM SIGSAC Conference on Computer and Communications Security, pp. 657–676 (2020)

[BHJ+21] Berk, R., Heidari, H., Jabbari, S., Kearns, M., Roth, A.: Fairness in criminal justice risk assessments: the state of the art. Sociol. Methods Res. **50**(1), 3–44 (2021)

[BPS19] Bagdasaryan, E., Poursaeed, O., Shmatikov, V.: Differential privacy has disparate impact on model accuracy. Adv. Neural Inf. Process. Syst. **32**, 1–10 (2019)

[BWD+22] Bietti, A., Wei, C.Y., Dudik, M., Langford, J., Wu, S.: Personalization improves privacy-accuracy tradeoffs in federated learning. In: International Conference on Machine Learning, pp. 1945–1962. PMLR (2022)

[CCKS22] Chen, W.N., Choo, C.A.C., Kairouz, P., Suresh, A.T.: The fundamental price of secure aggregation in differentially private federated learning. In: International Conference on Machine Learning, pp. 3056–3089. PMLR (2022)

[Cho17] Chouldechova, A.: Fair prediction with disparate impact: a study of bias in recidivism prediction instruments. Big Data **5**(2), 153–163 (2017)

[CSU+19] Cheu, A., Smith, A., Ullman, J., Zeber, D., Zhilyaev, M.: Distributed differential privacy via shuffling. In: Ishai, Y., Rijmen, V. (eds.) EUROCRYPT 2019. LNCS, vol. 11476, pp. 375–403. Springer, Cham (2019). https://doi.org/10.1007/978-3-030-17653-2_13

[CZZ+23] Chen, H., Zhu, T., Zhang, T., Zhou, W., Yu, P.S.: Privacy and fairness in federated learning: on the perspective of trade-off. ACM Comput. Surv. **56**, 1–37 (2023)

[DGK+22] Diana, E., Gill, W., Kearns, M., Kenthapadi, K., Roth, A., Sharifi-Malvajerdi, S.: Multiaccurate proxies for downstream fairness. In: Proceedings of the 2022 ACM Conference on Fairness, Accountability, and Transparency, pp. 1207–1239 (2022)

[DLC+20]  Duan, M., Liu, D., Chen, X., Liu, R., Tan, Y., Liang, L.: Self-balancing federated learning with global imbalanced data in mobile systems. IEEE Trans. Parallel Distrib. Syst. **32**(1), 59–71 (2020)

[DR+14]  Dwork, C., Roth, A., et al.: The algorithmic foundations of differential privacy. Found. Trends® Theor. Comput. Sci. **9**(3–4), 211–407 (2014)

[EFM+19]  Erlingsson, Ú., Feldman, V., Mironov, I., Raghunathan, A., Talwar, K., Thakurta, A.: Amplification by shuffling: from local to central differential privacy via anonymity. In: Proceedings of the Thirtieth Annual ACM-SIAM Symposium on Discrete Algorithms, pp. 2468–2479. SIAM (2019)

[EGLC22]  Esipova, M.S., Ghomi, A.A., Luo, Y., Cresswell, J.C.: Disparate impact in differential privacy from gradient misalignment. arXiv preprint arXiv:2206.07737 (2022)

[FMST20]  Farrand, T., Mireshghallah, F., Singh, S., Trask, A.: Neither private nor fair: impact of data imbalance on utility and fairness in differential privacy. In Proceedings of the 2020 Workshop on Privacy-Preserving Machine Learning in Practice, pp. 15–19 (2020)

[GDD+21]  Girgis, A., Data, D., Diggavi, S., Kairouz, P., Suresh, A.T.: Shuffled model of differential privacy in federated learning. In: International Conference on Artificial Intelligence and Statistics, pp. 2521–2529. PMLR (2021)

[GGK+21]  Ghazi, B., Golowich, N., Kumar, R., Pagh, R., Velingker, A.: On the power of multiple anonymous messages: frequency estimation and selection in the shuffle model of differential privacy. In: Canteaut, A., Standaert, F.-X. (eds.) EUROCRYPT 2021. LNCS, vol. 12698, pp. 463–488. Springer, Cham (2021). https://doi.org/10.1007/978-3-030-77883-5_16

[GKN17]  Geyer, R.C., Klein, T., Nabi, M.: Differentially private federated learning: a client level perspective. arXiv preprint arXiv:1712.07557 (2017)

[GMS+23]  Gehlhar, T., Marx, F., Schneider, T., Suresh, A., Wehrle, T., Yalame, H.: Mpc-friendly framework for private and robust federated learning. Cryptology ePrint Archive, Safefl (2023)

[GODC22]  Ganev, G., Oprisanu, B., De Cristofaro, E.: Robin hood and matthew effects: differential privacy has disparate impact on synthetic data. In: International Conference on Machine Learning, pp. 6944–6959. PMLR (2022)

[HEKL+21]  Hao, W., et al.: Towards fair federated learning with zero-shot data augmentation. In: Proceedings of the IEEE/CVF Conference on Computer Vision and Pattern Recognition, pp. 3310–3319 (2021)

[HPS16]  Hardt, M., Price, E., Srebro, N.: Equality of opportunity in supervised learning. Adv. Neural Inf. Process. Syst. **29** (2016)

[JKM+19]  Jagielski, M., et al.: Differentially private fair learning. In: International Conference on Machine Learning, pp. 3000–3008. PMLR (2019)

[JOK+18]  Jeong, E., Oh, S., Kim, H., Park, J., Bennis, M., Kim, S.L.: Communication-efficient on-device machine learning: federated distillation and augmentation under non-iid private data. arXiv preprint arXiv:1811.11479 (2018)

[KGK+18]  Kilbertus, N., Gascón, A., Kusner, M., Veale, M., Gummadi, K., Weller, A.: Blind justice: fairness with encrypted sensitive attributes. In: International Conference on Machine Learning, pp. 2630–2639. PMLR (2018)

[KKM+20]  Karimireddy, S.P., Kale, S., Mohri, M., Reddi, S., Stich, S., Suresh, A.T.: Scaffold: stochastic controlled averaging for federated learning. In: International Conference on Machine Learning, pp. 5132–5143. PMLR (2020)

[KLRS17]  Kusner, M.J., Loftus, J., Russell, C., Silva, R.: Counterfactual fairness. Adv. Neural Inf. Process. Syst. **30** (2017)

[KMA+21]  Kairouz, P., et al.: Advances and open problems in federated learning. Found. Trends® Mach. Learn. **14**(1–2), 1–210 (2021)

[LGR23a] Lowy, A., Ghafelebashi, A., Razaviyayn, M.: Private non-convex federated learning without a trusted server. In International Conference on Artificial Intelligence and Statistics, pp. 5749–5786. PMLR (2023)

[LGR23b] Lowy, A., Gupta, D., Razaviyayn, M.: Stochastic differentially private and fair learning. In: Workshop on Algorithmic Fairness through the Lens of Causality and Privacy, pp. 86–119. PMLR (2023)

[LLF+23] Li, X., et al.: Privacy enhancement via dummy points in the shuffle model. IEEE Trans. Depend. Secure Comput. (2023)

[LSBS19] Li, T., Sanjabi, M., Beirami, A., Smith, V.: Fair resource allocation in federated learning. arXiv preprint arXiv:1905.10497 (2019)

[LZMV19] Lamy, A., Zhong, Z., Menon, A.K., Verma, N.: Noise-tolerant fair classification. Adv. Neural Inf. Process. Syst. **32** (2019)

[MBS20] Martinez, N., Bertran, M., Sapiro, G.: Minimax pareto fairness: a multi objective perspective. In: International Conference on Machine Learning, pp. 6755–6764. PMLR (2020)

[MMR+17] McMahan, B., Moore, E., Ramage, D., Hampson, S., Aguera y Arcas, B.: Communication-efficient learning of deep networks from decentralized data. In: Artificial Intelligence and Statistics, pp. 1273–1282. PMLR (2017)

[MOS20] Mozannar, H., Ohannessian, M., Srebro, N.: Fair learning with private demographic data. In: International Conference on Machine Learning, pp. 7066–7075. PMLR (2020)

[PG20] Padala, M., Gujar, S.: FNNC: achieving fairness through neural networks. In: Proceedings of the Twenty-Ninth International Joint Conference on Artificial Intelligence,{IJCAI-20}, International Joint Conferences on Artificial Intelligence Organization (2020)

[PMK+20] Pujol, D., McKenna, R., Kuppam, S., Hay, M., Machanavajjhala, A., Miklau, G.: Fair decision making using privacy-protected data. In Proceedings of the 2020 Conference on Fairness, Accountability, and Transparency, pp. 189–199 (2020)

[RSL+08] Raskhodnikova, S., Smith, A., Lee, H.K., Nissim, K., Kasiviswanathan, S.P.: What can we learn privately. In: Proceedings of the 54th Annual Symposium on Foundations of Computer Science, pp. 531–540 (2008)

[SLS+23] Shao, J., et al.: A survey of what to share in federated learning: perspectives on model utility, privacy leakage, and communication efficiency. arXiv preprint arXiv:2307.10655 (2023)

[SMS22] Scheliga, D., Mäder, P., Seeland, M.: Precode-a generic model extension to prevent deep gradient leakage. In: Proceedings of the IEEE/CVF Winter Conference on Applications of Computer Vision, pp. 1849–1858 (2022)

[TFVH21] Tran, C., Fioretto, F., Van Hentenryck, P.: Differentially private and fair deep learning: a lagrangian dual approach. In: Proceedings of the AAAI Conference on Artificial Intelligence, vol. 35, pp. 9932–9939 (2021)

[WGN+20] Wang, S., Guo, W., Narasimhan, H., Cotter, A., Gupta, M., Jordan, M.: Robust optimization for fairness with noisy protected groups. Adv. Neural. Inf. Process. Syst. **33**, 5190–5203 (2020)

[WKL+21] Wu, Y., Kang, Y., Luo, J., He, Y., Yang, Q.: FEDCG: leverage conditional gan for protecting privacy and maintaining competitive performance in federated learning. arXiv preprint arXiv:2111.08211 (2021)

[WKNL20] Wang, H., Kaplan, Z., Niu, D., Li, B.: Optimizing federated learning on non-iid data with reinforcement learning. In: IEEE INFOCOM 2020-IEEE Conference on Computer Communications, pp. 1698–1707. IEEE (2020)

[WLD+20] Wei, K., et al.: Federated learning with differential privacy: algorithms and performance analysis. IEEE Trans. Inf. Forensics Secur. **15**, 3454–3469 (2020)

[XBJ21]  Xu, R., Baracaldo, N., Joshi, J.: Privacy-preserving machine learning: methods, challenges and directions. arXiv preprint arXiv:2108.04417 (2021)

[YLL+20]  Yu, H., et al.: A fairness-aware incentive scheme for federated learning. In: Proceedings of the AAAI/ACM Conference on AI, Ethics, and Society, pp. 393–399 (2020)

[ZVRG17]  Zafar, M.B., Valera, I., Rogriguez, M.G., Gummadi, K.P.: Fairness constraints: mechanisms for fair classification. In: Artificial Intelligence and Statistics, pp. 962–970. PMLR (2017)

[ZXW+22]  Zhou, Z., Xu, C., Wang, M., Kuang, X., Zhuang, Y., Yu, S.: A multi-shuffler framework to establish mutual confidence for secure federated learning. IEEE Trans. Depend. Secure Comput. 20, 4230–4244 (2022)

# Chinese Named Entity Recognition Within the Electric Power Domain

Jun Feng[1], Hongkai Wang[1], Liangying Peng[1], Yidan Wang[1(✉)],
Haomin Song[1], and Hongju Guo[2]

[1] State Grid Zhejiang Electric Power Corporation Information and
Telecommunication Branch, Hangzhou, China
{fengjun,wang_hongkai,peng_liangying,song_haomin}@zj.sgcc.com.cn,
demi0901@126.com
[2] Nanjing Duotuo Intelligent Technology Limited Liability Company,
Nanjing, China

**Abstract.** The field of electrical power encompasses a vast array of diverse information modalities, with textual data standing as a pivotal constituent of this domain. In this study, we harness an extensive corpus of textual data drawn from the electrical power systems domain, comprising regulations, reports, and other pertinent materials. Leveraging this corpus, we construct an Electrical Power Systems Corpus and proceed to annotate entities within this text, thereby introducing a novel Named Entity Recognition (NER) dataset tailored specifically for the electrical power domain. We employ an end-to-end deep learning model, the BERT-BiLSTM-CRF model, for named entity recognition on our custom electrical power domain dataset. This NER model integrates the BERT pre-trained model into the traditional BiLSTM-CRF model, enhancing its ability to capture contextual and semantic information within the text. Results demonstrate that the proposed model outperforms both the BiLSTM-CRF model and the BERT-softmax model in NER tasks across the electrical power domain and various other domains. This study contributes to the advancement of NER applications in the electrical power domain and holds significance for furthering the construction of knowledge graphs and databases related to electrical power systems.

**Keywords:** Electric power domain · Named entity recognition · Bidirectional encoder representations from transformers · Bidirectional long short-term memory · Conditional random fields

## 1 Introduction

Information Extraction (IE) is a pivotal field in natural language processing (NLP) that transforms unstructured textual information into structured data, catering to specific task requirements. Within the realm of Information Extraction, Named Entity Recognition (NER) [1] holds a central position. Its primary

J. Shao et al. (Eds.): EISA 2023, CCIS 2004, pp. 133–146, 2024.
https://doi.org/10.1007/978-981-99-9614-8_9

objective is to extract and categorize named entities such as names of persons, organizations, and specialized terms from text data.

NER plays a pivotal role in various applications across domains, including information retrieval, sentiment analysis, business opportunity discovery, and knowledge graph construction [2]. Particularly, in constructing Knowledge Graphs, NER extracts and categorizes entities from unstructured text, enabling advanced knowledge extraction, information integration, and data-driven decision-making [3].

Over the years, NER has witnessed significant advancements, transitioning from traditional rule-based approaches to state-of-the-art deep learning techniques. In recent years, deep learning has revolutionized NER. Deep neural networks, such as Convolutional Neural Networks (CNNs) [4], Recurrent Neural Networks (RNNs) [5], Long Short-Term Memory networks (LSTM) [6], and Gate Recurrent Units (GRUs) [7], have been deployed to tackle NER tasks. These models possess the remarkable ability to capture intricate semantic relationships, drastically reducing the need for manual feature engineering. The deep learning paradigm has garnered widespread adoption, making it the prevailing approach in NER. The emergence of large pre-trained language models like Bidirectional Encoder Representations from Transformers (BERT) [8] have revolutionized NER and other NLP tasks. BERT and its variants excel at capturing contextual information, making them versatile tools for NER across different domains.

While deep learning models, such as the BERT, have demonstrated remarkable performance in various NLP tasks on publicly available datasets [9], their efficacy in the domain of electric power remains unexplored. The unique characteristics and domain-specific nuances of electric power data demand specialized models and fine-tuning. In the context of the electric power system, the data landscape is characterized by its complexity, involving multiple sources, modalities, and data formats. This heterogeneity results in diverse and often unaligned semantic representations, making data integration, sharing, and mining challenging. The construction of a Knowledge Graph tailored to the electric power domain becomes imperative as it provides a unified framework for integrating and organizing domain-specific knowledge. NER, as the initial step in this process, holds the key to unlocking valuable insights from the vast corpus of electric power data.

To address this challenge, we have addressed the scarcity of labeled data in the electric power domain by curating a comprehensive NER dataset tailored to this specific domain. This dataset fills a critical gap in the availability of training data for electric power entity recognition. Leveraging this dataset, we have successfully employed the BERT-BiLSTM-CRF model to perform entity recognition tasks, demonstrating its applicability and effectiveness in the electric power domain. We also conducted extensive experiments across multiple domains, employing various BERT NER models, including the BERT-BiLSTM-CRF model. Through these experiments, we have provided empirical evidence showcasing the superior performance of the BERT-BiLSTM-CRF model in addressing the intricacies of entity recognition across diverse domains.

## 2    Related Work

The evolution of Named Entity Recognition research can be outlined in several phases, each marked by distinct methodologies and advancements.

Initially, rule-based and dictionary-based methods required domain experts to construct extensive knowledge bases and dictionaries, observing entity composition patterns and deducing templates based on grammar rules. While effective on specific corpora, these methods were highly domain- and language-specific, resulting in limited coverage, error-prone outcomes, and challenges in portability, high cost, and knowledge base maintenance [10].

Statistical machine learning methods marked the second phase, necessitating the integration of knowledge from machine learning, statistics, and linguistics to build models. These methods, essentially sequence labeling tasks, employed supervised training on manually annotated text corpora. Notable statistical models included Hidden Markov Models (HMM) [11], Maximum Entropy [12], Support Vector Machines (SVM) [13], and Conditional Random Fields (CRF) [14]. Among these, HMM utilized the Viterbi algorithm to search for the optimal labeling path, exhibiting relatively faster training and recognition speeds, making it suitable for tasks with extensive text data, such as short-text NER. On the other hand, CRF provided a flexible feature-rich framework for NER and facilitated global optimization.

The emergence of deep learning techniques ushered in the third phase. These methods harnessed the powerful nonlinear transformation, vector representation capabilities, and computational prowess of deep neural networks to obtain word and text embeddings, reducing the need for extensive feature engineering. These methods excelled at learning contextual semantic information to enhance NER performance and gradually became mainstream. Initial attempts, such as Ronan et al.'s application of CNN for NER in the general domain [15], were notable but suffered from issues like information loss over long distances. Huang et al. [16] introduced Bi-LSTM to capture past and future features but relied heavily on feature engineering. Ma et al. [17] proposed an end-to-end model by combining BiLSTM and CNN, eliminating the need for manual feature construction. Qiu's RD-CNN-CRF model [18] converted NER into a sequence labeling task, utilizing dilated residual convolutions to capture context efficiently, especially in the clinical domain. Yan et al. [19] addressed the Transformer's limitations in capturing directional information and relative positions, introducing the TENER (Transformer Encoder for NER) model, which incorporates relative positional encoding at both the word and character levels. Zeng et al. [20] introduced self-attention mechanisms, combining Bi-LSTM and CRF models to better handle long-distance dependencies between entities.

As NER technology matured, deep learning-based approaches found applications across various domains. For example, Qiu et al. [21] leveraged the BiLSTM-CRF model framework to extract contextual sequence information more effectively, aiding in historical domain information extraction. However, these models had their limitations: they focused on inter-word or inter-character features but neglected the context in which words appeared, resulting in static word embeddings that couldn't effectively capture varying semantic information across different contexts.

To address this issue, Google introduced the BERT (Bidirectional Encoder Representations from Transformers) pre-trained model [8]. BERT aims to enhance the representation of relationships between words or characters, effectively capturing different semantics that words carry in diverse contexts. The integration of large-scale pre-trained language models, such as BERT, into NER tasks has shown promise in various domains, with Wang et al. achieving notable results in Chinese entity recognition using a combination of BERT and BiLSTM-CRF models [22]. While BERT models have demonstrated impressive performance in general NLP tasks, their effectiveness in specialized domains is an ongoing area of exploration.

## 3 Method

### 3.1 Architecture

In this paper, we propose a novel approach that combines BERT with the traditional NER model, BiLSTM-CRF. The model architecture comprises three main components: the BERT layer, Bidirectional Long Short-Term Memory (BiLSTM) [16] layer, and Conditional Random Field (CRF) [14] layer. The detailed construction process of the model is illustrated in Fig. 1.

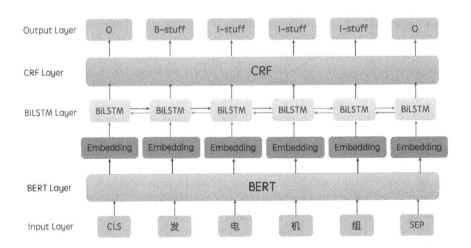

**Fig. 1.** BERT-BiLSTM-CRF model structure.

Input Layer: To illustrate our model's input sequence, let's consider the example "发电机组". We first split the input sequence into individual characters: "发", "电", "机", and "组". These characters are then mapped into vector representations using a vocabulary generated from our corpus.

BERT Layer: The vector representations of the characters are fed into the BERT layer. BERT, a pre-trained language model, captures contextual information and semantics effectively. It refines the initial character embeddings based on the surrounding context.

BiLSTM Layer: The output from the BERT layer is then processed by the BiLSTM layer. This step involves embedding concatenation, where the BERT output is combined and fed into both forward and backward LSTM layers. The LSTM layers encode the sequence bidirectionally and generate label probabilities for each word based on the context. Notably, the softmax function is used here to assign probabilities to word labels.

CRF Layer: Finally, the output from the BiLSTM layer is passed through the CRF layer. The CRF layer refines the output by considering the dependencies and relationships between labels. This results in the identification of the most probable and coherent sequence of labels. For example, it may produce labels such as "B-stuff", "I-stuff", "I-stuff", and "I-stuff" for the input sequence "发电机组".

In the following sections, we will delve into the principles and methodologies behind the BERT, BiLSTM, and CRF models to provide a comprehensive understanding of our proposed approach.

## 3.2   BERT Model

Devlin et al. [8] introduced the Bidirectional Encoder Representations from Transformers (BERT) model, which is based on the bidirectional Transformer architecture [11]. Its structure is shown in Fig. 2. BERT has achieved remarkable success across various Natural Language Processing tasks by pretraining on contextual information from all layers. This innovation has paved the way for cutting-edge models in tasks like question answering and language inference.

BERT serves as both a word embedding layer and a pretrained language representation model, building on the foundation of the Transformer architecture. In this approach, each character in the input text is initially treated as an individual unit. These characters are then transformed into one-dimensional vectors by querying a character embedding table. Subsequently, these vectors are fed into the model. The model's output comprises vector representations that amalgamate the semantic information of each character based on the entire text's context.

The Transformer model, first introduced by Google in 2017 [23], has played a pivotal role in BERT. It adopts an Encoder-Decoder architecture, with each Transformer unit encompassing key components such as multi-head attention layers, feedforward layers, residual connections, and normalization layers. What sets the Transformer architecture apart is its ability to parallelize language processing. Unlike traditional NLP models and models based on RNNs, which pro-

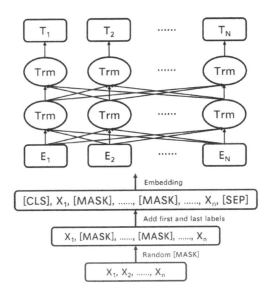

**Fig. 2.** BERT pre-trained model structure.

cess sequences sequentially either from left to right or right to left, Transformer can parallelize computations. This feature enables Transformer, particularly at the Encoder side, to process entire sequences concurrently, leading to substantial reductions in training time. The Transformer relies primarily on self-attention mechanisms 39], which adjust the weight coefficients for word importance by measuring the correlations between words within the same sentence. During the self-attention computation, three distinct matrix vectors are created for each word: the Query matrix Q, the Key matrix K, and the Value matrix V. The calculation formula is shown in (1).

$$Attention(Q, K, V) = softmax \left( \frac{QK^T}{\sqrt{d_K}} \right) V \tag{1}$$

$d_K$ represents the second dimension of the Value matrix $K$. The multi-head attention mechanism allows for obtaining multiple feature representations by setting different heads and then concatenating all these features together to form a comprehensive feature set. The calculation formulas are illustrated in (2) and (3):

$$head_i = Attention \left( QW_i^O, KW_i^K, VW_i^V \right) \tag{2}$$

$$Multi - head(Q, K, V) = concat \left( head_1, \cdots, head_h \right) W^Q \tag{3}$$

*concat* denotes the concatenation of the results from each head.

By incorporating BERT into our model architecture, we harness its prowess as an initial word embedding layer. This empowers our model to capture contextual information across the entire text, resulting in superior entity recognition performance within the Chinese text data of the electric power domain.

## 3.3 BiLSTM Model

Long Short-Term Memory (LSTM) [6] is a unique form of RNNs distinguished by its ingenious gate design, which adeptly mitigates the challenges of gradient explosion and long-term dependencies. However, the unidirectional nature of traditional LSTM models hinders their capacity to incorporate contextual information effectively. Consequently, Huang.et al proposed the Bidirectional LSTM (BiLSTM) neural network model to address issues arising from the inability to establish connections between sequences and their context.

The BiLSTM layer is a combination of both forward and backward LSTMs. Its structure is shown in Fig. 3. For each sentence, the BiLSTM model conducts forward and reverse computations, resulting in two distinct sets of hidden layer representations. These representations are then concatenated into the final hidden layer representation. Here, we elucidate the underlying principles and computational workflow.

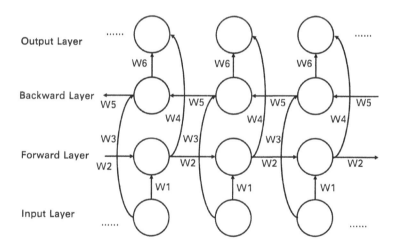

**Fig. 3.** BiLSTM model structure.

In the forward pass, computations advance from time step 1 to time step t, generating and preserving forward hidden layer outputs at each time step. Simultaneously, in the backward pass, computations progress from time step t to time step 1, resulting in and preserving backward hidden layer outputs. The outputs from the forward and backward hidden layers at corresponding time steps are amalgamated to derive the final output. This fusion effectively integrates information from both directions, thereby enhancing the contextual understanding of each word within the sequence. The process is indicated by Eqs. (4), (5), and (6):

$$h_t = f\left(w_1 x_t + w_2 h_{t-1}\right) \tag{4}$$

$$h'_t = f\left(w_3 x_t + w_5 h'_{t+1}\right) \tag{5}$$

$$o_t = g\left(w_4 h_t + w_6 h'_t\right) \tag{6}$$

Mathematically, the computations involve key steps. First is the calculation of the Forget Gate, which determines what information within the cell state should be forgotten or retained. It incorporates the computation of the forget gate, denoted as $f_t$, which assumes values between 0 and 1. A value of 0 signifies complete forgetting, while 1 implies complete retention of information. It receive the previous hidden state $h_{t-1}$ and the current time $X_t$ input through the sigmoid function $\sigma$ and output the value, which is indicated by Eqs. (7):

$$f_t = \sigma * \left( W_f * \left[ h_{t-1}, x_t \right] + b_f \right) \tag{7}$$

$b_f$ is the forgetting gate bias vector.

Then, the input gate ascertains which new information should be added to the cell state. Firstly, it receives the hidden state $h_{t-1}$ from the previous moment and $X_t$ from the current moment, and outputs a value it between $(0, 1)$ to indicate which information in the unit state $C_{t-1}$ needs to be updated. Then, create a new candidate vector $C_t$ from the tanh layer and add it to the unit state. The process is indicated by Eqs. (8), (9):

$$i_t = \sigma * \left( W_i * \left[ h_{t-1}, x_t \right] + b_i \right) \tag{8}$$

$$\tilde{C}_t = \tanh * \left( W_c * \left[ h_{t-1}, X_t \right] + b_c \right) \tag{9}$$

$b_i$ is the update gate bias vector, and $b_c$ is the memory unit bias vector. Subsequently, the cell state is updated from $C_{t-1}$ to $C_t$ as Eqs. (10):

$$C_t = f_t * C_{t-1} + i_t * \tilde{C}_t \tag{10}$$

Finally, the output gate and hidden state $h_t$ determine what information should be output. it receives the hidden state $h_{t-1}$ from the previous moment and $X_t$ from the current moment, and outputs a value $o_t$ between $(0, 1)$ to indicate which information in the unit state $C_{t-1}$ needs to be output. Then input the unit state $C_t$ into the tanh layer for processing, and finally perform a product operation with $o_t$ to output the information we need. The process is indicated by Eqs. (11), (12):

$$o_t = \sigma * \left( W_o * \left[ h_{t-1}, x_t \right] + b_o \right) \tag{11}$$

$$h_t = \sigma * \tanh\left( C_t \right) \tag{12}$$

By conducting these computations at each time step, a sequence of outputs $(h_1, h_2, ..., h_t, ..., h_n)$ is generated, aligning in length with the input sentence. This BiLSTM layer significantly bolsters the model's capacity to capture contextual information from both forward and backward directions, a crucial attribute for our entity recognition task within the domain of Chinese text in the power sector.

### 3.4  CRF Model

CRF is a probabilistic graphical model used to address sequence labeling problems. The model takes an observation sequence $(X_1, X_2, ..., X_n)$ and, through probability calculations, outputs a sequence of states ( $Y_1, Y_2, ..., Y_n$ ). The computation involves the emission scores generated by the BiLSTM and transition scores. The calculation formula is depicted in Eq. (13):

$$score(\text{x}, \text{y}) = \sum_{i=1}^{n} P_{i,y_i} + \sum_{i=1}^{n} A_{y_i,y_{i+1}} \tag{13}$$

$P_{i,y_i}$ is the score for predicting the i-th character as the $y_i$ label. $A_{y_i,y_{i+1}}$ is the score for transitioning from label $y_i$ to label $y_{i+1}$.

CRF models find extensive applications in natural language processing, particularly in entity recognition tasks. While BiLSTM effectively handles long-distance text information, it struggles with identifying dependencies between adjacent labels. CRF models, on the other hand, can correctly recognize certain features between adjacent characters based on specific constraints. For example, recognizing that sentences should start with "B-" or "O" rather than "I-," or predicting "I-label1" after "B-label1" instead of an entity of a different type like "I-label2." This reduces the occurrence of label prediction errors, thereby improving recognition accuracy.

## 4  Experiments

### 4.1  Electric Power Domain Dataset

To address the scarcity of datasets tailored for entity detection in the electrical power domain, we embarked on an extensive data collection and annotation effort. We carefully curated a corpus of 150 Chinese documents comprising legal regulations and reports relevant to the electrical power sector. These documents were meticulously selected to encompass a broad spectrum of topics and scenarios within the domain.

Before creating the dataset, we subjected the collected documents to rigorous preprocessing steps. These included:

Data Cleaning: Removal of non-textual elements, headers, footers, and extraneous information to ensure the dataset's cleanliness and consistency.

Deduplication: We conducted a deduplication process to eliminate any redundant documents, ensuring that each document in the dataset contributed unique textual content.

Sentence Segmentation: The processed documents were then segmented into individual sentences. This granulation facilitated entity annotation at a more fine-grained level.

The resulting dataset consisted of a total of 8586 sentences. To facilitate model training and evaluation, we divided this dataset into two subsets: Training set comprised 6713 sentences, utilized for training our entity recognition models. The training set serves as the foundation for our model's understanding of electrical power-related entities. Test Set, consisting of 1973 sentences, was reserved exclusively for evaluating the performance of our models. This separation ensures an unbiased assessment of our models' capabilities.

The cornerstone of our dataset construction was the meticulous annotation of entities. We systematically labeled entities in each sentence, categorizing them into four distinct classes, each of which holds significant relevance within the electrical power domain: • Stuff: This category encompasses entities that represent tangible objects or items directly related to the electrical power sector. Examples include "输电线", "供电箱".

• Location: Entities categorized under "location" represent specific places or geographic points pertinent to the electrical power industry. Such as "供电公司", "电力局".

• Law: The "law" category pertains to entities associated with legal and regulatory aspects governing the electrical power domain. Examples include " 《华东电力系统调度规程》 ".

• Event: Entities in the "event" category denote actions, operations, or events that occur within the electrical power sector. Such as "自检", "调度". The distribution of entities across the four categories is outlined in Table 1.

**Table 1.** Number of entities of electric power dataset.

| Classification | number |
|---|---|
| Stuff | 3828 |
| Law | 1167 |
| Event | 5049 |
| Location | 2214 |
| **Total** | 12258 |

## 4.2   Performance of Electric Power Dataset

In our experiments, we rigorously evaluated the performance of the BERT-BiLSTM-CRF model on the Electrical Power Systems Named Entity Recognition dataset, as described in Sect. 4.1. Our evaluation metrics included precision, recall, and F1-score. The comprehensive results, as well as those for each specific entity class, are presented in Table 2.

**Table 2.** Electric power dataset experimental results of each classifications on BERT-BiLSTM-CRF model.

| Classification | Precision (%) | Recall (%) | F1-score (%) |
|---|---|---|---|
| Stuff | 98.22 | 97.79 | 98.00 |
| Law | 86.67 | 86.06 | 86.36 |
| Event | 99.30 | 99.42 | 99.36 |
| Location | 92.80 | 97.02 | 94.86 |
| **Total** | 97.13 | 97.78 | 97.45 |

The overall performance of the model was impressive, achieving an outstanding F1-score of 97.45%. Notably, each individual entity class exhibited high recognition rates. The "Law" class, characterized by longer entity content and increased recognition complexity, demonstrated slightly lower overall performance, yet it still attained an F1-score of 86.36%.

To further contextualize the superiority of the BERT-BiLSTM-CRF model, we conducted comparative experiments with two alternative models: BiLSTM-CRF and BERT-softmax. The comparative results are summarized in Table 3, revealing the remarkable advantages of the BERT-BiLSTM-CRF model. Across all three evaluation metrics, this model consistently outperformed the alternatives, underscoring its significant efficacy in the task of Named Entity Recognition within the electrical power systems domain.

**Table 3.** Different NER model results of electric power dataset.

| Model | Precision (%) | Recall (%) | F1-score (%) |
|---|---|---|---|
| BiLSTM-CRF | 93.24 | 95.11 | 94.16 |
| BERT-softmax | 96.50 | 96.63 | 96.57 |
| BERT-BiLSTM-CRF | **97.13** | **97.78** | **97.45** |

These results affirm the potential and robustness of the proposed BERT-BiLSTM-CRF model in accurately identifying named entities in the electrical power systems domain, further validating its applicability in knowledge graph construction and knowledge base development.

## 4.3  Performance Comparison of NER Models

In order to thoroughly assess and compare the performance of several NER models across multiple domains, this study meticulously selected diverse open-source NER datasets. These datasets were employed for comprehensive comparative experiments involving multiple NER models, including BiLSTM-CRF, BERT-softmax, and BERT-BiLSTM-CRF. The experiments were conducted using identical training and testing sets to provide a clear and consistent basis for performance evaluation, with a particular focus on validating the performance of the BERT-BiLSTM-CRF model. The datasets used are as follows:

- CLUENER Fine-Grained NER [24]: Derived from THUCTC, an open-source text classification dataset provided by Tsinghua University. It was meticulously crafted by selecting a subset of data from THUCTC and annotating it for fine-grained named entity recognition. This dataset offers detailed annotations and covers a wide array of entity types.
- TCM-NER (Traditional Chinese Medicine - Named Entity Recognition Dataset): The data source is traditional Chinese medicine drug instructions. It comprises a total of 1,997 documents, segmented into training, validation, and test sets containing 1,000, 500, and 497 documents, respectively. The dataset encompasses a rich annotation of 59,803 named entities within the domain of Traditional Chinese Medicine.
- Music Domain NER: Data source is task-oriented dialogues in the music domain. It is designed for tasks related to music and comprises 21,352 samples. It encompasses a diverse set of 15 entity categories, making it particularly suitable for evaluating NER models in the context of music-related information extraction.

These datasets were utilized to conduct a comprehensive suite of experiments, evaluated on the same training and testing sets across multiple domains. The results of these experiments are meticulously detailed in Table 4.

**Table 4.** Results of each datasets on different NER model.

| Dataset | Model | Precision (%) | Recall (%) | F1-score (%) |
|---|---|---|---|---|
| CLUENER | BiLSTM-CRF | 65.19 | 66.21 | 65.70 |
|  | BERT-softmax | 79.07 | 79.92 | 79.49 |
|  | BERT-BiLSTM-CRF | **79.77** | **81.77** | **80.76** |
| TCM-NER | BiLSTM-CRF | **87.69** | 62.35 | 72.88 |
|  | BERT-softmax | 83.59 | 65.92 | 73.71 |
|  | BERT-BiLSTM-CRF | 84.20 | **69.43** | **76.10** |
| Music Domain NER | BiLSTM-CRF | 86.70 | 82.08 | 84.32 |
|  | BERT-softmax | 88.62 | 90.19 | 89.40 |
|  | BERT-BiLSTM-CRF | **90.88** | **91.28** | **91.08** |

The outcomes of these experiments unequivocally demonstrate the effectiveness of the BERT-BiLSTM-CRF model in extracting specific entities from textual data. This model exhibited superior performance across various domain-specific tasks, outperforming alternative models. The results underscore the versatility and robustness of the BERT-BiLSTM-CRF model in named entity recognition tasks, providing compelling evidence of its efficacy in diverse domains.

## 5    Conclusions

In this paper, we delve into the techniques and strategies for utilizing various BERT-based models for NER in Chinese text. Our contributions in this research are twofold: Firstly, recognizing the scarcity of Chinese text data in the power sector and the absence of entity recognition datasets, we introduce a new annotated dataset tailored to entity recognition in the Chinese electric power domain. Secondly, we conduct extensive experiments employing multiple BERT NER model variants across various domains, demonstrating the adaptability and robustness of NER models in the context of Chinese text.

The significance of this research extends beyond the electric power industry. It showcases the potential of combining state-of-the-art deep learning techniques with domain-specific knowledge to tackle complex NER challenges in specialized domains. By achieving notable results in the electric power sector, our approach sets a precedent for similar advancements in other technical and domain-specific fields. By addressing these issues, we contributes the ongoing evolution of Chinese NER techniques and underscores the potential for deep learning models to revolutionize information extraction in specialized domains. As NER continues to play a crucial role in various applications, including information retrieval, knowledge graph construction, and more, our work sets the stage for continued advancements in this vital field.

**Acknowledgments.** This work was supported by the Science and Technology Project of State Grid Zhejiang Electric Power Co., Ltd. (Project number: B311XT220007).

## References

1. Nadeau, D., Sekine, S.: A survey of named entity recognition and classification. Lingvisticae Investigationes **30**(1), 3–26 (2007)
2. Xie, T., Yang, J.A., Liu, H.: Chinese entity recognition based on BERT-BiLSTM-CRF model. Comput. Syst. Appl. **29**(7), 48–57 (2020)
3. Ji, S., Pan, S., Cambria, E., et al.: A survey on knowledge graphs: representation, acquisition, and applications. IEEE Trans. Neural Netw. Learn. Syst. **33**(2), 494–514 (2021)
4. Kim, Y.: Convolutional neural networks for sentence classification. arXiv preprint arXiv:1408.5882(2014)
5. Elman, J.L.: Finding structure in time. Cogn. Sci. **14**(2), 179–211 (1990)
6. Hochreiter, S., Schmidhuber, J.: Long Short-Term Memory. Neural Comput. **9**(8), 1735–1780 (1997)
7. Chung, J., Gulcehre, C., Cho, K.H., et al.: Empirical evaluation of gated recurrent neural networks on sequence modeling. arXiv preprint arXiv:1412.3555 (2014)

8. Devlin, J., Chang, M.W., Lee, K., et al.: Bert: pre-training of deep bidirectional transformers for language understanding. arXiv preprint arXiv:1810.04805 (2018)

9. Baigang, M., Fan, Y.: A review: development of named entity recognition (NER) technology for aeronautical information intelligence. Artif. Intell. Rev. **56**(2), 1515–1542 (2023)

10. Jiao, K.N., Li, X., Zhu, R.C.: A review of named entity recognition in Chinese domain. Comput. Eng. Appl. **57**(16), 1–15 (2021)

11. Eddy, S.R.: Hidden Markov models. Curr. Opin. Struct. Biol. **6**(3), 361–365 (1996)

12. Berger, A., Della Pietra, S.A., Della Pietra, V.J.: A maximum entropy approach to natural language processing. Comput. Linguist. **22**(1), 39–71 (1996)

13. Isozaki, H., Kazawa, H.: Speeding up named entity recognition based on support vector machines. IPSJ SIG Notes NL-149 **1**, 1–8 (2002)

14. Lafferty, J., Mccallum, A., Pereira, F.C.N.: Conditional random fields: probabilistic models for segmenting and labeling sequence data (2001)

15. Collobert, R., Weston, J., Bottou, L., et al.: Natural language processing (almost) from scratch. J. Mach. Learn. Res. **12**, 2493–2537 (2011)

16. Huang, Z., Xu, W., Yu, K.: Bidirectional LSTM-CRF models for sequence tagging. arXiv preprint arXiv:1508.01991 (2015)

17. Ma, X. Hovy, E.: End-to-end sequence labeling via bi-directional LSTM-CNNS-CRF. arXiv preprint arXiv:1603.01354 (2016)

18. Qiu, J., Zhou, Y., Wang, Q., et al.: Chinese clinical named entity recognition using residual dilated convolutional neural network with conditional random field. IEEE Trans. Nanobiosci. **18**(3), 306–315 (2019)

19. Yan, H., Deng, B., Li, X., et al.: TENER: adapting transformer encoder for named entity recognition. arXiv preprint arXiv:1911.04474 (2019)

20. Zeng, Q.X., Xiong, W.P., Du, J.Q., et al.: Named entity recognition of electronic medical records with BiLSTM-CRF combined with self-attention. Comput. Appl. Softw. **38**(3), 159–162 (2021)

21. Qiu, Q., Xie, Z., Wu, L., et al.: BiLSTM-CRF for geological named entity recognition from the geoscience literature. Earth Sci. Inf. **12**(4), 565–579 (2019)

22. Lample, G., Ballesteros, M., Subramanian, S., et al.: Neural architectures for named entity recognition. arXiv preprint arXiv:1603:01360 (2016)

23. Vaswani, A., Shazeer, N., Parmar, N., et al.: Attention is all you need. In: Advances in Neural Information Processing System, vol. 30 (2017)

24. Xu, L., Tong, Y., Dong, Q., et al.: CLUENER2020: fine-grained named entity recognition dataset and benchmark for Chinese. arXiv preprint arXiv:2001.04351 (2020)

# Adversarial Example Attacks and Defenses in DNS Data Exfiltration

Izabela Savić[1], Haonan Yan[1,2], Xiaodong Lin[1(✉)], and Daniel Gillis[1]

[1] School of Computer Science, University of Guelph, Guelph, Canada
{savici,xlin08,dgillis}@uoguelph.ca
[2] School of Cyber Engineering, Xidian University, Xi'an, China

**Abstract.** The Domain Network System (DNS) protocol is used on a daily basis to access the internet. It acts as a phone book that allows users to access websites using words rather than remembering address numbers. In recent years it has become clear that there are serious vulnerabilities in the DNS protocol, and the lack of attention to these vulnerabilities (e.g. data exfiltration) is concerning. The widespread use of the DNS protocol opens a door that could possibly allow for companies and users to have their data stolen through data exfiltration. Machine learning is a popular tool for malicious traffic detection, however they are vulnerable to adversarial examples. This leads to the security arms race, where researchers aim to accurately detect and counter new malicious threats exploited by malicious actors. In this work, we demonstrate the success of adversarial examples of DNS exfiltration packets in bypassing machine learning detection techniques. We then propose a voting ensemble method to improve adversarial attack detection. The voting ensemble proposed increases the accuracy of adversarial detection, providing a new level of protection against adversarial example attacks.

**Keywords:** DNS protocol · data exfiltration · machine learning · adversarial attack · network traffic analysis

## 1  Introduction

The DNS protocol is arguably one of the most well known protocols by computer scientists, networking enthusiasts, as well as common folk. The DNS Protocol is described as a protocol that "helps Internet users and network devices discover websites using human-readable hostnames, instead of numeric IP addresses." [1]. This idea began in 1970 with ARPANET (the DNS predecessor) at the Stanford Research Institute [1]. In 1984, BIND (the first DNS implementation) was created for Unix, and DNS was officially finalized in 1987 [1].

It is noted that the DNS protocol has not had any significant changes since its first invention [2], which leaves open questions such as "Is it sufficiently secure? Is it vulnerable to data breaches?" [2]. Due to the fact that DNS is not intended for data transfer, it has lead to the DNS protocol being vulnerable due to receiving

J. Shao et al. (Eds.): EISA 2023, CCIS 2004, pp. 147–163, 2024.
https://doi.org/10.1007/978-981-99-9614-8_10

"less attention in terms of security monitoring than other protocols" [3], and is naively assumed to be safe due to its daily usage. This allows for DNS to be used for data exfiltration by malware-infected devices or malicious insiders [2]. In a DNS security survey it was found that 46% of respondents were victims of DNS exfiltration [2]. Where a successful data exfiltration attack can result in data theft, with types of data being: personally identifiable information (e.g. social security numbers), data protected by the Health Insurance Portability and Accountability Act (HIPPA), intellectual property (personal or from an organization), etc. [2].

Due to the widespread use of the DNS protocol, data exfiltration leaves all companies and devices at risk, which is concerning if those devices are part of critical company infrastructure or belong to actors of high importance. Machine learning is an emerging and successful technique of detecting data exfiltration along with other types of malicious traffic. However, commonly used machine learning algorithms are significantly less effective against adversarial examples (a method of placing a small perturbation on input data to cause misclassification). This leaves a large hole in machine learning detection systems and devices still at risk. This novel idea introduces an arms race between non-malicious and malicious threat actors, as non-malicious actors aim to combat new malicious methodologies quickly and efficiently. To our knowledge, the use of adversarial examples in data exfiltration packets does not receive much attention.

In this work, we make the following contributions:

(A) An optimization technique for adversarial DNS exfiltration packet generation.
(B) A search approach for generating adversarial packets when using irreversible feature extraction.
(C) A voting ensemble method for the detection of adversarial DNS exfiltration network traffic.

The remainder of this paper is organized as follows: we begin with a review of related work in Sect. 2. In Sect. 3, we begin discussing existing detection methods for data exfiltration. In Sect. 4, we introduce our novel contribution of constructing DNS packets, which are capable of bypassing data exfiltration detection mechanisms by using adversarial example methodologies. In Sect. 5, we present a voting ensemble method to defend against the adversarial example method proposed in Sect. 4. Finally, in Sect. 6 we conclude our work with a summary of material presented.

## 2    Background and Related Work

In this section, we take a deeper look into the DNS protocol, and discuss the basics of the data exfiltration attack. This will provide the reader with an understanding of where vulnerabilities in the DNS protocol occur, as well as an understanding of how serious the exfiltration attacks are. We will first begin with the discussion on the DNS protocol, followed by the attack method.

## 2.1   A Deeper Look into the DNS Protocol

As previously mentioned, DNS messages are not intended for data exchange. Instead, it is meant to act as a forward lookup to find the IP address(es) corresponding to a given domain name [3]. DNS uses the UDP server port 53 and TCP server port 53, where UDP is preferred over TCP, which is used for zone transfers or payloads over 512 bytes [3].

DNS messages are primarily categorized into two main types, queries and responses, both of which have the same format [2]. DNS messages are short and responses are not guaranteed to arrive in the same order as the requests [4]. A single DNS message has a header and four sections: question, answer, authority, and additional [2]. The flags in the header of the message control the content of the four sections [2]. Each of the parameters in DNS have a size limit: labels are 63 bytes or less, names are 255 bytes or less, time to live is a positive signed 32-bit number, and UDP messages are limited to 512 bytes or less [2]. This means that a packet constructed by a hacker or malicious user is limited to 512 bytes at most for an exfiltration attack. We can see an example DNS query in Fig. 1.

```
Domain Name System (query)
  Transaction ID: 0xdbe2
> Flags: 0x0100 Standard query
  Questions: 1
  Answer RRs: 0
  Authority RRs: 0
  Additional RRs: 0
˅ Queries
  ˅ q+Z8AnwaBA.hidemyself.org: type TXT, class IN
    Name: q+Z8AnwaBA.hidemyself.org
    [Name Length: 25]
    [Label Count: 3]
    Type: TXT (Text strings) (16)
    Class: IN (0x0001)
  [Response In: 40]
```

Fig. 1. DNS Query in WireShark

## 2.2   Data Exfiltration

Data exfiltration is a method used by malicious actors "to target, copy, and transfer sensitive data" [7]. It can be done remotely via malicious network traffic or physically (e.g. physically stealing property from a workplace). A remote data exfiltration attack is difficult to detect due to the normal looking network traffic [7]. The consequences of a successful data exfiltration can lead to: loss of intellectual property/sensitive information, financial loss in incident response process cost, information abuse, lawsuits, reputational damage, and so on [8]. The data exfiltration vulnerability has gained such attention that Lockheed Martin lists data exfiltration as part of its Cyber Kill Chain diagram (Fig. 2), a military concept used to identify an attack structure [9].

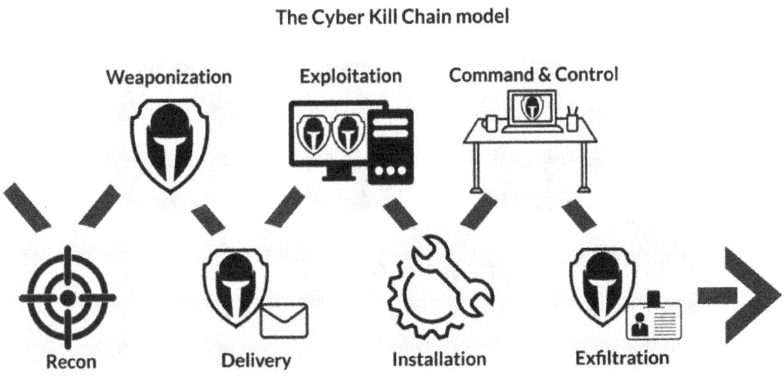

**Fig. 2.** Lockheed Martin Cyber Kill Chain Diagram from [8]

In a remote attack, the attacker would exploit the vulnerabilities of the DNS protocol for data exfiltration. It is shown that port 53 is often utilized for data exfiltration if it is left open [10]. The most common data targets include: usernames, passwords, cryptographic keys, and security numbers [10]. The remote data exfiltration attack method has a variety of different methodologies which use current network infrastructure to steal data [11]. The attack methods are: direct download, passive monitoring, timing channels, virtual machine vulnerabilities, spyware and malware, phishing, cross site and cross site scripting [11].

Over the years there has been a steady growth in the number of data exfiltration attacks. In 2017 there were 1,632 breaches, and in 2018 there were 2,216 successful data exfiltration attempts (out of a total 53,000 data exfiltration attempts) [10]. These attacks targeted companies such as Google, Facebook and Tesla, and breached in total around 100 million user accounts (between Facebook and Google+ combined) [10]. A Verizon report from 2019 stated that external actors were responsible for 69% of data exfiltration incidents [10]. It was also found that exfiltration incidents were no longer being carried out only by individuals but by groups as well [10]. In 2019, 23% of data exfiltration attacks came from nation-state actors. This is an 11% increase from the 12% recorded in 2018 [10]. In Figure 2 of [11], we can view some data exfiltration incidents from 2017 along with the type of data that was stolen, and the number of affected individuals. This includes incidents such as the 'America's Job Link Alliance' incident, which resulted in the theft of names, birth dates, and SIN numbers of 4.8 million account members [11].

# 3 Preliminaries

In this section we present current research and detection methods for data exfiltration. There are a variety of methods involving machine learning, network analysis, and additional technologies. We provide the reader with a broad understanding of the various technologies and options available. There are two main techniques for detecting the malicious network traffic: payload analysis and traffic analysis. A majority of detection methods are built using these two analysis methods.

## 3.1 Payload Analysis

Payload analysis uses techniques borrowed from Domain Generation Algorithms [3] to detect abnormal traffic. There are a variety of features used in payload analysis which will be discussed below.

**Size of Request and Response.** It is noted that the attack will typically have long labels and long names [3]. This is due to trying to fit as much exfiltrated information as possible into the queries.

**Entropy of Hostnames.** It is found that non malicious DNS names typically include dictionary words [3]. Names which are encrypted receive a higher entropy value [3].

**Statistical Analysis.** This method analyzes information such as the number of unique characters, number of numerical characters, the length of the longest meaningful substring, or even the number of repeated consonants [3].

## 3.2 Traffic Analysis

This method involves analyzing request and response pairs over time [3]. There are a variety of features used in traffic analysis which are discussed below. These features include:

- Volume of DNS traffic per IP address: Data exfiltration will require numerous data requests to forward data [3]. An IP address with a high amount of DNS traffic could be suspicious [3].

- Volume of DNS traffic per domain: Data exfiltration will commonly tunnel data through one specific domain name [3]. A domain with a high level of DNS traffic could possibly be malicious activity.
- Number of hostnames per domain: Data exfiltration will often "request a unique hostname on each request" [3], this can lead to having a much larger number of hostnames than typical DNS traffic.
- Geographic location of the DNS server
- Domain history: Data exfiltration requires the attacker to control the domain, one can check when a domain was acquired as it may have been acquired for the purpose of data exfiltration [3].

### 3.3    Data Exfiltration Detection Methods

In this subsection we will cover the current data exfiltration detection methods used in various research. Most sampled detection methods use analysis techniques discussed in Sect. 3.1 and/or Sect. 3.2 in support to additional techniques. Detection methods for data exfiltration can use a variety of different technologies. Some detection methods even work in real time, like [4]. We will not be able to cover all detection methods, as it is beyond the scope of this paper, but we will discuss a few below.

**Machine Learning.** The research presented in [4] focuses on the detection of low throughput malware exfiltration. Researchers in [4], collected a single week of DNS traffic with the assumption that all traffic was benign for the dataset. The two data exfiltration frameworks used were: FrameworkPOS (used in 2014 Home depot incident) and Backdoor.Win32.Dennis (discovered in 2017 by Kaspersky) [4]. The model used for training is unsupervised, and was only given benign traffic in its training [4]. The malicious traffic was injected in the testing data [4]. However, every 60 min, domains with at least 10 subdomains within the last 360 min are subject to classification [4]. As time progressed, the number of false positives gradually decreased, and most misclassified domains were "legitimate security services that mis-use the DNS protocol for data exchange" [4]. The model chosen allows for learning on a real-time basis. This allows traffic to be analyzed and categorized in real time, then a program can then shut down connections that are labelled as malicious [4].

The research presented in [16] provides another real time analysis tool for data exfiltration detection. Ahmed et al. do so by implementing machine learning categorization on collected data [16]. To begin, DNS traffic is collected from two enterprise networks and the characteristics of the traffic are analyzed [16]. This resulted in the capturing of a total of over 830 million DNS packets from both enterprises [16]. Data containing queries from unqualified domains are removed from the data set [16]. For malicious traffic, DNS exfiltration queries were created with the open-source tool called "DNS Exfiltration Toolkit" [16]. The features chosen for extraction were: total count of characters in the fully qualified domain name (FQDN), count of characters in sub-domain, count of upper case characters, count of numerical characters, (Shannon) entropy, number of labels, maximum label length, and average label length [16]. In this case labels are strings separated by periods (e.g. "www.scholar.google.com" has four labels) [16].

# 4   Problem Formulation

Machine learning is an effective and popular approach to the data exfiltration detection problem. However, machine learning is vulnerable to adversarial examples, which are described as small perturbations of the input that can change the decision of a classifier [16]. Adversarial methods are most heavily applied to image misclassification problems in machine learning. Our work exposes an open vulnerability in the DNS protocol, and machine learning applications in cyber security, by generating adversarial examples of data exfiltration DNS network packets. This contribution is novel as to our knowledge there is no adversarial packet generation on DNS packets. [19] demonstrates the use of adversarial examples on TCP packets, and currently adversarial example research is primarily focused on image classification. The vulnerability our contribution exposes has the potential to affect the security of data in businesses and personal devices worldwide.

Adversarial example generation in DNS packets presents two major challenges: packet limitations, and irreversible translation from packet to features. Our solution to the two challenges is also novel. The packet limitations include: packet functionality, packet length and name length. As discussed in Sect. 2.1, DNS subdomains are limited to 63 characters, packet names are limited to 255 bytes, with the packet being limited to 512 bytes. When applying these perturbations, the functionality of the packet must be maintained otherwise the packet will no longer be a functioning data exfiltration packet. In this section, we discuss our data exfiltration detection method and testing. We present our adversarial packet generation method in a formal optimization problem.

## 4.1   Data Exfiltration Detection Using Machine Learning

To begin our research, we use [20] as our dataset, which includes benign DNS packets, and DNS packets from 4 data exfiltration attack methods: dns2tcp, dnscapy, iodine and tuns. The packets underwent feature extraction to extract 23 features, 10 features from the query, and 13 features from the response. The choice of features to extract was influenced by the detection methods discussed in [3]. The following features were extracted from query and response:

- **Query features:** domain name length, subdomain name length, number of subdomains, ratio of special characters, entropy of characters, number of consonants, number of numbers, number of unique characters, length of the request and type

- **Response features:** domain name length, subdomain name length, number of subdomains, ratio of special characters, entropy of characters, number of consonants, number of numbers, number of unique characters, length of the request, type, entropy of data, length of data and time to live

If a query packet did not have a corresponding response, the response feature values were set to 0. All data was labeled with 0 for malicious packets, and 1 for benign packets. Data was cropped for uniform sampling, shuffled, and then split into 80:20 for training and testing. A LeNET5 CNN was implemented due to its popularity, simplicity and easy customizability to fit the shape of our feature vector. Using the LeNET5 CNN, and data sets previously discussed, the accuracy was 99.97%.

Although using machine learning to identify malicious packets is not a novel contribution, the accuracy presented will act as a baseline which can be used to calculate the effectiveness of our adversarial example packet generation.

## 4.2 Optimization Approach to Adversarial Example Packet Generation of Data Exfiltration Packets

The use of the optimization approach allows us to present our findings in a more theoretical, or mathematical, manner. The previously discussed constraints can be represented as:

$$\forall c \in C : c \in [a - z, A - Z, 0 - 9] \tag{1}$$

In Eq. 1, c represents a character in a subdomain C, and C represents the set of subdomains in a DNS packet.

$$\forall l \in L : l <= 63 \tag{2}$$

In Eq. 2, l represents the length of a subdomain in a name L, and L represents the set of subdomains in a DNS packet.

$$\forall n \in N : n <= 255 \tag{3}$$

In Eq. 3, n represents the length of a name in a DNS packet N, and N represents the set of DNS packets.

$$\forall p \in P : P_{advDNSPktSubdomains} \\ = p_{advSubdomains} + p_{origSubdomains} \tag{4}$$

In Eq. 4, P represents the set of all adversarial DNS packets, and p represents the subdomains of a packet. The equation signifies how adversarial DNS packets are created, the adversarial subdomains generated are prepended to the original subdomains of the packet.

From here forward we denote: $X^0$ as benign DNS packet features, $X^*$ as adversarial DNS packet features, and X' as malicious DNS packet features. We use the following formulas to create an adversarial packet:

$$X^* = \underset{d(X^0,X)<=\varepsilon}{argminL(X)} \tag{5}$$

$$X' = \underset{X' \in set(X^0)}{arg\,min\,d(X',X^*)} \tag{6}$$

In Eq. 5, the L(X) represents the cross entropy loss function with an input packet X. In Eq. 6, the d(X', X*) represents the Euclidean distance between the two feature vectors.

Finally, to ensure that the adversarial generated packet meets the constraints in Eqs. 1, 2 and 3, we can write the following equation:

$$X' \in set(X) \tag{7}$$

where X is the set of all valid DNS packets.

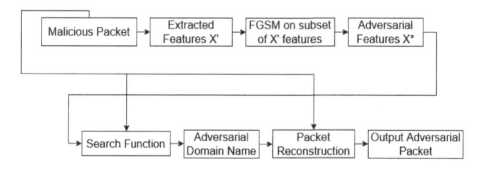

**Fig. 3.** Diagram of our Adversarial Packet Generation Steps

The optimization technique presented in Sect. 4 highlights a limitation in traditional optimization problem-solving techniques in the network field. The optimization technique presented uses feature extraction, which is an irreversible process. Moreover, different features can be correlated with each other. Therefore, we can not directly construct an adversarial DNS packet from the adversarial features. Thus, a traditional mathematical solution is not feasible. To address this limitation, we present a search based solution algorithm in Algorithm 1. Furthermore, Fig. 3 illustrates the key processes of the algorithm.

Algorithm 1 only uses 4 of the 23 features for feature perturbation and packet generation as these features are the most independent features, and can be modified easily. The 4 modified features in the query are: number of unique characters,

---

**Algorithm 1:** Method for Generating Adversarial Packets

---

1 **Function** buildPacket(*advQname, originalPkt*):

    /* Function takes the original malicious packet and newly calculated adversarial qname and creates a new DNS packet. This packet is written to a PCAP file.     */

2 **Function** buildPacket(*packet, filename*):

    /* Function takes the pertubed packet and file name and appends the packet to the PCAP file.     */

3 **Function** getAdvQname(*originalQname, advFeatures*):

    /* Function to generate adversarial packets, takes in the extracted query name of the original malicious packet and adversarial feature vector. The function modifies the qname by adding characters and subdomains. For each modified qname, the features of the qname are calculated. These features are compared to the advFeatures list and a subset of features is chosen: number of subdomains, number of consonants, number of numbers, number of unique characters. The qname with the smallest Euclidean distance between the two feature subsets is returned.     */

4 **Function** generateAdversarialPackets():

5     $model \leftarrow$ LeNET5 model trained on data set;

6     $mask \leftarrow$ list of which features to pertube (number of subdomains, number of consonants, number of numbers, number of unique characters);

7     $attack \leftarrow$ FastGradientMethod(...);

8     **for** $pkt \in subsetOfMaliciousDNSqueries$ **do**

9         $advFeat \leftarrow$ attack(*pkt features, mask*);

10         $advQname \leftarrow$ getAdvQname(*pkt extracted query name, advFeat*);

11         $advPkt \leftarrow$ buildPacket(*advQname, pkt*);

12         writeToFile(*advPkt, fileName*);

---

number of subdomains, number of numbers, and number of consonants. The algorithm is a search based algorithm which takes as input the original packet query name and the adversarial feature vector, which is the solution of the above optimization problem. The algorithm then appends alphanumeric characters until it reaches a new query name with the minimal feature distance to the input adversarial feature vector. The algorithm output is an adversarial query name, which is then used to rebuild the malicious packet into an adversarial packet, and finally the packet is written to a file which can be referenced for later use.

To verify the optimization approach, the algorithm was applied to the first 501 packets of dnscapy, tuns and dns2tcp data sets. When provided with a testing data set containing only the 1503 adversarial example packets, the accuracy of the LeNET5 CNN was 35.46%. When mixing the adversarial example packets with the previous test data, the accuracy of the LeNET5 CNN was lowered to 77.26% in comparison to the 99.97% accuracy in baseline testing. This lowered accuracy also demonstrates the effectiveness of the proposed search problem approach.

### 4.3  Our Findings

The work presented in Sect. 4.2 clearly demonstrates that adversarial examples are an effective mechanism for bypassing the malicious data exfiltration detection method. To further improve the attack's probability of success, the distance algorithm selected can be replaced, additional features can be included, or certain features can be weighted. Depending on data sets and input, the modifications can improve the success of the attack.

We can once again conclude that our work is novel, as the closest related research is [19], which uses adversarial examples on the TCP, UDP and ICMP protocols to misclassify traffic related to a DDoS or Remote to Local (R2L) attack. Moreover, [22] which uses adversarial examples to defeat traffic analysis attacks on Tor traffic. [23] uses adversarial examples to defeat traffic characterization. [24] uses adversarial examples to defeat ML-based IDSs (with regards to attacks such as DDoS). In addition, [25] uses adversarial examples from a defense perspective to cause the attacker to misclassify network traffic. Our work instead allows for a malicious actor to create adversarial examples of data exfiltration packets which are able to be successfully misclassified.

## 5  Defense Against Malicious Evasion of DNS Exfiltration Detection

Adversarial examples in DNS exfiltration pose a threat to ML-based DNS exfiltration detection techniques and its effectiveness is clearly demonstrated in Sect. 4.2. To counter the techniques introduced in Sect. 4, we introduce an ensemble voting technique, a strategy which combines multiple models, to strengthen the accuracy of adversarial example classification. The aim is that the majority of ensembles should be able to detect the adversarial attack, as the attack may be catered specifically towards or only effective against one (or a minority) of the used classifiers. We then introduce adversarial training as an additional support method for the voting ensemble method proposed.

### 5.1  Ensemble Voting Approach

The majority voting approach, also called an ensemble method, is a technique of combining multiple models to create a single optimal model [26]. An ensemble voting approach uses multiple classifiers which can be trained on the same data set, or different data subsets. The goal of the ensemble voting technique is to rely on multiple machine learning algorithms to classify the same input data and make a classification decision based on a majority vote. One of the main challenges in voting classifiers is selecting which classifiers to use, and how many classifiers to use. The selection of classifiers used in a voting ensemble is incredibly important. The voting ensemble has M number of classifiers to train and use for testing. The use of a slower or more resource consuming classifier (e.g. VGG-16) in the ensemble can increase testing and training times. It is important to select the right number of classifiers, and efficient classifiers, to ensure that testing and training can be done in a feasible manner. An example diagram of a voting ensemble model can be seen in Fig. 4-B. This approach is quite different to the more traditional approach of a single classifier, which can be seen in Fig. 4-A.

In our voting ensemble, we propose the use of 3 classifiers to classify data exfiltration packets to combat against adversarial attacks. The classifiers chosen were LeNET5 CNN, MLP Classifier, and a linear SVM. SVM was chosen due to the mention of SVM usage in network traffic analysis in [21]. The use of 3 classifiers together aims to increase classification accuracy without the requirement of additional data training. An odd number of classifiers was chosen to avoid a tie in decisions, and all classifiers were given the same weight. The classifiers were all trained on the same data set, and voted on the labels for the testing data. The most popular label was chosen as the final label. A diagram demonstrating the process of label calculation on a test input can be seen in Fig. 5.

The voting ensemble was given a data set with an 80:20 split for training and testing. The 1503 adversarial example packets were then mixed into the test data, and also inserted into their own separate testing file. When encountered with the mixed test file (adversarial and non-adversarial) the voting ensemble had a slightly better performance than the LeNET5 CNN with an accuracy of 80%. When encountered with the adversarial only testing file the voting ensemble had much better performance with 55% accuracy.

The results previously mentioned (also included in Table 1) demonstrate the effectiveness of having multiple models working together in identifying adversarial examples. The ensemble model can also be easily strengthened by adding or removing the machine learning models within it. However, one must take care to make sure that the models used do not create an unreasonable cost on resources. The current implementation comes at a slightly elevated cost in comparison to simply using the LeNET5 CNN classifier, but it is still able to classify data in a reasonable time. Our work introduced in this section is novel as we are not currently aware of any other research using voting ensembles to protect against adversarial examples of DNS exfiltration attacks. To further improve the accuracy results, we propose the use of adversarial training in Sect. 5.2.

### 5.2   Adversarial Example Training

The use of adversarial examples in training data is a method that is often called adversarial training, and is used to increase the robustness of the neural network [22,24]. For the robustness training, the first 1001 packets of the dnscapy, tuns, and dns2tcp packets are taken and converted to adversarial examples using the optimization approach mentioned above. The adversarial examples are given an 80:20 data split and mixed into both the training and testing data set. A third

## An Illustration of Our Evasion Attack and Defense in Data Exfiltration on DNS

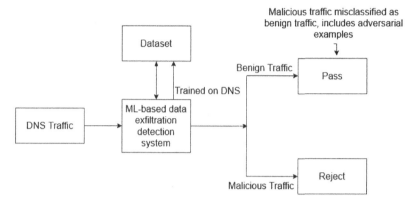

**A - ML Based Detection**

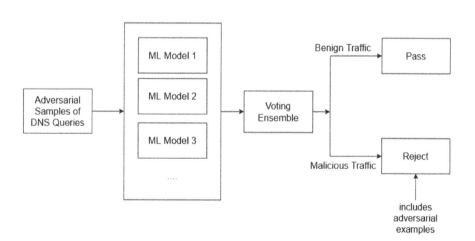

**B - Proposed Ensemble-based Detection**

**Fig. 4.** Diagram of our Voting Ensemble Model vs Traditional Models

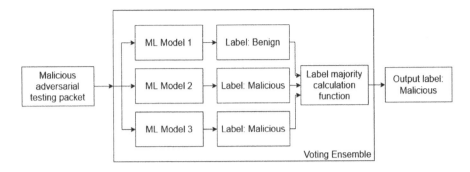

**Fig. 5.** Example Test Flow of Ensemble Model

file including only adversarial examples from the testing data set is also created. The ensemble voting model is trained using the training set with adversarial examples included. When given the mixed testing set, the voting ensemble is able to achieve 86% accuracy. However, given the adversarial testing set, the voting ensemble is able to identify adversarial data with an impressive accuracy of 88%. These results clearly demonstrate the effectiveness of adversarial training to support the classification accuracy of a voting ensemble approach. However the proposed support measure has a few limitations:

1. **Uniqueness:** The included adversarial examples are crafted using packets from 3 attacks (dnscapy, tuns and dns2tcp). Considering the results in Sect. 5.1 it is safe to assume that a new adversarial attack will have a higher chance of success if it is an attack that does not have similar characteristics to adversarial attacks included in the training set.
2. **Data Sets:** There are few data sets including data exfiltration traffic, and even fewer data sets including adversarial examples of data exfiltration packets. This means that data sets will be the responsibility of the victim, or victim's network management company/employee(s), and will need to be created and kept up to date accordingly.

The results above clearly demonstrate the effectiveness of adversarial training in the robustness of a voting ensemble. Regardless of the limitations, it provides a level of assurance that adversarial examples are not as undetectable as assumed, so long as the neural network has adequate training and uses multiple models for a majority vote for classification.

**Table 1.** Machine Learning Model Classification Results

| ML Model | Testing Approach | Accuracy |
|---|---|---|
| LeNET5 CNN | Mixed Testing Data | 77.26% |
| LeNET5 CNN | Adversarial Data Only | 35.46% |
| Majority Vote | Mixed Testing Data | 80% |
| Majority Vote | Adversarial Data Only | 55.02% |
| Majority Vote | Adv Training, Mixed Testing Data | 86.26% |
| Majority Vote | Adv Training, Adversarial Data Only | 88.3% |

# 6    Conclusion

In this paper, we introduced a methodology of developing adversarial examples of DNS exfiltration packets using a novel search approach for packet generation after obtaining the adversarial features using the optimization method we proposed. We presented the effectiveness of adversarial packets for bypassing machine learning detection methods. Our adversarial packet generation algorithm can be applied to multiple kinds of DNS exfiltration attack types (e.g. tuns, dnscapy).

We then propose the use of ensemble learning as a counter method to the previously discussed attack method, which is also a novel idea in countering the adversarial DNS packet attack. Our implementation of the ensemble learning marginally increases the classification time and cost of a packet, and demonstrates the importance of selecting models which are efficient and relatively inexpensive. Finally, we discuss the use of adversarial training as a support method to the ensemble learning detection method.

Future directions of this work include applying the adversarial DNS packet generation method to other DNS attacks (e.g. DNS tunneling and DNS amplification attacks), and the creation of a general framework to detect adversarial attacks for various protocols.

**Acknowledgments.** This work was supported in part by the Natural Sciences and Engineering Research Council of Canada (NSERC). Part of Haonan Yan's work is done when he visits the School of Computer Science at the University of Guelph.

# References

1. Unknown, DNS protocol, NS1. https://ns1.com/resources/dns-protocol. Accessed 01 Aug 2022
2. Unknown, Data exfiltration and DNS closing back-door access to your sensitive data, Infoblox, Unknown
3. Farnham, G., Atlasis, A.F.: Detecting DNS tunneling (2019)

4. Nadler, A., Aminov, A., Shabtai, A.: Detection of malicious and low throughput data exfiltration over the DNS protocol. arXiv (2017)
5. Unknown, What is DNS tunneling? Paloalto network. https://www. paloaltonetworks.com/cyberpedia/what-is-dns-tunneling. Accessed 01 Aug 2022
6. Markova, V.: DNS tunneling attack - what is it, and how to protect ourselves? Cloudns.net. https://www.cloudns.net/blog/dns-tunneling-attack-what-is-it-and-how-to-protect-ourselves/. Accessed 01 Aug 2022
7. Unknown, Data exfiltration, arista networks. https://aristanetworks.force.com/ AristaCommunity/s/article/Data-Exfiltration. Accessed 01 Aug 2022
8. Diana, Data exfiltration: most common techniques and best prevention tactics, xorlab (2022). https://www.xorlab.com/en/blog/data-exfiltration-most-common-techniques-and-best-prevention-tactics. Accessed 01 Aug 2022
9. Unknown, Kill chain, Wikipedia. https://en.wikipedia.org/wiki/Kill_chain. Accessed 01 Aug 2022
10. Sabir, B., Ullah, F., Babar, M.A., Gaire, R.: Machine learning for detecting data exfiltration: a review. arXiv (2020)
11. Ullah, F., Edwards, M., Ramdhany, R., Chitchyan, R., Babar, M.A., Rashid, A.: Data exfiltration: a review of external attack vectors and countermeasures. J. Netw. Comput. Appl. **101**, 18–54 (2017)
12. Sakarkar, G., et al.: Advance approach for detection of DNS tunneling attack from network packets using deep learning algorithms. ADCAIJ: Adv. Distrib. Comput. Artif. Intell. J. **10**(3), 241–266 (2021)
13. Altuncu, M.A., et al.: Deep learning based DNS tunneling detection and blocking system. Adv. Electr. Comput. Eng. **21**(3), 39–48 (2021)
14. Almusawi, A., Amintoosi, H.: DNS tunneling detection method based on multilabel support vector machine. Secur. Commun. Netw. **2018**, 1–9 (2018)
15. D'Angelo, G., Catiglione, A., Palmieri, F.: DNS tunnels detection via DNS-images. Inf. Process. Manag. **59**, 102930 (2022)
16. Ahmed, J., Gharakheili, H.H., Raza, Q., Russel, C., Sivarman, V.: Monitoring enterprise DNS queries for detecting data exfiltration from internal hosts. IEEE Trans. Netw. Serv. Manag. **17**(1), 265–279 (2020)
17. Croce, F., Hein, M.: Reliable evaluation of adversarial robustness with an ensemble of diverse parameter-free attacks. arXiv (2020)
18. Madry, A., Makelov, A., Schmidt, L., Tsipras, D., Vladu, A.: Towards deep learning models resistant to adversarial attacks. arXiv (2019)
19. Sheatsley, R., McDaniel, P., Papernot, N., Weisman, M.J., Verma, G.: Adversarial examples in constrained domains. arXiv (2022)
20. Bubnov, Y.: netrack/learn, Github. https://github.com/netrack/learn. Accessed 21 Apr 2022
21. Du, X., et al.: SoK: exploring the state of the art and the future potential of artificial intelligence in digital forensic investigation. arXiv (2012)
22. Nasr, M., Bahramali, A., Houmansadr, A.: Defeating DNN-based traffic analysis systems in real-time with blind adversarial perturbations. In: 30th USENIX Security Symposium (USENIX Security 2021), pp. 2705–2722 (2021)
23. Sadeghzadeh, A.M., Shiravi, S., Jalili, R.: Adversarial network traffic: towards evaluating the robustness of deep learning-based network traffic classification. arXiv (2020)
24. Yan, H., et al.: Automatic evasion of machine learning-based network intrusion detection systems. IEEE Trans. Dependable Secure Comput. 1–16 (2023)

25. Hu, Y., Tian, J., Ma, J.: A novel way to generate adversarial network traffic samples against network traffic classification. Wireless Commun. Mob. Comput. **2021** (2021)
26. Lutins, E.: Ensemble methods in machine learning: what are they and why use them?, Towards Data Science. https://towardsdatascience.com/ensemble-methods-in-machine-learning-what-are-they-and-why-use-them-68ec3f9fef5f. Accessed 5 June

# CONNECTION: COvert chaNnel NEtwork attaCk Through bIt-rate mOdulatioN

Simone Soderi[1,2]($\boxtimes$) (ID) and Rocco De Nicola[1,2] (ID)

[1] IMT School for Advanced Studies Lucca, Lucca, Italy
{simone.soderi,rocco.denicola}@imtlucca.it
[2] Cybersecurity National Laboratory, CINI - Roma, Rome, Italy

**Abstract.** Covert channel networks are a well-known method for circumventing the security measures organizations put in place to protect their networks from adversarial attacks. This paper introduces a novel method based on bit-rate modulation for implementing covert channels between devices connected over a wide area network. This attack can be exploited to exfiltrate sensitive information from a machine (i.e., covert sender) and stealthily transfer it to a covert receiver while evading network security measures and detection systems. We explain how to implement this threat, focusing specifically on covert channel networks and their potential security risks to network information transmission. The proposed method leverages bit-rate modulation, where a high bit rate represents a '1' and a low bit rate represents a '0', enabling covert communication. We analyze the key metrics associated with covert channels, including robustness in the presence of legitimate traffic and other interference, bit-rate capacity, and bit error rate. Experiments demonstrate the good performance of this attack, which achieved 5 bps with excellent robustness and a channel capacity of up to 0.9239 $^{bps}/_{Hz}$ under different noise sources. Therefore, we show that bit-rate modulation effectively violates network security and compromises sensitive data.

**Keywords:** Covert channel · Network security · Cyber range · Bit-rate

## 1 Introduction

In today's digital era, information exchange via networks is widespread and diverse, covering voice, text, images, and video [13,25]. Despite its vital role in modern society, networked communication is vulnerable to security breaches. Malicious actors can exploit communication channels, conducting covert attacks to extract sensitive data or establish hidden backdoors [36]. Indeed, *covert network channels*, concealing unauthorized information transfer, present a substantial security risk. These channels can be crafted by manipulating network protocols or using steganography to hide data within innocuous information. Their primary aim is discreet information transfer, evading detection and network disruption. This stealthy nature makes covert channels a potent tool for attackers, allowing them to access data secretly. Examining covert network channels

© The Author(s), under exclusive license to Springer Nature Singapore Pte Ltd. 2024
J. Shao et al. (Eds.): EISA 2023, CCIS 2004, pp. 164–183, 2024.
https://doi.org/10.1007/978-981-99-9614-8_11

is vital for network security. Enhancing detection and mitigation strategies is crucial to prevent data leaks and unauthorized access. Covert channels pose tangible threats to networks and data processes [32]. Their goal is hidden infiltration, increasingly challenging in evolving security landscapes. Incorporating covert channel detection tools in network defence is essential. Data can be surreptitiously transferred via various methods, often exploiting well-known internet protocols [8]. Monitoring covert channel actions can prevent future attacks. This paper introduces a novel technique relying on bit-rate modulation for covert communication between networked devices. The approach aims to evade detection systems by exploiting bit-rate variations. To the best of our knowledge, this mechanism is new and calls for further research to curb its impact.

**Contribution.** The main contribution of this paper is the design of a new covert channel to attack enterprise networks under different noise sources. The basic intuition is that the attacker is not interested in intercepting the data transiting the network; rather, she/he wants to control the bit-rate at which it is transmitted. By modulating the bit-rate appropriately, the attacker can associate some pieces of information with a high bit-rate and others with a low bit-rate. Although simple, this technique is new in the covert channel scenario. Other contributions of this paper include the *artefact* implementation of the covert sender and receiver and the description of experiments on the performance of the proposed attack in a cyber range that emulates an enterprise data network.

The rest of the paper is organized as follows. Section 2 describes the main background concepts used in this work, while Sect. 3 contains a short overview of revising the literature about covert channels. Section 4 introduces the attacker model, while Sect. 5 describes the actual implementation of the covert sender and receiver. Section 6 presents our experiments and its results. Finally, Sect. 8 concludes the paper.

## 2    Background

This section provides the basic concepts for understanding covert channels and how we exploited them during our experiments. Furthermore, it provides the basic concepts of network architectures that span wide geographical areas, which will be used in an emulated environment (a *cyber-range*) to assess our attack model.

### 2.1    Covert Channel Characteristics

The creation, maintenance, and effective operation of covert channels depend on balancing fundamental characteristics: anonymity, robustness, bit error rate, and channel capacity. These prerequisites collectively serve as crucial factors in assessing the effectiveness of a covert channel, as they determine its ability to transmit information while eluding network monitoring security systems [37]. The paramount consideration in crafting a successful covert channel is skillfully achieving and harmonizing all these essential features.

**Anonymity.** This feature, often synonymous with unobservability, is essential in establishing the covert nature of the channel. To ensure evasion from potential detection mechanisms, the communication via a covert channel must adeptly mimic ordinary network traffic. This requirement extends beyond simple masquerading; the channel's data patterns and behavioural characteristics must not show statistically significant deviations compared to normal traffic patterns. Additionally, the channel must remain immune to various intrusion detection techniques, including anomaly-based and signature-based detection systems.

**Robustness.** This attribute of a covert channel represents its resilience to alterations, noise, and data losses. Covert channels should exhibit high data integrity and guarantee accurate and reliable data transmission despite potential disruptions. For instance, channels must be resilient against network jitter, packet loss, or intentional disruptions. Furthermore, the channel should be robust against varying network conditions, such as changes in network load or transmission rates.

**Bit Error Rate (BER).** The bit error rate measures the frequency of transmission errors or bit errors during communication. It is crucial to evaluate the error rate of the covert channel as it can affect the reliability and accuracy of the transmitted data. Higher error rates can lead to information loss or corruption, compromising covert communication.

**Coexistence with Legitimate Traffic.** Analyzing the behaviour of a covert channel when it coexists with legitimate network traffic is essential. This investigation helps uncover potential interference or congestion issues that may arise when covert communication overlaps with regular network traffic. Understanding these coexistence characteristics is instrumental in designing covert channels that are not only efficient but also highly stealthy.

**Channel Capacity.** When designing a covert communication channel using unintended mechanisms, understanding its capacity is crucial. This capacity signifies the maximum reliable information rate transmitted, a vital metric for assessing efficiency. We use the Binary Symmetric Channel (BSC) model [31], shown in Fig. 1, a discrete variant of the Discrete Memoryless Channel (DMC) model. It has binary input/output symbols, $X, Y \in 0, 1$, and accounts for noise-causing errors ($p$). For instance, a '0' or '1' could be sent, with $p$ probability of receiving the opposite due to noise ($P(1|0)$ or $P(0|1)$). Conversely, $(1 - p)$ is the probability of correct reception ($P(0|0)$ or $P(1|1)$). This models symmetric errors. In this case, the channel capacity, $C$, can be mathematically determined using the following equation [31]. It quantifies optimal error-free data transfer while optimizing efficiency and minimizing detection risk and is expressed in $bps/Hz$.

$$C = \max_{P} \mathbb{I}(X; Y) = 1 - H(p) = 1 - p \log_2 \left( \frac{1}{p} \right) - (1 - p) \log_2 \left( \frac{1}{1 - p} \right), \quad (1)$$

where $\mathbb{I}(X; Y)$ is the mutual information between the input $X$ and output $Y$, $H(p)$ is the binary entropy function, and $p$ is the error probability.

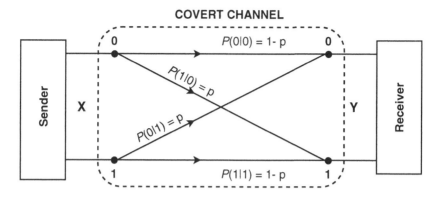

**Fig. 1.** Binary Symmetric Channel model.

## 2.2 Brief Overview of Enterprise Networks

In computer networks and communication infrastructures, service and enterprise networks emerge as two distinct interconnected types [9], with the Multi-Protocol Label Switching (MPLS) protocol playing a central role. MPLS governs large Internet Service Providerss (ISPs) networks and enterprise network backbones, utilizing various routing protocols like Open Shortest Path First (OSPF), internal Border Gateway Protocol (iBGP), and Border Gateway Protocol (BGP) between different Autonomous Systems (ASs) [10,12]. MPLS employs labelling mechanisms for efficient packet routing, ensuring rapid and deterministic switching. For example, consider routing an IP packet through a Layer 3 Virtual Private Network (L3VPN) from a CE device at *remote Site 1* to *remote Site 2*, as depicted in Fig. 2. The packet is labelled at the ingress PE device, dictating its path. P routers forward the packet using its label, and the label is removed at the egress PE device before reaching the destination CE device at *Site 2*. This process is controlled by Virtual Routing and Forwarding (VRF) instances at the PE devices, segregating network traffic based on Virtual Private Network (VPN) membership. MPLS plays a crucial role in modern network architecture by efficiently routing data packets using labels. This approach facilitates streamlined routing across remote sites within networks, avoiding the complexities of destination-based routing algorithms. With VRF instances, MPLS ensures secure and efficient connectivity between different network sites, highlighting its pivotal contribution to managing data flows within intricate network structures [7].

## 3 Related Works

In 1973, Lampson defined the *covert channel* as a communication channel not intended for information transfer [27]. Such type of communication falls within a more general discipline of data manipulation known as *information hiding* or

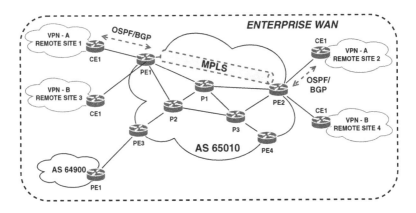

**Fig. 2.** Overview of service and enterprise networks.

*data hiding.* Nowadays, covert channels are carefully engineered to evade detection and circumvent network security policies by establishing new communication paths, causing the disruption of security mechanisms and making their creation and maintenance challenging [11,17,43]. Since covert channels exploit unconventional aspects, it is easy to imagine that there are different types of them. It is, therefore, important to mention a couple of them.

**Covert Timing Channels.** These covert channels transmit information based on the packet arrival times rather than the actual packet content [28,30,33]. They can be subdivided into two types: *timing* and *sorting* channels. In the first, the sender uses predefined time intervals to convey information; for instance, the reception of a packet could represent a binary '1', and the absence of a packet could represent a '0'. More sophisticated timing channels might use inter-packet arrival times to convey data. In such a scenario, a long delay may signify a '0' while a short delay indicates a '1'. Whereas in sorting channels, the sequence of packet arrivals forms the transmitted message. Given that such channels secretly exploit temporal data to forward information, they face significant challenges, such as synchronization between the sender and receiver, especially when the network introduces jitters or noise. However, despite their relatively low throughput, the high anonymity makes them efficient enough for covert communication. Multiple techniques aim to enhance statistical detection's resilience, such as mimicking genuine traffic patterns or employing randomized inter-packet delays [29].

**Covert Network/Storage Channels.** These channels manipulate different layers of the Internet Protocol stack to facilitate covert communication. The sender, who can control parts of the network stack, modifies protocol headers, fragments, checksum values, or packet transmission timing to conceal the information [34,42]. The hidden messages could be embedded in unused bits or fields of protocol headers, such as the IP identification field, the IP fragment offset, the TCP sequence number field, and TCP timestamps [22,35]. While embedding messages in packet headers provides an easy way to create a covert channel, these channels are equally simple to detect and prevent. An adversary can monitor specific fields of packet headers for detection or sanitize these fields for prevention. Furthermore, it is worth noting that payload embedding is generally avoided in the spirit of maintaining covert communication, as this could reveal the existence of the covert channel. For instance, a spread-spectrum watermarking technique can track data covertly flows through a network [24].

Covert channels, characterized as *policy-violating* and unconventional stealthy communication mediums in a system's design, are habitually employed to secretly transfer sensitive information, potentially for data exfiltration or malware communications. Moreover, these channels can serve as vehicles for circumventing cybersecurity policy in companies' perimeter. Covert channels have been observed in many environments, ranging from networks, cyber-physical systems [5], and local processes/systems to out-of-band scenarios like ultrasonic sound [21], light [17], power supply [19], radio frequency [23,39], magnetic fields [16], or temperature [14,20]. Overall, each type of covert channel has advantages and drawbacks, and the choice between them often depends on the specific requirements of covert communication and the constraints imposed by the network environment. Furthermore, a prevalent characteristic among covert channels is the low data transfer rate, exploiting the potential of protracted hiding. Covert channels achieving speeds of 100 bps are classified as fast in this context [44].

In addition to timing and storage channels, other types of covert channels are worth mentioning, even if they are less important in the context of this paper:

(*i*) *covert thermal channels* use a process to modulate the CPU usage and change the machine's temperature, which is then sensed by a thermal sensor controlled by another process [20];

(*ii*) *covert acoustic channels* leverage the audible or ultrasonic sound spectrum for data exfiltration [15,21].

## 4   Attacker Model

In this section, we illustrate the proposed model of our attacker. The attacker's main objective is to illegally establish a communication conduit, herein termed a *covert channel* between two specific entities: the *sender* and the *receiver*. They must be intended as equipment interconnected via a WAN, as described in Sect. 2.2. In the assumptions of our adversarial model, both the sender and the receiver fall under the attacker's control. To illustrate, consider the situation wherein the sender and the receiver are devices that malware deployed by the attacker has compromised. This malware can execute arbitrary code on the infected devices, creating a *connection*. It is important to emphasize that when constructing our attack model for establishing covert channels, we control and integrate features of both senders and receivers, exactly like in many other approaches to the same issue. Many studies focusing on covert channels have incorporated an attack model that, like ours, is characterized by a transmitter-receiver structure in which the attacker requires the same control

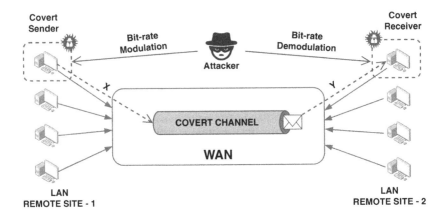

**Fig. 3.** Attack model where the WAN can be an enterprise network or the Internet. Sender and Receiver are two devices connected through the WAN.

capabilities. Some examples from recent literature can be found in these references [6,11,17,18,38], but none of the considered approaches relies on bit-rate modulation.

The concept of an Advanced Persistent Threat (APT) delineates an attack campaign whereby an adversarial entity maintains an unauthorized presence within a targeted network, thereby gaining high-sensitivity access to data [41]. The attacker model we propose, named CONNECTION - "COvert chaNnel NEtwork attaCk Through bIt-rate mOdulatioN", involves both sender and receiver elements, as illustrated in Fig. 3. This attack falls into the category of a covert timing channel. The compromise of the two entities can be achieved through various methods, including but not limited to supply chain attacks, the use of social engineering techniques, or the exploitation of hardware with pre-installed software or firmware. The attacker does not require special permissions to carry out this attack once the machines have been infected. It's worth noting that even highly secure facilities, including air-gapped ones, are not immune to such exploits, as demonstrated in recent years, with Stuxnet [26] being one of the most famous examples.

After successfully infecting the two designated devices, the malicious software initiates a process to identify the communication partners of the sender. In this scenario, the attacker may not need to know the exact address of the sender; the target network's address range or the IP address subnet could be sufficient.

Under the attacker's control, the sender initiates covert communication attempts with each IP address within the target network's address space. Upon successfully detecting this covert communication, the (infected) receiver responds to the sender by modulating its bit-rate. To be more precise, when the sender selects a specific IP address, it begins transmitting a bitstream (represented as $X$ in Fig. 3), using bit-rate variation as the communication method: a high bit-rate indicates the transmission of a '1' bit, while a low bit-rate indicates the transmission of a '0' bit.

Conversely, the receiver using a traffic dump can demodulate the encoded information, resulting in receiving the message $Y$. By observing the traffic shape, often referred to as the *envelope*, exchanged between these two devices, an amplitude modulation such as a Pulse Amplitude Modulation (PAM) or an On-Off Keying (OOK) modulations [31] could be identified. However, in our case, this is achieved by controlling the *network throughput*. Implementing this type of covert channel depends on the specifications of the victim device. The following section will discuss how to carry out this attack.

## 5   Bit-Rate Modulation as Covert Channel

Let us, therefore, consider the context described in Sect. 4, i.e., a threat actor operating on two devices communicating over a WAN (see Fig. 2). Given its extensive use, at this time, we will use the MITRE ATT&CK framework [40] as a reference to frame the activities of the attacker. In particular, he/she must plan tactics and use techniques to implement the covert channel. There will be a pre-attack phase in which the attacker will conduct a *reconnaissance* phase to acquire useful information to *weaponize* and adapt the malware that will create the covert channel between the sender in *Site 1* and the receiver in *Site 2*. The techniques needed to effectively realize this covert communication, and in particular, how the covert channel between the *sender* and the *receiver* is established, are explained in the following.

### 5.1   Covert Sender

Algorithm 1 outlines a procedure for transmitting a *bitstream* over a covert network. The process employs the principles of bit-rate modulation, effectively performing an amplitude modulation (e.g., PAM) of the throughput. This technique ingeniously hides the communication, making it robust against conventional detection strategies.

The procedure begins with identifying the essential elements required to execute the algorithm, which includes the amplitude modulation parameters $b1$ and $b0$, i.e., the high bit-rate levels to transmit 1 and the low bit-rate levels to transmit 0. The only information the sender must have is the IP address (or the addressing of the destination LAN) and port of the receiver. An attacker can potentially obtain this information in the reconnaissance phase through social engineering operations such as phishing or other means. It is, however, assumed that the sender and receiver are already connected via the WAN.

Upon initiation, the algorithm processes each bit in the *bitstream*. Depending on whether the current bit is '1' or '0', the payload is generated using the modulation parameters $b1$ or $b0$, respectively. This operation is performed by the *GeneratePayload* function, which generates random data at the corresponding bit rate, i.e., $b0$ or $b1$. Once the payload is generated, the algorithm encapsulates it into a network UDP packet using the *ConstructPacket* function. This packet, intended for the receiver, contains the payload and is routed to the specified

---

**Algorithm 1:** Sender's Transmission using Bit-rate Modulation

---

**Input:** $b1, b0, bitstream, receiverIP, receiverPORT$
**Output:** Transmit $bitstream$ covertly over the network
**Function** GeneratePayload($b$):
    $payload \leftarrow$ empty byte array
    **for** $i \leftarrow 1$ **to** $b$ **do**
        $rand\_byte \leftarrow$ random integer from 0 to 255
        append $rand\_byte$ to $payload$
    **return** $payload$
**Function** ConstructPacket($receiverIP, receiverPORT, payload$):
    $pkt \leftarrow$ Ether / IP(dst $= receiverIP$) / UDP(dport $= receiverPORT$) /
    Raw($payload$)
    **return** $pkt$

**Function** Main():
    **for** $bit \in bitstream$ **do**
        **if** $bit = 1$ **then**
            $payload \leftarrow$ GeneratePayload ($b1$)
        **else**
            $payload \leftarrow$ GeneratePayload ($b0$)
        $pkt \leftarrow$ ConstructPacket ($receiverIP, receiverPORT, payload$)
        $frags \leftarrow$ FragmentPacket($pkt, fragSize$)
        **for** $frag \in frags$ **do**
            TransmitFragment($frag$)
**End**

---

receiver's IP and port number. We have used the UDP protocol without losing generality to maximize control over the timing of the data sent.

To comply with Maximum Transmission Unit (MTU) constraints, specifically in Ethernet networks, and to avoid unintended fragmentation at the network layer, the constructed packet is fragmented into smaller pieces of a predetermined size, which here is set at 1472 bytes. The fragmentation is implemented using the *FragmentPacket* function. After the fragmentation, each fragment is sent in a sequence using the *TransmitFragment* function. This phase represents the transportation of each bit in the bitstream as an independent network packet. In essence, this algorithm executes the covert transmission of the bitstream over the WAN. Applying the bit-rate modulation mechanism modulates the amplitude of the network throughput, such as an PAM signal modulation. This mechanism, combined with the fact that the algorithm does not modify the content of the packets, makes the transmission highly resistant to detection, thereby improving the stealth and reliability of the covert channel.

### 5.2  Covert Receiver

In the covert communication scenario, the receiver starts by passively monitoring or sniffing UDP network traffic on a specific port, e.g., using the network traffic capture utility, *tcpdump* [3]. It saves it in a PCAP file for further processing, i.e., demodulation.

---

**Algorithm 2:** Covert receiver's demodulation and synchronization

---

**Input:** $PCAP\_FILE, receiverIP, receiverPORT, PREAMBLE$
**Output:** Demodulated bitstream and bitstream synchronization

**Function** FilterPacket(*pkt, receiverIP*):
    **Input:** *pkt* (packets from the PCAP file)
    **Output:** Packets considered for further processing
    $fpkts \leftarrow$ Ether in pkt and IP in pkt and pkt[IP].src == receiverIP and pkt[IP].proto == 17
    **return** $fpkts$

**Function** DemodulatePacket(*all_packets_counts*):
    **Input:** *all_packets_counts* (a list of packets with the same id)
    **Output:** Demodulated bitstream
    $threshold \leftarrow$ 0.8 * max($all\_packets\_counts$)
    $demodulated \leftarrow$ Empty list
    **for** *rate* in *all_packets_counts* **do**
        **if** $rate \geq threshold$ **then**
            | Append 1 to *demodulated*
        **else**
            | Append 0 to *demodulated*
    **return** *demodulated*

**Function** SyncCommunication(*demodulated, PREAMBLE*):
    **Input:** *demodulated* (the bitstream), $PREAMBLE$
    **Output:** $start\_bitstream\_index$ (after the preamble)
    $preamble\_index \leftarrow$ SynchPreamble($demodulated, PREAMBLE$)
    **if** $preamble\_index is not empty$ **then**
        | $start\_bitstream\_index \leftarrow$ last element of preamble_index + 1
    **return** $start\_bitstream\_index$

**Function** Main():
    $packets \leftarrow$ ReadCaptureFile(PCAP_FILE)
    $filtered\_packets \leftarrow$ FilterPacket ($packets, receiverIP$)
    $all\_packets\_counts \leftarrow$ CountPacketsByIdOnPort($filtered\_packets, receiverPORT$)
    $demodulated \leftarrow$ DemodulatePacket($all\_packets\_counts$)
    $start\_bitstream\_index \leftarrow$
    SyncCommunication($demodulated, PREAMBLE$)
    **return** $demodulated, start\_bitstream\_index$
**End**

---

The receiver analyses the network traffic it has just captured following the procedure in Algorithm 2. It filters only those packets that might contain secret information, demodulates the bits, and synchronizes to a known *preamble*. The preamble needed to synchronise the communication is also sent using bit-rate modulation. Thus, after acquiring incoming packets, the receiver's algorithm applies a filter (*FilterPacket*) to discard all packets irrelevant for transmission, retaining only those received that use UDP for transport (indicated by protocol number 17).

As mentioned earlier, during transmission, the sender can employ packet fragmentation. When transmitting a '1', which uses a high bit-rate, it will generate numerous fragments, while when transmitting a '0', it will use a much lower bit-rate and, therefore, fewer fragments or even no fragments if the payload is shorter than the MTU. After the filtering process, it becomes necessary to group the packets based on their identification (ID) and count the number of packets in each group arriving at a specific port The resulting count serves as an indicator for the bit-rate, thus acting as an implicit representation of the value of the bit originally transmitted. The *DemodulatePacket* function analyzes this counter, and the higher the packet count, the more likely it is that the corresponding bit value in the original bit stream was a '1' and vice versa. To translate these counts into a demodulated bit stream, a threshold comparator is used, and then a threshold value is defined, for example, 80% of the maximum observed count. Counts that meet or exceed this threshold are interpreted as '1', while those that fall below are interpreted as '0'. The demodulated bit stream is scanned for this sequence, and the index immediately following the end of the sequence is taken as the starting point for the actual data in the bit stream.

This algorithm provides a robust and ingenious approach to covert communication by exploiting the underlying characteristics of network transmissions and their inherent variability in the number of packets to encode and transmit data secretly. Though this method operates with low throughput, the most significant advantage is the possibility that it offers a method for exfiltrating valuable information from within an organization. For example, one could send externally the file */etc/passwd*, which in a few bytes (typically < 100 B) contains the accounts and associated passwords of Unix computers.

## 6    Evaluation of the Covert Channel

In this section, we will evaluate the usefulness of the implemented covert channel, which uses bit-rate modulation, in a virtual scenario (see Fig. 4). This evaluation aims to understand the potential risks associated with the covert channel and assess its effectiveness as a means of unauthorized communication. For our experiments, we relied on a controlled environment known as a cyber range, where we set up a secure network infrastructure comprising an MPLS backbone connecting two remote sites. The cyber range provides a controlled environment to evaluate the covert channel's utility while considering achievable bit-rate, BER, robustness, and coexistence with legitimate traffic.

We deployed the attack model sketched in Fig. 3 in the cyber range using the Graphical Network Simulator-3 (GNS3) [1]. This network software emulator combines virtual and real devices to simulate complex networks. In this virtual environment, we established an MPLS backbone based on OSPF and BGP protocols. The backbone consisted of three routers P, two PE, and two CE, all running on the VyOS open-source network operating system [4]. The cyber range connected two remote sites, each with an infected machine as the covert sender (PC1-1) and the covert receiver (PC1-2). The aim is to use the malicious covert channel to exfiltrate sensitive information from PC1-1. To achieve this, the covert sender implements Algorithm 1 using a Python script that uses *Scapy* [2], a Python program for network packet manipulation. Scapy facilitated

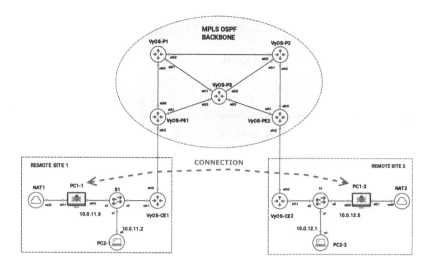

**Fig. 4.** Covert channel (CONNECTION) deployed in a cyber-range.

the generation, modulation, and transmission of covert payloads. The covert receiver implements Algorithm 2 using tcpdump, Python, and Scapy. Tcpdump allowed real-time network traffic capture, while Python and Scapy enabled the demodulation and analysis of received packets. Algorithm 2 decoded the covert bitstream, recovering the transmitted information.

## 6.1   Results of Adversary Emulation in the Cyber Range

We conducted a comprehensive set of experiments to evaluate the performance of the covert channel. The experiments considered the metrics outlined in Sect. 2.1, providing valuable insights into the channel's behaviour and capabilities. The parameters and details of these tests are summarized in Table 1. In particular,

**Table 1.** Scenario parameters for the covert channel experiments.

| Parameter | Value |
|---|---|
| Modulation type | PAM |
| Amplitude ratio ($AR$) | 6, 4.5, 3, 2 |
| Bitstream (with 16 bits of preamble) | $48 \div 144$ bits |
| Jitter | $(5, 10)$ ms |
| Delay | $(10, 20)$ ms |
| Packets loss | $(1, 2, 5, 10, 15)\%$ |
| Packets corruption | $(10, 20)\%$ |
| Frequency dropping threshold | $(21, 51, 101, 201, 301)$ |

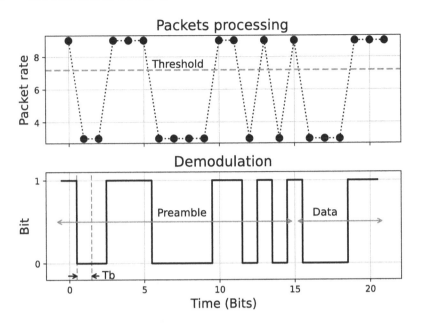

**Fig. 5.** Transmission of a bitstream (preamble and data) over the covert channel.

we investigated the influence of the Amplitude Ratio (AR) in the bit-rate modulation technique. The AR represents the ratio between the number of bytes used to transmit bit '1' ($b1$) and the number used to transmit bit '0' ($b0$). For instance, if we allocated 6000 bytes for bit '1' and 1000 bytes for bit '0', the resulting AR would be 6. To capture a comprehensive perspective, we collected statistical data on transmitting multiple bitstreams with varying lengths ranging from 48 to 144 bits (including the 16 preamble bits). We computed the mean and standard deviation of the bit-rate and BER by analyzing these measurements. These statistical measures allowed us to gain deeper insights into the channel's performance and robustness.

Figure 5 shows the covert channel in action when transmitting a short bitstream (i.e., 16 bits of preamble and 6 bits of data) and how demodulation (Algorithm 2) is done by assessing whether the packet rate is above or below the threshold.

To evaluate the covert channel's capacity, we conducted measurements to determine its maximum bit-rate. Initially, we set a fixed payload size for transmitting bit '1' ($b1$) and explored various scenarios using smaller payloads to represent bit '0' ($b0$). This approach allowed us to achieve amplitude modulation with variable amplitude ratios (AR). Figure 6 illustrates two cases where b1 is set to 6000 bytes in one group of tests and 4000 in another. The results revealed that the maximum achievable bit-rate is approximately 5 bps. Interestingly, Fig. 6 shows that the throughput remains constant when the AR is such that the payload size of bit zero is smaller than the MTU.

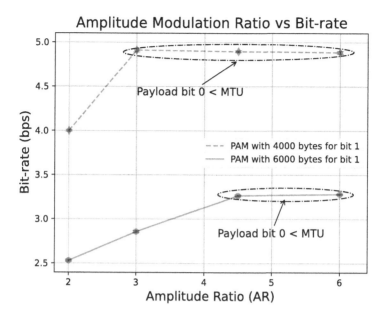

**Fig. 6.** Bit-rate evaluation at varying amplitude modulation depth, i.e., AR.

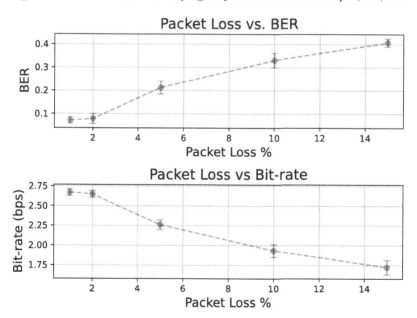

**Fig. 7.** Transmitting a bitstream over the covert channel under packet loss.

In Fig. 7, we examined the impact of packet loss on the covert channel using an PAM scheme with b1 set to 6000 bytes. Notably, for high packet loss rates, specifically around 5%, the BER reached approximately 20%. Similarly, Fig. 8

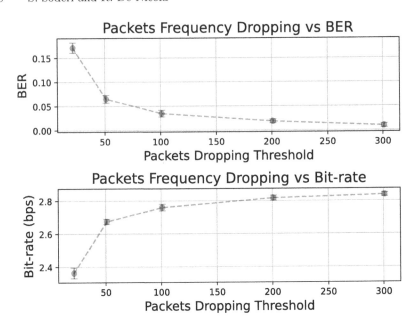

**Fig. 8.** Transmitting a bitstream over the covert channel under packet dropping.

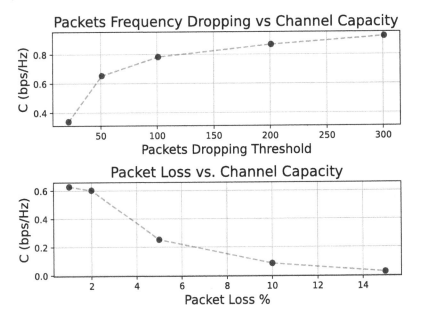

**Fig. 9.** Channel capacity (C) under packets dropping and packet loss.

illustrates the effect of dropping packets periodically, where the threshold denotes the number of packets dropped. For example, with a drop rate of 1 packet per 50, the BER was approximately 15%. With the same settings, Fig. 9 shows the relation between the channel capacity (C) expressed by (1) and packets dropping and packet loss, respectively. With the covert channel proposed here, we achieved a spectral efficiency of 0.9239 $^{bps}/_{Hz}$.

In addition, we conducted further tests to evaluate the other characteristics of covert channels by considering UDP traffic of up to 10 Mbps between PC1-1 and PC1-2 and experienced no interference of the covert channel. We also introduced variations in latency, jitter, and corrupted packets (values used for these tests are in Table 1). Remarkably, none of these operations disrupted the covert channel's transmission. GNS3 allowed us to vary packet loss, frequency drop, latency, jitter, and corruption by operating on the communication link between the two machines.

These results demonstrate the robustness of the covert channel in a typical enterprise network scenario. Moreover, the channel exhibits a sufficient bit-rate for effective information exfiltration. Its inherent anonymity poses significant challenges for detection since the transmitted bursts exhibit very low throughput, thus avoiding the microburst phenomenon typically mitigated by modern network devices. Additionally, using random payload data and commonly employed UDP services further contribute to the channel's elusive nature, making it difficult to detect.

## 7   Discussion

Covert channels have been an area of significant research interest, with various techniques being proposed over the years. The proposed attack offers a novel approach in this domain. As described in the previous sections, the throughput achieved is comparable with other solutions proposed in the literature. In addition, the simplicity of the attack, based on bit-rate modulation, could prospectively make it applicable even in contexts where devices with low computational capabilities operate.

**Comparison with Other Schemes.** While there is a limited number of studies in the literature that employ a similar scheme to our attack, it remains appropriate to compare our performance with those existing contributions. In [44], the authors introduced a covert channel mechanism in a virtualized environment that posed serious security risks in the cloud. Their method achieved a throughput of 100 bps on average. In [22], authors create a unique covert timing channel to exfiltrate data utilizing Internet of Things (IoT) devices. The TCP/IP throughput of the Stealth mode is 4.61 bps, while the ZigBee throughput is 3.90 bps. Recently, Hou *et al.* [23] published an innovative approach, exploiting the LoRa physical layer to establish a covert channel with a throughput of 30 bps. This approach is the closest work to our contribution. The authors implemented the covert channel by modulating the amplitude of the LoRA radio signal.

**Mitigation.** The detection of the attack we propose is challenging without prior knowledge. Nevertheless, if the network-controlling team possesses specific information, it is plausible that by analyzing network traffic variations (such as observing the network traffic envelope), they could potentially detect an amplitude modulation and trigger an alert.

**Ethical Aspects.** Our research aims to signal a new class of vulnerabilities within network traffic, thereby hardening defences against exploiting such channels to leak sensitive data by adverse entities. To effectively identify and cancel bit-rate modulation covert channels, network devices must incorporate advanced monitoring capabilities to monitor and respond to anomalous throughput fluctuations.

## 8     Conclusions

We have presented a novel covert timing channel that exploits bit-rate modulation as a new attack vector on enterprise networks. An advantage of this technique is that it uses a light and simple algorithm to implement the sender and receiver, making it suitable also for hacking those resource-limited devices belonging to two Local Area Networks (LANs) communicating via an enterprise network.

We conducted extensive experiments in a controlled cyber range environment to validate our approach, allowing us to manipulate network parameters and thoroughly evaluate our model. The results demonstrated the effectiveness of our covert channel, achieving a data transmission rate of 5 bps and a channel capacity up to $0.9239\ bps/Hz$. Although the bit-rate may seem low, let us remember that it is a typical value for a covert channel and sufficient to exfiltrate sensitive data before being discovered. Furthermore, our solution shows resilience against common network challenges such as jitter, latency, and coexistence with legitimate traffic and maintains complete anonymity. Through a comprehensive understanding of covert channel attacks, we can defend our networks, preserving the integrity and privacy of data and, ultimately, fostering trust in our digital world.

**Acknowledgments.** The authors thank Niccolò Maggioni for his insightful comments. This work was partly supported by Consorzio Interuniversitario Nazionale per l'Informatica (CINI) through a Research Project under Grant CA 01/2021 a.i. 2 and by project SERICS (PE00000014) under the NRRP MUR program funded by the EU - NGEU.

## References

1. Graphical Network Simulator 3 (GNS3). https://www.gns3.com/
2. Scapy. https://scapy.net/
3. TCPdump. https://www.tcpdump.org/
4. VyOS. https://vyos.io/
5. Abdelwahab, A., Lucia, W., Youssef, A.: Covert channels in cyber-physical systems. IEEE Control Syst. Lett. 5(4), 1273–1278 (2021). https://doi.org/10.1109/LCSYS.2020.3033059

6. Amro, A., Gkioulos, V.: From click to sink: utilizing AIS for command and control in maritime cyber attacks. In: Atluri, V., Di Pietro, R., Jensen, C.D., Meng, W. (eds.) ESORICS 2022, Part III. LNCS, vol. 13556, pp. 535–553. Springer, Heidelberg (2022). https://doi.org/10.1007/978-3-031-17143-7_26

7. Behringer, M.H., Morrow, M.: MPLS VPN Security. Cisco Press (2005)

8. Cabaj, K., Caviglione, L., Mazurczyk, W., Wendzel, S., Woodward, A., Zander, S.: The new threats of information hiding: the road ahead. IT Prof. **20**(3), 31–39 (2018). https://doi.org/10.1109/MITP.2018.032501746

9. Cisco Systems: MPLS in the DCN (2007). https://www.cisco.com/c/en/us/td/docs/ios/solutions_docs/telco_dcn/Book/telco5.html

10. Cisco Systems: Configuring a Basic MPLS VPN (2020). https://www.cisco.com/c/en/us/support/docs/multiprotocol-label-switching-mpls/mpls/13733-mpls-vpn-basic.html

11. Costa, G., Pinelli, F., Soderi, S., Tolomei, G.: Turning federated learning systems into covert channels. IEEE Access **10**, 130642–130656 (2022). https://doi.org/10.1109/ACCESS.2022.3229124

12. Ghein, L.D.: MPLS Fundamentals. Cisco Press (2016)

13. Gui, G., Liu, M., Tang, F., Kato, N., Adachi, F.: 6G: opening new horizons for integration of comfort, security, and intelligence. IEEE Wirel. Commun. **27**(5), 126–132 (2020). https://doi.org/10.1109/MWC.001.1900516

14. Guri, M.: HOTSPOT: crossing the air-gap between isolated PCs and nearby smartphones using temperature. In: 2019 European Intelligence and Security Informatics Conference (EISIC), pp. 94–100 (2019). https://doi.org/10.1109/EISIC49498.2019.9108874

15. Guri, M.: CD-LEAK: leaking secrets from audioless air-gapped computers using covert acoustic signals from CD/DVD drives. In: 2020 IEEE 44th Annual Computers, Software, and Applications Conference (COMPSAC), pp. 808–816 (2020). https://doi.org/10.1109/COMPSAC48688.2020.0-163

16. Guri, M.: MAGNETO: covert channel between air-gapped systems and nearby smartphones via CPU-generated magnetic fields. Future Gener. Comput. Syst. **115**, 115–125 (2021). https://doi.org/10.1016/j.future.2020.08.045. https://www.sciencedirect.com/science/article/pii/S0167739X2030916X

17. Guri, M.: ETHERLED: sending covert Morse signals from air-gapped devices via network card (NIC) LEDs. In: 2022 IEEE International Conference on Cyber Security and Resilience (CSR), pp. 163–170 (2022). https://doi.org/10.1109/CSR54599.2022.9850284

18. Guri, M.: Near field air-gap covert channel attack. In: 2022 IEEE International Conference on Trust, Security and Privacy in Computing and Communications (TrustCom), pp. 490–497 (2022). https://doi.org/10.1109/TrustCom56396.2022.00074

19. Guri, M.: *POWER-SUPPLaY*: leaking sensitive data from air-gapped, audio-gapped systems by turning the power supplies into speakers. IEEE Trans. Dependable Secure Comput. **20**(1), 313–330 (2023). https://doi.org/10.1109/TDSC.2021.3133406

20. Guri, M., Monitz, M., Mirski, Y., Elovici, Y.: BitWhisper: covert signaling channel between air-gapped computers using thermal manipulations. In: 2015 IEEE 28th Computer Security Foundations Symposium, pp. 276–289 (2015). https://doi.org/10.1109/CSF.2015.26

21. Guri, M., Solewicz, Y., Elovici, Y.: MOSQUITO: covert ultrasonic transmissions between two air-gapped computers using speaker-to-speaker communication. In:

2018 IEEE Conference on Dependable and Secure Computing (DSC), pp. 1–8 (2018). https://doi.org/10.1109/DESEC.2018.8625124

22. Harris, K., Henry, W., Dill, R.: A network-based IoT covert channel. In: 2022 4th International Conference on Computer Communication and the Internet (ICCCI), pp. 91–99 (2022). https://doi.org/10.1109/ICCCI55554.2022.9850247

23. Hou, N., Xia, X., Zheng, Y.: CloakLoRa: a covert channel over LoRa PHY. IEEE/ACM Trans. Netw. **31**(3), 1159–1172 (2022). https://doi.org/10.1109/TNET.2022.3209255

24. Jia, W., Tso, F.P., Ling, Z., Fu, X., Xuan, D., Yu, W.: Blind detection of spread spectrum flow watermarks. In: IEEE INFOCOM 2009, pp. 2195–2203 (2009). https://doi.org/10.1109/INFCOM.2009.5062144

25. Katz, M., Matinmikko-Blue, M., Latva-Aho, M.: 6Genesis flagship program: building the bridges towards 6G-enabled wireless smart society and ecosystem. In: 2018 IEEE 10th Latin-American Conference on Communications (LATINCOM), pp. 1–9 (2018). https://doi.org/10.1109/LATINCOM.2018.8613209

26. Kushner, D.: The real story of stuxnet. IEEE Spectr. **50**(3), 48–53 (2013). https://doi.org/10.1109/MSPEC.2013.6471059

27. Lampson, B.W.: A note on the confinement problem. Commun. ACM **16**(10), 613–615 (1973). https://doi.org/10.1145/362375.362389

28. Lee, K.S., Wang, H., Weatherspoon, H.: PHY covert channels: can you see the idles? In: 11th USENIX Symposium on Networked Systems Design and Implementation (NSDI 2014), pp. 173–185. USENIX Association, Seattle (2014). https://www.usenix.org/conference/nsdi14/technical-sessions/presentation/lee

29. Luo, X., Chan, E.W.W., Chang, R.K.C.: TCP covert timing channels: design and detection. In: 2008 IEEE International Conference on Dependable Systems and Networks with FTCS and DCC (DSN), pp. 420–429 (2008). https://doi.org/10.1109/DSN.2008.4630112

30. Luo, X., Zhou, P., Zhang, J., Perdisci, R., Lee, W., Chang, R.K.C.: Exposing invisible timing-based traffic watermarks with backlit. In: Proceedings of the 27th Annual Computer Security Applications Conference, ACSAC 2011, pp. 197–206. Association for Computing Machinery, New York (2011). https://doi.org/10.1145/2076732.2076760

31. Massoud Salehi, P., Proakis, J.: Digital Communications, 5th edn. McGraw-Hill Education (2007). ISBN: 9780072957167

32. Mazurczyk, W., Caviglione, L.: Information hiding as a challenge for malware detection. IEEE Secur. Priv. **13**(2), 89–93 (2015). https://doi.org/10.1109/MSP.2015.33

33. Mazurczyk, W., Smolarczyk, M., Szczypiorski, K.: On information hiding in retransmissions. Telecommun. Syst. **52**(2), 1113–1121 (2013). https://doi.org/10.1007/s11235-011-9617-y

34. Mazurczyk, W., Szczypiorski, K.: Steganography in handling oversized IP packets. In: 2009 International Conference on Multimedia Information Networking and Security, vol. 1, pp. 559–564 (2009). https://doi.org/10.1109/MINES.2009.246

35. Mazurczyk, W., Szczypiorski, K.: Steganography in handling oversized IP packets, vol. 1, pp. 559–564 (2009). https://doi.org/10.1109/MINES.2009.246

36. Mazurczyk, W., Wendzel, S.: Information hiding: challenges for forensic experts. Commun. ACM **61**(1), 86–94 (2017). https://doi.org/10.1145/3158416

37. Ondov, A., Helebrandt, P.: Covert channel detection methods. In: 2022 20th International Conference on Emerging eLearning Technologies and Applications (ICETA), pp. 491–496 (2022). https://doi.org/10.1109/ICETA57911.2022.9974878

38. Ovadya, A., Ogen, R., Mallah, Y., Gilboa, N., Oren, Y.: Cross-router covert channels. In: Proceedings of the 13th USENIX Conference on Offensive Technologies, WOOT 2019, p. 2. USENIX Association (2019)
39. Soderi, S., Dainelli, G., Iinatti, J., Hämäläinen, M.: Signal fingerprinting in cognitive wireless networks. In: 2014 9th International Conference on Cognitive Radio Oriented Wireless Networks and Communications (CROWNCOM), pp. 266–270 (2014). https://doi.org/10.4108/icst.crowncom.2014.255374
40. Strom, B.E., Applebaum, A., Miller, D.P., Nickels, K.C., Pennington, A.G., Thomas, C.B.: MITRE ATT&CK: design and philosophy. Technical report, The MITRE Corporation (2018)
41. Ussath, M., Jaeger, D., Cheng, F., Meinel, C.: Advanced persistent threats: behind the scenes. In: 2016 Annual Conference on Information Science and Systems (CISS), pp. 181–186 (2016). https://doi.org/10.1109/CISS.2016.7460498
42. Wendzel, S., Zander, S., Fechner, B., Herdin, C.: Pattern-based survey and categorization of network covert channel techniques. ACM Comput. Surv. 47(3), 1–26 (2015). https://doi.org/10.1145/2684195
43. Ying, X., Bernieri, G., Conti, M., Bushnell, L., Poovendran, R.: Covert channel-based transmitter authentication in controller area networks. IEEE Trans. Dependable Secure Comput. 19(4), 2665–2679 (2022). https://doi.org/10.1109/TDSC.2021.3068213
44. Zhenyu, W., Zhang, X., Wang, H.: Whispers in the hyper-space: high-speed covert channel attacks in the cloud. In: USENIX Security Symposium, pp. 159–173 (2012)

# Author Index

J. Shao et al. (Eds.): EISA 2023, CCIS 2004, p. 185, 2024.
https://doi.org/10.1007/978-981-99-9614-8

Printed in the United States
by Baker & Taylor Publisher Services